TAXSCAM

How The Internal Revenue Service Swindles You And What You Can Do About It

Alan Stang

Mount Sinai Press

Cover illustration and lettering by Joe Taylor Design, Crosbyton, Texas

Typesetting by Thoburn Press, Tyler, Texas

Printed in the United States of America

Library of Congress Catalog Card No. 88-60843

ISBN 0-9620089-0-7

$9.95

To order by mail, send $9.95 per copy, plus $1.50 per order for postage and handling, to Research Publications, P.O. Box 84902, Phoenix, AZ 85071. (Enclose check or money order payable to *Taxscam-Research Publications*.)

To order by telephone call 1-800-528-0559

For more information about *Taxscam*, call (714) 980-3165, or write Mount Sinai Press, P.O. Box 1220, Alta Loma, California 91701.

Books on the subject of income taxes have, for too long now, been written primarily for the specialists such as attorneys and CPAs, to the exclusion and detriment of many Americans. Now, Alan has written a very understandable, humorous and entertaining book which explains both the practical and the legal impact of this tax in terms capable of comprehension by the ordinary layman.

The IRS in express terms considers most, if not all, taxpayers as "Dingbats," ever willing to do what the taxman commands. If you want to take yourself out of this "Edith Bunker" class, read this delightful and thought-provoking book.

Lowell H. Becraft, *Trial Attorney*

Alan Stang's book—*Taxscam*—goes to the root of the I.R.S. tree. It is the most documented and massive volume concerning the corruption of this unconstitutional system and injustice to the American people. I strongly urge all to read this book before it is too late.

Dr. Greg Dixon, *Pastor, Indianapolis Baptist Temple*
National Chairman, American Coalition of Unregistered Churches

Every freedom-loving American should read *Taxscam*! Alan Stang brilliantly nails the hide of the Internal Revenue Service to the wall, demonstrating beyond question their illegal power grabs and abusive administration of the Income Tax.

I can personally attest to the ruthless and unconstitutional methods used by the I.R.S. to shake down taxpayers. *Taxscam* tells it like it is through the great courage and unique experiences of a fearless American.

The Bible counsels us to seek the truth and the truth will make us free. The truths of Alan Stang's words are just that powerful—for those who will read and heed!

George Hansen, *Member of Congress (1965-69; 1975-85)*
Chairman, Free America

This is a brilliant piece of literature, written by a man (Alan Stang) of more than adequate capabilities, a person whom I have come to admire because of his tenacity, which I have personally observed. This tells it all in a fast-paced, easy to read and understand (non-boring) book. Alan, in a manner equated to genius, exposes the problem, tells us why we have it, explains how it developed, suggests alternative solutions, and points out how one person can have a tremendous impact.

Leo Masters, *Independent paralegal*

Taxscam is a superb analysis of the ruthless tactics of the Internal Revenue Service. I applaud Alan Stang, who performs a great service for the American people in his frightening revelation of the IRS.

Ron Paul, *M.D.*
Member of Congress, 4 terms
Presidential nominee, Libertarian Party, 1988

Having been an I.R.S. agent—and secret whistleblower—for many years, I can testify personally to the fact that I.R.S. officials break the law every day, and thereby promote totalitarianism. They tried to shut Alan Stang up. Happily, they failed.

Name Withheld in Fear of I.R.S. Retaliation

Other books by Alan Stang

It's Very Simple:
The True Story of Civil Rights, 1965

The Actor:
The True Story of John Foster Dulles, 1968

The Highest Virtue (A Novel), 1974

To

RUTH STUDLEY and **NANCY BRODIE**

Two Good Men

THE UNITED STATES GOVERNMENT GENEROUSLY FINANCED THIS BOOK

Our gratitude goes to the Department of Justice, which liberally provided the office, the typewriter, the word processor, the supplies and the library that made it possible.

TABLE OF CONTENTS

Decency, security, and liberty alike demand that government officials shall be subjected to the same rules of conduct that are commands to the citizen. In a government of laws, existence of the government will be imperiled if it fails to observe the law scrupulously. Our government is the potent, the omnipresent teacher. For good or for ill, it teaches the whole people by its example. Crime is contagious. If the government becomes a lawbreaker, it breeds contempt for law; it invites every man to become a law unto himself; it invites anarchy. . . .

Supreme Court Justice Louis Brandeis
Olmstead v. United States, 277 U.S. 438, 485 (1928)

FOREWORD

We have lost our country. If you don't know that, or won't believe it, you either don't know what's going on, or you don't want to. We have lost it to a relatively small gang of immensely powerful totalitarians, whose goal is the total subjugation of the American people in a world government. We have lost it because of our own default. The only question worth asking now is: How can we get it back?

Some people claim to believe we can win it back without risk. They insist on being "respectable" even if it kills them—which it probably will. They really believe—or pretend to—that we American victims can defeat the most awesome power and technology ever assembled, already so close to victory, without facing danger. They meet, don tuxedos, speechify, eat and retreat, convincing themselves that because they have gone through the motions they have accomplished something.

They are Pharisees. They care more for themselves than they do for the Mission. They don't want to get down into the ditch and go toe-to-toe with the enemy, because they might get mud on their shoes. They would have told Patton not to go to Bastogne because he might be attacked. They would have told Jesus to pass the good word, but to be "respectable," to avoid danger; to reject Paul, the jailbird. Or, while the situation continues to degenerate, some fine, immensely patriotic, people continue to believe they have "influence" with an allegedly "conservative" White House which covertly derides them.

This is a fantasy, a dangerous fantasy that is worse than nothing, because it creates the illusion of progress, thereby neutralizing Americans. We are not going to win our country back until enough victims are willing to talk publicly and do something about the instrumentality of the Conspiracy that is at once most dangerous and most vulnerable.

Which instrumentality is that? You can talk about the U.N., the National Debt, Washington corruption or Afghanistan all day without repercussions. Yes, they are all very important; but they are just legs on the bug. They are not the bug itself. Chances are you would not be ruined financially if you complain about them. You would not be thrown into prison.

On the other hand, those things could well happen to you if you sufficiently expose the machinations of our friends at the Internal Revenue Service, who presently are using the income tax to transform and subvert our government from a republic of strictly limited powers, into a world Socialist dictatorship in which the Constitution would be cancelled and all American rights annulled. How important is a disaster even as genuinely important as Nicaragua besides this? What good to us would freedom be in Nicaragua, if we lose ours?

As we shall see, the power-lusters who threaten our liberty now, daily break laws with impunity. Indeed, they have turned our God-ordained government into the greatest lawbreaker in history, a totalitarian juggernaut that makes the Mafia look sick. As we shall see, they take children hostage, drive businessmen to ruin, routinely commit perjury, pervert the courts, spit at the Bill of Rights—and even terrorize Congress.

Could a battle with such an enemy be won without taking risks and facing danger? Much easier could George III have been persuaded to see reason. If the advocates of "meet, eat and retreat" lack the courage to quit playing at revolution, the least they could do if they have the principles they claim, is to pay silent homage to people who have what they don't. Instead, they whisper to each other that Congressman George Hansen, for instance—whom U.S. marshals kidnapped on April 15, 1987 on behalf of I.R.S.—is "not respectable." Typically, they don't even have the courage to say it out loud.

Along these lines, consider the hypocrites at the other end of the spectrum in the American Civil Liberties Union. They pride themselves on protecting people from governmental oppression. Does a rapist or a Nazi have a problem? The A.C.L.U. is there. However, the A.C.L.U. hypocrites have not a word to say about this severest threat to liberty in the history of our nation. Indeed, on one occasion Ramona Ripston, then head of the influential Southern California chapter of A.C.L.U., told your reporter's national radio audience, in response to a question about the discrepancy, that her organization was considering it. We have yet to hear from A.C.L.U., and don't expect to.

Why is the income tax so important to the power-lusters? This book will answer that among many other questions. It will prove the true purpose of the income tax in what we call Taxscam. It will prove, from the mouths of the collectivists themselves, that the income tax is not needed to finance the government. It will prove, from the mouths of Congress and the Supreme Court, what kind of tax it is. It will prove that, while the tax the Congress passed is legal—if the Sixteenth Amendment was ratified, which we doubt—the Internal Revenue Service's administration of that legal tax is illegal. It will prove that very few Americans are subject to the tax.

More important than anything else, this book will show you how we can win our country back, by way of a sensible program to restore the law and to bind down with the chains of the Constitution an agency that is the closest thing to a gestapo America has ever had, and is getting closer every day.

PREFACE

The income tax is dead. If you are suffering from a jeopardy assessment, or a lien, or a midnight raid, or some other Internal Revenue Service outrage as you read this, you may well find that hard to believe; but, it's true. Indeed, we believe that the present outrages are symptoms of the system's demise. It's dead, but, like the dinosaurs, it has a pea brain and a primitive nervous system, which is taking too long to send the message. It's dead, but doesn't know it; and its death throes make it more dangerous than it was when alive.

How did it die? It committed suicide. It died because its administrators—the Internal Revenue Service and the Department of Justice—perverted it into something the Congress never intended it to be. It died because the Treasury Department encouraged the collection of a tax that is different from the tax the Constitution permits—different and, therefore, illegal. It was Lincoln who said that no enemy soldier would ever take a drink from the Ohio; that if we die we shall die by our own hand, by suicide, by usurpation. The trouble is that not enough Americans know this yet. Not enough Americans realize that, as in "The Invasion of the Body Snatchers," the income tax has been secretly supplanted; that it looks like itself, but isn't.

That is the rationale of this book. It will conduct an autopsy on the corpse, to show you how and why it was replaced. When enough Americans understand, they will bury it. There is hope. Political commentators tell us that our country is divided today as never before; divided by race, by religion and politics, even by gender. Those divisions disappear in the face of the so-called "income tax," which has a unifying effect even more influential than World War Two. Then, people boasted about how much income tax they had paid—when they were galvanized by wholesome, patriotic feeling, and when the tax had only recently been perverted. Today, it is not easy to find someone who speaks of the so-called "income tax" without sneering. People who have worked on the inside tell us that even I.R.S. workers hate I.R.S. The obvious exceptions include Communists and other Socialists; limousine liberals who feed at the tax trough; I.R.S. officials; some C.P.A.s; and other beneficiaries of the perversion's Socialist largesse. These include Fortune 500 companies ("Socialism for the rich"), and poverty officials ("Socialism for the poor").

Indeed, the swelling ranks of those Americans who have stopped filing returns—because they have discovered they never had to—is another proof of our thesis. Our friends at I.R.S. call these scores of millions the Tax Rebellion; but this book will prove that the Tax Rebellion—an organized, willful refusal to obey tax laws—is the Internal Revenue Service; and that the "tax rebels" are top officials of I.R.S., the Department of Justice and the courts; along with the totalitarian, Socialist billionaires who control them.

To neutralize discontent, and to exacerbate the problem, they permitted passage of the Reagan "reforms," which, as we write—in the fall of 1987—are percolating through the economy. We believe that this "solution," however well meant, will turn out to be worse than the problem it was allegedly designed to "solve," because it sets the stage for another tax increase—and another and another—without the protection of deductions, many of which are gone. Already the chill wind from Washington brings word of new taxes, including Ronald Reagan's acquiescence in a tax increase after the biggest stock market crash in history. When this latest betrayal hits the people's pocketbooks, the movement to restore the law will explode even more.

The reader has seen that, from time to time, we use the term "income tax," inside quotation marks. When we do, we refer to the imaginary tax I.R.S. has concocted, as opposed to the tax the

Congress passed. A word should also be said about the cases and other documents we refer to. As your obedient servant sat in various law libraries for many months, we found ourselves gasping over page after page, wondering whether the people would believe it. The things we refer to should be easily accessible—most of them. Please go and see for yourself. They tell the story of perhaps the biggest fraud ever perpetrated.

This book makes just one claim: When you finish, you will finally understand. It offers no legal advice, except to encourage you to pay all the taxes the law requires you to pay, and to file all the forms the law requires you to file. Indeed, it shows you how to restore the law—the law on the books that has been perverted.

Welcome to Alice In Revenueland—where things are not what they seem.

The Internal Revenue Record

AND

CUSTOMS JOURNAL.

VOLUME XIII.—NUMBER 4. WHOLE NUMBER 317. | NEW YORK, SATURDAY, JANUARY 28, 1871. | FIVE DOLLARS A YEAR.

Register of U. S. Official Revenue and Customs Decisions.

W. C. & F. P. CHURCH, 39 Park Row, N. Y.

THE INTERNAL REVENUE RECORD AND CUSTOMS JOURNAL publishes OFFICIALLY, every Saturday, for the guidance of Government officers and taxpayers, the latest Internal Revenue and Customs Decisions, Regulations, and Law Reports.

TERMS—Five dollars per annum; three dollars for six months.

A few sets of the back volumes from I. to XI.—from April, 1865, to July, 1870—for sale, bound, at $40 a set.

THE *United States Jurist* is the title of a monthly law periodical which makes its appearance in Washington with the opening of the new year. James Schouler is the editor, and W. H. & O. H. Morrison are the publishers.

THE Secretary of the Treasury, in a letter to the Collector of Customs of New York, relative to the proper rate of duty to be assessed on rum, gin, and whiskey imported into the United States since January 1, 1871, says:

The act of July 14, 1870, imposes a duty of two dollars per proof gallon on brandy and on other spirits manufactured and distilled from grain or other material and "not otherwise provided for." The question presented is as to what the words "not otherwise provided for," in this paragraph, include; and it the opinion of the Department that they apply only to the "other spirits" manufactured or distilled from grain and other material, and that, consequently, brandy of first proof is entitled to entry at two dollars a gallon; but that rum, gin, and whiskey being specially provided for by name in the act of March 3, 1865, which imposes thereon fifty cents a gallon in addition to the duties imposed by the act of June 30, 1864, which were "on other spirits manufactured or distilled from grain or other materials for first proof two dollars per gallon." are excluded from the said act of July 14, 1870, and are liable to duty at the rate of $2 50 a gallon under the said acts of 1864 and 1865 before mentioned, and you will be governed accordingly in securing the duties at those rates on all entries of rum, gin, and whiskey passed at your port since the 1st instant.

TREASURY DEPARTMENT.

OFFICIAL—PUBLISHED BY AUTHORITY.

OFFICE OF INTERNAL REVENUE.

ALFRED PLEASONTON, COMMISSIONER.

THE INCOME TAX.

THE following letters on the subject of the repeal of the income tax have been addressed by the Commissioner of Internal Revenue to the chairman of the Committee of Ways and Means of the House of Representatives:

OFFICE OF INTERNAL REVENUE,
WASHINGTON, Jan. 20, 1871.

Hon. Samuel Hooper, Chairman of Ways and Means Committee.

SIR: In view of the very general discussion by the public at large of the income tax, and of the introduction in Congress of several measures looking to its repeal, and presuming that the formal consideration of the subject may shortly arise in your honorable committee, I deem it not improper briefly to express to the committee, through you, the conclusions which I have myself reached. I regard the tax as the one of all others most obnoxious to the genius of our people, being inquisitorial in its nature and dragging into public view an exposition of the most private pecuniary affairs of the citizen. Such an exposition can only be compulsorily effected, through a maintenance of the most expensive machinery, and both the nature of the tax and the means necessarily employed for its enforcement appear to be regarded by the better class of citizens with more and more disfavor from year to year. It is furthermore most difficult of exact statement, and especially in large business examinations and where long periods of time are involved in extended commercial affairs. There is some question as to its constitutionality, but as to that I express no opinion. The amount derived from that service has, under the legislation already had, been greatly diminished, and I am so well satisfied that the evils more than counterbalance the benefits derived from its longer retention that I recommend its unconditional repeal.

I have the honor to be very respectfully your obedient servant,

A. PLEASONTON, Commissioner.

OFFICE OF INTERNAL REVENUE,
WASHINGTON, Jan. 25, 1871.

Hon. Samuel Hooper, Chairman Committee Ways and Means.

SIR: I have the honor to transmit herewith an approximate estimate of the annual receipts from income under act of July 14, 1870, based on the average returns of the last four years. The number of persons assessed for income in each of the classes below named, as returned to this office by the assessors of the several collection districts, from 1867 to 1870 inclusive is as follows:

First-class tax, $20 or less—In 1867, 101,219; in 1868, 100,558; in 1869, 107,997; in 1870, 112,424; average, 105,550.

Second-class tax, over $20 and not over $50—In 1867, 68,680; in 1868, 55,949; in 1869, 69,184; in 1870, 68,501; average, 65,578.

Third-class tax, over $50 and not over $100—In 1867, 40,899; in 1868, 38,957; in 1869, 41,196; in 1870, 40,484; average, 40,449.

Fourth-class tax, over $100 and not over $500—In 1867, 46,055; in 1868, 51,188; in 1869, 45,002; in 1870, 44,496; average, 46,685.

Fifth-class tax, over $500—In 1867, 9,282; in 1868, 7,965; in 1869, 9,464; in 1870, 9,243; average, 8,988.

Total—In 1867, 266,135; in 1868, 254,617; in 1869, 272,843; in 1870, 275,248, exclusive of the returns of the Eleventh district of New York, not yet received; average, 267,210.

These returns are made under the act of March 2, 1867, which provides that the amount of exemption shall be $1,000. The first two classes are entirely relieved from tax under the act of July 14, 1870, by the raising of the exemption from $1,000 to $2,000. If we suppose the average tax of the first class to be $15, and of the second class $40 per head, we have 105,550 at $15, $1,583,250; 65,578 persons at $40, $2,623,120—a total of $4,206,370 as the aggregate tax lost on the first and second classes. Each person in the three remaining classes will pay $50 less per annum under $2,000 exemption than under $1,000 exemption; then, losing $50 each on 96,082 persons, $4,804,100 is lost in the third, fourth, and fifth classes, which, added to $4,206,370, gives $9,010,470, the aggregate tax lost on incomes, "salary tax excepted," by the change in the amount of exemption.

After reducing this half, for the change in the rate of tax, there remains $8,369,794 as the aggregate tax from individuals under act of July 14, 1870. The aggregate five per cent. tax returned on the dividends and additions to surplus funds of banks, railroad companies, etc., enumerated in sections 120 and 122 act of June 30, 1864,

1

THE NATURE OF THE BEAST

The Internal Revenue Service thrives on outrage. Injustice is the life-blood of the so-called "income tax." From time to time, someone exposes the crimes of I.R.S. From time to time, there are hearings in Congress. Not only do our friends at I.R.S. not fear such exposure; they welcome it. It feeds the terror they want you to feel. Are you aware of any basic change—just one—such exposure has inspired? On the contrary, the more terrible our friends at I.R.S. are shown to be, the better they like it. So it is that every year, in February and March, you read a new crop of stories about victims whom I.R.S. is throwing into prison for so-called "tax crimes." You are not reading real journalism. You are reading press releases prepared by our friends at I.R.S. As your reporter sets this down, they are preparing the roster of the Class of '88.

In any other controversy, from Watergate to Abscam to Iranamok, the Prostitute National Press superficially covers all the issues at tedious length. Every day, you hear speculation by certified pundits about who didn't know what, and when he didn't know it. Eventually, the weight of detail produces stupor. When the issue is income tax, however, the media behave like the Nazi press when Dr. Goebbels "requested" that something be printed. All you need do is look at the coverage, to see the biggest transformation of lions into lambs since Isaiah. Everything calculated to inspire fear is broadcast. Everything involving unafraid Americans winning victories is suppressed. Not a word is ever printed about what the law really says. Not a word is broadcast about the *details* of the Reign of Terror.

Since horror stories in a book about the income tax are obligatory, and since your obedient servant is exactly that, here are some horror stories, stories they haven't told you.

Our friends at I.R.S. assessed a $500 penalty against Charles P. Streich, of Elwood, Illinois, allegedly for filing a so-called "frivolous" W-4. Mr. Streich, it should be said in passing, was married and had three young children, including an infant who was ten months old, when I.R.S. hit the fan. He was also a veteran of the Vietnam War, during which he won a Bronze Star, a National Defense Medal, a Navy Unit Commendation and a Vietnam Campaign ribbon. Then he worked at Caterpillar Tractor, in Joliet, Illinois, for ten years. He had been on layoff for more than a year, on June 14, 1983, when an old, unmarked, green car, containing five people in plain clothes, pulled into his driveway.

The five were I.R.S. agents, but they did not identify themselves. Mrs. Streich started screaming. Her four-year-old, Johnny, mysteriously developed a bloody nose. Charles Streich noticed that at least one of the unidentified strangers was armed, and this was a neighborhood in which there had been numerous incidents of violent crime. In just the few months prior to this I.R.S. invasion, there had been four multiple murders.

Mr. Streich armed himself with an AR-15, just in case. Even the Special Agents themselves testified that he did not point it at them, but Mr. Streich was arrested. At the trial, his semi-automatic AR-15 showed up with M-16 parts; our friends at I.R.S. presumably had arranged for someone to alter it. Victim Streich was convicted of assault and possession of an unregistered machine gun.

Every aspect of the government's case reeked of criminality. The law under which the I.R.S. agents tried to collect that $500 penalty was the Economic Recovery Tax Act of 1981, the $500 penalty provision of which took effect on January 1, 1982. The trouble is that Mr. Streich had filed the W-4 at issue during 1981, *before* the law took effect.

Andrew B. Spiegel, Mr. Streich's attorney, wrote as follows in the appeal: "Under what has become known as TEFRA, Congress empowered the I.R.S. to act as judge, jury and executioner by allowing I.R.S. personnel to determine whether a particular form is false, whether the $500 civil penalty is warranted and if so, whether the I.R.S. should seize a person's wages, automobiles, bank accounts or other property to satisfy the $500 penalty. Each of those determinations was made without a judicial determination and without a judicial hearing, the right to confront witnesses, to have a trial by jury as required by the Seventh Amendment or to have a day in court."

Yet, Mr. Streich wound up convicted of two felonies, because unidentified I.R.S. agents had arrived in an unmarked car to enforce a law that didn't yet exist, and would be illegal anyway; while the government agents who had committed the felony of manufacturing evidence—the doctored rifle—were not charged.

On October 28, 1983, Assistant District Counsel Gerald Leland wrote a letter for I.R.S. District Counsel Robert F. Cunningham, to Glenn Archer, Assistant Attorney General, Tax Division, Department of Justice, Washington, D.C., to the attention of the Criminal Section. The letter concerned a South Dakota businessman, and Leland said this: "You should note that some of the evidence contained in the exhibits to the special agent's report was received by the special agent from inspectors of the United States Postal Service. . . . The exhibits are not intended to be introduced in the criminal trial, and they should not be disclosed to anyone outside the Department of Justice and the Internal Revenue Service. To disclose the above-referenced exhibits could jeopardize a confidential source, as well as expose an undercover investigative technique."

This boils down to mean that the government is illegally looking at your mail. If they were doing it legally, they wouldn't have to hide it, and you can bet they would have planned to introduce it at the trial. Remember that in our great system the government has no more rights than you do. That is the case, because the only powers it has are the ones you delegate. Do you have the power to read someone else's mail? Isn't that a serious felony? Notice that Post Office people are accessories to the crime.

Along these lines, a San Francisco man says our friends at I.R.S. grabbed his $1,300 mortgage check, changed it and cashed it. How could they do that without reading his mail? Victim Donald Thurow owed no taxes, and our friends at I.R.S. never claimed he did. A story printed in *The Washington Times* on April 28, 1987 tells us this: "Mr. Thurow mailed his mortgage check to California Federal in Los Angeles last July 2. After being notified that his payment was late, Mr. Thurow discovered that his check had cleared the bank on which it was drawn, Hibernia. The check had 'Internal Revenue Service' stamped on the payee line—over Mr. Thurow's handwritten 'California Federal.'" At last word, Mr. Thurow's lawyer, Montie Day, of Oakland, had filed suit to get the money back. What would the government do to you if you stole a check from the U.S. mail, rewrote it to yourself and cashed it?

Suppose you thought someone owed you money, so, to put pressure on him, you held someone else's children hostage. What would the government do to you? The answer is that you would be thrown into a jail so deep, your family would have to visit you in a diving bell. Day after day, the media would explain, rightly, what a bad man you are.

On November 28, 1984, at about 4 P.M., a couple of cars containing seven or eight armed I.R.S. agents from Detroit arrived at Engleworld, a day-care center in suburban Allen Park. They brought a locksmith, who changed all the locks, so that no one but the agents could get in or out. Isn't this a violation of the fire laws, especially where children are involved? Meanwhile, the agents hustled most of the twenty children into Room C, sealed it and put a table across the door. When the unsuspecting parents and grandparents arrived to get their children, they found our friends from I.R.S. sitting at the table, demanding that they sign Notices of Levy and pay what they owed Engleworld—so that the agents could confiscate it to satisfy the day-care center's alleged $14,000 tax liability. The agents made clear that, until they did so, the parents could not have their kids.

Did you hear about this outrage on the network news; on the national wires; in the big magazines and newspapers? Neither did we. The Prostitute National Press bombed again.

Sue Stoia was one of the parents. She went to Engleworld to pick up Catherine, her seven-year-old daughter. According to a story by Greg Kaza, in the *Wyandotte News-Herald*, of January 16, 1985, Mrs. Stoia said this: "They indicated you could not take your child out of the building until you had settled your debt with the school, and you did that by signing a form to pay the I.R.S. What we were facing was a hostage-type situation. They were using the children as collateral."

Catherine Rawson was another Engleworld parent, coming to get her daughter, Carla, nine. Mrs. Rawson says the agents demanded payment "on the spot." The children "were crying. It was apparent they were extremely afraid over what was occurring. I'm extremely resentful that they subjected these children to the kind of action you would only be subjected to in a police state. In retrospect, I'm sorry now that I let them intimidate me as they did."

Marilyn Derby was the Director of Engleworld, and was our guest on our radio talk show. She said this: "It was a very scary situation, like the *Gestapo* was here. Children were crying. Parents were trembling. I told one woman whose hands were shaking that she shouldn't sign anything she didn't want to. She signed anyway."

No one at I.R.S. was punished. For all we know, the raiders were rewarded. Engleworld was closed. The victimized parents no doubt innocently spread word through the community about what I.R.S. will do to you if your day-care center allegedly owes taxes.

The reader may wonder what your reporter would have done as an Engleworld parent. Among other things, we would have called their bluff and told them to keep our children. We suspect the situation would have degenerated into a sequel to "The Ransom of Red Chief," especially after a couple of grocery bills.

Ed Lambert has a doctorate in economics. He has run a plastics company. He is a C.P.A., whose Hollywood company's clients included Tom Jones, Engelbert Humperdinck and others like them. Ed Lambert paid $2.2 million in personal income taxes in 1977-79. Yes, Pilgrim, you read that right: $2.2 million! In 1986-87, Ed Lambert was a convicted felon at the federal prison in Terminal Island, California. Why? One of Dr. Lambert's returns included a mistake amounting to $6,000. Remember, he had paid $2.2 million over the three years, so his mistake amounted to a little more than .002727% of what he had paid.

Dr. Lambert offered to pay the $6,000, or $12,000, or any multiple of those numbers the government chose to take. He was refused. The government's answer was: "We want you." Dr. Lambert has it in writing. As usual, our friends at I.R.S. wanted to send his clients a message. Dr. Lambert tells your reporter that he received many messages of support in prison, but the writers were afraid to put their return addresses on the envelopes. They didn't know that all incoming mail is opened and read by the authorities.

In the spring of 1987, Senate Finance subcommittees conducted hearings on a proposed "taxpayers' bill of rights." Among other things, the legislation wanted to shift the burden of proof from the people to the Internal Revenue Service in most court proceedings, and limit I.R.S. power to seize property. It also proposed preventing I.R.S. from promoting employees on the basis of their collections. On April 21, 1987, I.R.S. Commissioner Lawrence Gibbs testified before the Senate Finance Subcommittees on Private Retirement Plans and Oversight of the I.R.S. Gibbs strongly criticized the proposal to hold I.R.S. employees personally liable for the deprivation of any rights secured by the Constitution. What's wrong with holding government officials responsible when they violate your rights? Isn't such responsibility a basic element of the American idea? Gibbs also attacked a proposal that I.R.S. be required to issue the Miranda warning in any civil case, whether or not there is an indication of fraud. This raises the question of whether our friends at I.R.S. are trying to collect taxes, or to trick Americans into prison. If you still don't know the answer, you will when you finish this book. Such a provision is necessary, because our friends at I.R.S. love to launch a "friendly, civil" investigation, and then suddenly metastasize it into a criminal proceeding.

At another hearing in June, the subcommittee produced a memo from an I.R.S. field branch chief, which suggested that he would promote employees according to the number of seizures they had made. This of course is a violation of written I.R.S. policy. Rose Gutfeld reported in *The Wall Street Journal* on June 23, 1987 that the memo came from Baltimore, and was dated February 17, 1987. In it, the manager complained about low numbers of referrals to criminal investigations and seizures: "Your midyear evaluations will be prepared in approximately one and one-half months. You will be evaluated on your accomplishments or lack of accomplishments. Need I say more?" Our friends at I.R.S. routinely deny they have a quota system. As you can see, they lie. Indeed, for about twelve years, John Hargett, a C.P.A., was a Revenue Agent in Tupelo, Mississippi. He confirms there is a quota system in I.R.S. He was also President of the local chapter of the National Treasury Employees Union, but because he opposes such things as quotas he was driven from his job.

Among the witnesses was Pennsylvania businessman Thomas Treadway. The agent said he owed the government $247,000, so our friends at I.R.S. seized his *girl friend's* farm and bank accounts. She had to borrow to feed her horses. Mr. Treadway himself was ruined. Later, I.R.S. said he had owed nothing after all; but, at last word, our friends at I.R.S. were threatening to nail him again.

In the Believe It Or Not department, Rose Gutfeld reports that Robert Brown, a 26-year I.R.S. veteran, testified that "his performance evaluation as an instructor suffered after he urged employees to be courteous to taxpayers." Would you have believed that courtesy is against I.R.S. policy? It is. Are we dealing with a tax collector, or with a mad dog?

Subcommittee Chairman Senator David Pryor, of Arkansas, a chief sponsor of the "taxpayers' bill of rights," said "that some lawmakers declined to help sponsor the bill out of fear that they would be audited."

So, Senator Pryor himself admits that *our friends at I.R.S. even have intimidated Congress*. That is why nothing substantial ever comes from such hearings. Congress conducts them once in a while, to let the people blow off steam. Then, our friends at I.R.S. return to their crimes.

Along these lines, there is the truly incredible case of George Hansen, for many years an Idaho Congressman, who is cut from the same cloth as the Founding Fathers. Time after time, when Americans needed help—and when no one else in government would stick his neck out—George was there. George uncovered a scandal in the Immigration and Naturalization Service, in which officials of that agency brought illegal aliens to Idaho farmers, and then nailed those farmers for hiring them.

George flew to Teheran, to try to free the hostages seized at the American Embassy by mobs loyal to the dictator installed by Jimmy Carter. George arranged the Congressional hearings on Iran Khomeini wanted, and Foreign Minister Abolhassan Bani-Sadr said he could take some hostages home as proof of good faith; but Carter queered the arrangement by rejecting hearings, and George went home empty-handed. Later, Chase Manhattan bankers arranged a deal. George told the American people that David Rockefeller and Henry Kissinger, of Chase Manhattan, should have been sitting in the hostages' place.

When the State of Nebraska threw Pastor Everett Sileven into jail for using "uncertified" teachers in the Faith Baptist Church, in Louisville, George Hansen went there to help. No other national, political leaders did so, even after the State Police invaded the Church, where about seventy preachers from around the country were on their knees praying. The police picked the preachers up, carried them out, threw them on the lawn—and *padlocked* the church. Typically, the Prostitute National Press squelched the story for a long time. Your reporter gave it substantial coverage, in our daily, nationally syndicated, radio news commentary; and was told by many listeners with vehemence that no such outrage had happened or could happen in America.

More specifically for our present purpose, George Hansen also exposed not just the crimes, but the internal machinations, of our friends at I.R.S.; in his lectures, in interviews, in a best-selling book entitled *To Harass Our People* (Washington, D.C., Positive Publications, 1984). They decided to destroy George, no matter how long it took.

On April 15, 1987, your obedient servant was back at the Louisville church, to preach at an annual conference on liberty organized by Dr. Sileven. So was George. After his message, George returned from the telephone to tell the congregation that he had just talked with his wife, Connie, back in northern Virginia, outside Washington, and that two U.S. marshals had come to his home. Mrs. Hansen had told them that George was flying home from Omaha that night, and would land at Dulles International after midnight. The marshals had said they would "pick him up and take him home," whatever that meant.

They lied. Don't they always? They arranged for other marshals to arrest George—without the warrant the law requires—as he arrived to board his plane at Eppley Airport in Omaha. They threw George into the Douglas County Jail. The next morning, Dr. Sileven mounted a demonstration of believers around the jail, so the marshals rented a Lear jet at National Airport in Washington, flew to Omaha and back, feasting on gourmet sandwiches while George sat in chains. That little flight cost you $10,000. Remember that Congressman Hansen had been trying to fly back to Washington *at his own expense*. Our friends at I.R.S. didn't let him do it, because *they wanted to lock him up on April 15*. Indeed, they took the risk of illegally seizing him without a warrant, to prevent him from testifying at those hearings on the "taxpayers' bill of rights." George had been planning to do that, which was no surprise since he was the original author of the bill.

Back in Washington, the marshals booked him into the Alexandria City Jail under an assumed name: "Fred Smith." If you thought they did this only in Nazi Germany and Soviet Russia, you were wrong. Congressman Hansen didn't know he was "Fred Smith" for the better part of a day. Neither did his wife and attorney. Later, the marshal in charge explained that he had done it to avoid a repetition of the demonstration in Omaha.

George was thrown into a dark basement cell full of cockroaches and lice, surrounded by drunks who shook with delirium tremens. He had to sleep in a bunk too narrow to contain him, and wear his Omaha coveralls for ten days, until jail officials found clothing that fit. George is 6′6″ tall, and weighed 270 pounds when the daymare began.

Under pressure from Members of Congress, Justice Department officials met with George in the Alexandria, Virginia courthouse. After the meeting, U.S. marshals kept him in a holding cell there for four hours, trying to outwait the press. Later, sixteen Members of Congress wrote as follows to Attorney General Ed Meese, in a letter you will find on page S 7031 of the *Congressional Record* of May 21, 1987: "When it became clear that two of the cameras were not going to leave before Mr. Hansen was transferred, the marshals took Mr. Hansen in chains, but without the leg irons, so that he could be compelled to run to a car in an alley leading to a parking lot behind the courthouse. While this occurred, other marshals pulled a van in front of the television cameras in order to block their view. The car with Mr. Hansen then careened out of the parking lot, tires squealing and nearly colliding with the van. These reckless actions endangered the safety of the TV cameramen, nearby pedestrians, street traffic, the marshal who was trying to coordinate the vehicles in the parking lot, and Mr. Hansen himself. Enclosed is a video tape of the news coverage of this fiasco."

The ostensible reason for all this was a parole violation stemming from a so-called "ethics violation," in which the Congressman had not only cleared all his actions in advance with his own counsel, but also with the attorneys for the House, with whose approval he made some personal, financial arrangements. Indeed, according to page S 7027, of the *Congressional Record* of May 21, 1987, Utah Senator Orrin Hatch explains that the Ethics in Government Act "was never intended to subject any living soul to criminal prosecution." The only punishment in the law is a $5,000 fine. "As for the notion of imposing a criminal penalty, the idea was specifically discussed, debated and rejected by Congress.

One of the early proposals of the act contained a criminal penalty, but it met with such widespread criticism that it was deleted from the final bill. There is virtually no disagreement on this point. Anyone who cares to take the time to talk to persons involved or simply to read the *Congressional Record* will find out with very little effort that Congress intended that the new Ethics Act would not subject government officials to criminal penalties."

In short, Congressman Hansen was imprisoned under a law that contains no criminal penalties. After his conviction, a sizeable bunch of Members of the House rushed to change their "ethics" declarations, but, so far, no one else has been brought to trial, despite daily revelations of truly criminal behavior. Former New York Congresswoman Geraldine Ferraro, whose ties to the Mob rival the Godfather's, defied the ethics committee and spit at the law, unlike George. She did so with impunity and went home to sulk.

What about George's "parole violation?" One of the conditions of parole required him to make a living. Another forbade him to leave the Washington, D.C. area. However, George makes his living these days by lecturing around the country, so something had to give. He told the Parole Commission, "If I have to be limited to the area of Alexandria, Virginia, I then am unable to carry out my responsibilities. Take me back to prison, because I cannot comply with this." He noted on the permanent parole certificate that he couldn't obey the terms; to which the Board replied that he should find other work.

The real reason for these outrages was George's exposure of the machinations of our friends at I.R.S. Already in 1976, they were revealing the information on his tax returns to his opponent in his race for reelection to the House. Need we add that such an impropriety is a felony? Paul DesFosses, for almost twenty years an I.R.S. agent, who retired as senior revenue agent in eastern Idaho, confirms that our friends at I.R.S. handed the information to the wife of George's opponent, and did so at I.R.S. headquarters. Ten days before the election, the government announced that George was not properly paying his taxes. Criminal investigators from I.R.S. went to work. The publicity almost caused George's defeat. Later, there were a couple of years of audits. Finally the government was forced to send Congressman Hansen a refund of $10,000. Don't you wish you had been there when they put the check into the mail?

George Hansen told your reporter this: "There is a desperate struggle for the right to privacy. Any Congressman who gets in the way of cradle-to-the-grave falls out of favor. He doesn't even have to be a Republican. They leaked Senator Montoya's taxes to the *Washington Post*. After the election, it turned out his taxes were in order. They ruined Senator Long. Congressman Ken Gray, of Illinois, and Congressman Jack McDonald, of Michigan, denied I.R.S. a computer center in Detroit. The next morning, they got notices of audit by telegram."

Meanwhile, the chances are excellent that your local Internal Revenue "Service Center" is riddled with petty crime. A story in the *Los Angeles Times* on April 15, 1983, said as follows: "In the 1982 fiscal year ended last September 30, I.R.S. employee transgressions included embezzlements, thefts and bribe acceptances, as well as the wholesale discovery of a group of 250 seasonal workers at a Georgia service center who were wrongly collecting state unemployment checks."

In 1986, a local television station uncovered the widespread use of cocaine and other narcotics at the huge I.R.S. headquarters in Fresno. If you are a private citizen who deals in coke, you should expect to be locked up. Not if you work for I.R.S. Paul DesFosses tells your reporter that our friends at I.R.S. also burned his house down, to persuade him to desist from his revelations.

As your reporter sets this down, our friends at I.R.S. are pushing to require banks to report all cash transactions of $3,000 or more. With many such transactions, you would be investigated secretly. Under the recent Reagan "reform," you must file a tax compliance certificate with I.R.S. to get a passport. This of course is unconstitutional. The Supreme Court has ruled under the Fifth Amendment that the right to travel is inviolable, but the Reagan "reform" says otherwise. Also under the law, children over four must have Social Security numbers, without which you are forbidden to deduct them as dependents.

For more than thirty years, our friends at I.R.S. have been pushing for a system without returns, in which they would simply assess your taxes, and deduct them from your accounts. If you don't like what they do, you could appeal. This change is now well in the works, and it was the allegedly "conservative" Reagan Administration that finally gave them the funding.

Indeed, now they are pushing for federal identity cards, that would contain your Social Security, driver's license, passport and credit card numbers; along with insurance and medical information—and your fingerprints, handprints, retina patterns, voice prints and signature. Whatever you do, the government would know. Along these lines, the Senate passed a bill entitled, "The Computer Matching and Privacy Protection Act of 1987," which, typically, would further crush your privacy. It would allow federal agencies to crossmatch their computer records with other federal, state and even local data banks. With strong backing from the Reagan Administration, it passed the Senate by a voice vote, and when your reporter set this down, in the fall of 1987, a House version was in the works.

Indeed, your reporter forced the government to reveal in court that it had been subjecting him to criminal investigation since 1966, so you are reading a book by a man who was under criminal investigation for twenty one years, and no doubt still is. The print-out the government reluctantly delivered was in I.R.S. code, but we are now able to decode it. In that official record, our friends at I.R.S. had your reporter already married to his wife in 1966, when she was still a child, an arrangement that would have sent her father looking for your intrepid correspondent with a shotgun.

In the face of all this, Attorney General Ed Meese has reversed a long-standing policy. Reporter Ronald Ostrow wrote in the *Los Angeles Times* on August 13, 1986 (Part I, page 18), that henceforth, F.B.I. and federal drug agents, U.S. marshals and other Justice Department employees who lose court judgments over actions taken in the "the line of duty," will be reimbursed. The decision "seeks to still fears of agents who hesitate to take 'reasonable' actions against suspects and others that might lead to suits against them, department officials said."

This boils down to mean that our friends at I.R.S. can intensify their reign of terror against you, with even more impunity than they enjoyed before. Why should someone be reimbursed for denying your rights; for breaking the law; for violating the Constitution? Indeed, the harsh fact is that the "conservative" Reagan Administration has given our friends at I.R.S. considerably more power—totalitarian power—than did any of its predecessors. Protected by the benign imprimatur of Ronald Reagan, they are using the laws on conspiracy and mail fraud—under which anyone can be charged with anything for making a telephone call, conducting a conversation or mailing a letter—and the Racketeer-Influenced and Corrupt Organizations (R.I.C.O.) Act, to steal property and throw Americans into prison. Anything goes, the vaguer the "better." The *Communist Manifesto* preaches the theft of property of people who oppose Marx. With the implementation of these policies, all the planks of the *Manifesto* now have been installed as the official, public policy of the United States.

The fact that some genuine criminals no doubt are being jailed is irrelevant; akin to the famous paradox in which Hitler loved his dog. No doubt Hitler too locked up some genuine criminals. The truth is found in the rule, not the exception; in the effect of such policies on the people, not the criminals; in the direction we are going. The purpose of law is to protect the innocent, even more than it is to punish the guilty.

Consider the well-known "war on drugs." For many years, your obedient servant supported the harshest possible criminal penalties for pushers. As your reporter sets this down, accusations that top U.S. government officials themselves have been pushers all that time, are starting to surface. Is this standard Soviet "disinformation?" Is it true to some extent? We don't know. We do know that former Green Beret Colonel Bo Gritz says he has a videotape that proves it. We do know that the more the "war on drugs" is fought, the more drugs—and the more profits—there are. Indeed, the worst aspect of the "war" is the fact that our liberties are being crippled in its name. The "war on drugs" is one of the biggest reasons cited to justify currency controls; the approaching new currency itself, allegedly designed to flush out the "underground economy"; the destruction of bank privacy; and restrictions on travel, such as searches at airports, not for bombs but for financial instruments. The trouble is that the multi-national pushers are aware of all this and have their own aircraft and ships. They are not going to trundle their merchandise wholesale through Miami International. Instead, the Administration's totalitarian policies will hit Mom and Pop. There was no drug problem when there were no drug laws.

The people are displeased. In a letter to a Congressman, dated December 20, 1982, Tully Miller, Acting District Director for I.R.S. in Georgia, wrote as follows: "Recently, employees in our Augusta office were subjected to disturbances and harassment by protesters who came in mass to our office. Twice, they had to be removed by the local police. Our agent who is coordinating the investigation in the Augusta area was subjected to late night telephone calls and was visited at his home by a group at 1:30 A.M. Also, unordered merchandise is being received through the mail by employees in the Augusta office." Such deliveries apparently can range from pornography to a couple of yards of gravel dumped in a driveway by an unsuspecting dealer who sends a bill.

Threats and assaults against I.R.S. agents in recent years have been increasing. Indeed, we know of three executions. Were there more? In the fall of 1983, Buffalo I.R.S. agent Michael Dillon tried to seize property to satisfy a $1,600 lien. He was killed by three shots from a rifle, allegedly fired by a man who had worked for I.R.S. Is that what is meant by "poetic justice?"

In 1984, a citizen who apparently had had enough broke into Cleveland I.R.S. headquarters and began shooting at random. A tax collector was killed.

On the morning of August 12, 1984, at 6:30, Miss Heidi Berg, a program analyst at I.R.S. headquarters in Washington, D.C., was jogging in northern Virginia, when she was assassinated. According to the police, she was shot six times. Before she became a program analyst, Miss Berg had been a Revenue Officer at the I.R.S. field operations office in Virginia. Informed sources there say she asked to be transferred "after receiving death threats related to her job."

No doubt all this is why your local "I.R.S. Servicenter" is protected by as much security as a U.S. Army base, and resembles the headquarters of an occupying power, which, in a painfully real sense, it is. We said earlier that our friends at I.R.S. revel in stories about what they do to you in court. They don't like stories about what you do to them. That is why you may be hearing them now for the first time. Such stories tend to tarnish the carefully burnished myth of their invincibility, and could give copy cats ideas. Needless to say, we tell them here for no such purpose. We tell them only because the Prostitute National Press, always grovelling before government, has not told them; and because "the people have a right to know."

Permit us to conclude this brief introduction with a quiz. Who said this?: "Thirty and forty years ago, you didn't hear people brag at social get-togethers about how they got their tax bill down by exploiting this loophole and engineering that credit. But now you do. And it's not considered bad behavior. After all, goes this thinking, what's immoral about cheating a system that is itself a cheat? That isn't a sin, it's a duty.

"Our federal tax system is, in short, utterly impossible, utterly unjust, and completely counter-productive. It's earned a rebellion, and it's time we rebelled."

As you see, the man who said this is not at all an extreme moderate, like your obedient servant. We can guarantee that such a statement would routinely be introduced as evidence by the prosecution, in any Soviet-style income tax show trial. Was the man who said it a "tax rebel," or an "illegal tax protester?" Someone in prison? Someone the President has said should be there?

No, the author of this inflammatory statement—unlike anything your diffident reporter would ever say—was the President himself. He said it in the Capitol Building, in Williamsburg, Virginia, on May 30, 1985, when he introduced his proposed "reforms." Is the President a "tax rebel?" Does this remarkable endorsement by the President himself mean that "tax rebellion" is now officially accepted? Remember that our friends at I.R.S. no doubt would call the nation's Founding Fathers "illegal tax protesters," because Jefferson and Henry and the other mighty men of valor took military action against taxes—taxes so low that we, today, struggling half the year and more to pay ours, would welcome the colonial tax burden as perfect liberty.

The trouble is that the Reagan "reform" changed nothing basic; and, as we have seen, will soon exacerbate the problem. Is that why our friends at I.R.S. suddenly reversed themselves and allowed it to pass? The trouble with the so-called "income tax" is too basic, too chronic and degenerative, to be solved by mere cutting and pasting. Major surgery is needed to excise this important element of the biggest fraud in history.

2

ILLEGITIMATE ANCESTRY

In 1894, Congress gave us an income tax. Why? Did Washington need the money? Would our wonderful, God-ordained government have collapsed without it? No, on the contrary, not only did Washington *not* need the money; the fact is that, before the income tax, one of Washington's big worries was what to do with all the money that was pouring in. That's right! Before the income tax, the federal government usually took in more tax money than it could figure out how to use.

Of course, that was before somebody decided that Washington could solve every problem from dandruff to loneliness. Frightening newspaper cartoons showed a bloated beast labelled, "Surplus Monster," about to crush the Congress. The emergency was real. A way was needed to protect our government from the rising tax tide before it was engulfed.

Since the income tax, Washington has accumulated more than a two-trillion dollar debt; and that's just the *official* figure. If you add such unfunded liabilities as Social Security, which you should, the unofficial debt adds up to several times as much. This proves that the income tax wasn't needed to run the government. Indeed, since we had little or no debt without the income tax, and a gargantuan debt with it, you can make a good case that the income tax is one of the reasons our government today is going broke. The higher the tax, the bigger the debt; the lower the tax, the smaller the debt. The reason is that today's typical Congressman is dedicated to spending us into bankruptcy to win brownie points for himself. He does it and lies about it, even passing resolutions and legislation against it, which he promptly ignores. We shall have more to say about this later, when we discuss the proper financing of government.

Harvard Professor F. W. Taussig was also Chairman of the U.S. Tariff Commission, so he was a first-hand expert on the nation's revenues. In *The Tariff History of the United States* (New York, G. P. Putnam's Sons, 1931), he wrote as follows about the period after the War Between the States: "Added to all this, the state of the finances demanded immediate attention. In 1872, as later in 1883 and in 1890, a redundant revenue compelled Congress to take action of some sort on the tariff as the chief source of federal income. In each of the fiscal years 1870-71 and 1871-72, the surplus revenue, after paying all appropriations and all interest on the public debt, amounted to about $100,000,000, a sum greatly in excess of any requirement of the sinking fund. The government was buying bonds in the open market in order to dispose of the money that was flowing into the treasury vaults."

So, the fact is that the government had *too much money*, and was devising ways to get rid of it. Consider also that we are talking about a time that began only a few years after a typically expensive war; and that $100,000,000, which to us seems like chicken feed when discussing government, was in fact a gargantuan sum, worth many billions in today's inflated, monopoly paper.

"*. . . And Ladies Of The Club*," by Helen Hooven Santmyer (New York, G. P. Putnam's Sons, 1982), was recently a best-seller. On page 647, a character says as follows of President Grover Cleveland, in 1888: "That Democrat's hanged himself. He proposes to cut the tariff because in the past three years a dangerous surplus, one hundred and twenty-two million dollars, has accumulated in the Treasury, a surplus over government expenses. And the only way we can rid ourselves of the menace is by cutting the tariff. . . ."

Ah, the dear, dead days of long ago! Notice also that President Cleveland was a *Democrat*, indicating that the traditional Demo-

THE OPENING OF THE

TARIFF MONSTER.—*Here I am again.*

CONGRESSIONAL SESSION
What are you going to do with me?

PUCK: *The Comic Weekly*—12/7/1887

crat Party was quite different from the blood-sucking monster it has become.

This should irrevocably lay to rest the absurd idea that Congress gave us the income tax because the government needed revenue. Indeed, Professor Taussig says this of the period just before 1890: "In that period the United States were embarrassed by a large surplus in the revenue, the situation in this respect being again similar to that in 1870-72."

Notice in passing that Professor Taussig uses the plural construction ("the United States *were*"), which reflected the fact that, from the beginning until relatively recently, the United States were understood to be exactly that: a federal union of originally independent states. When the United States were demoted from "they" into an "it," they took a long step from free government to totalitarianism and from republic to empire.

Along these lines, Simeon E. Baldwin wrote as follows in the *Harvard Law Review* of January 25, 1899 (Vol. XII, No. 6), at page 409: "The United States of America is a plural term. The union of separate States in one political body does not extinguish their separate existence, nor vary the force of their having formed this 'more perfect union' in order to promote their several as well as their common interests. . . ."

John Clark Ridpath's nine-volume *History Of The World* (Cincinnati, Jones Brothers, 1910) is another work that has the advantage of proximity to these events. In volume nine, Ridpath writes that, around 1890, "the revenues of the United States were swollen to mountainous proportions. The treasury at Washington became engorged, and at length the necessity was developed of doing something in the nature of reform."

Why was all that money in the hands of the government so dangerous? Ridpath has a remarkable answer: "The state of the National treasury—depending as it did upon the protective tariff system—entailed two prodigious evils: In the first place the surplus served as a temptation and motive in Congress for all manner of jobbery and extravagant expenditures. In the second place, it enabled the combined monopolies of the country to uphold themselves by influencing national legislation in favor of the protected industries and against the common interest of the people as a whole. . . ."

Doesn't this buttress your reporter's conclusion that the cause of debt is too much tax; and that the cause of the nation's present suicidal debt is the crushing taxes? Notice Ridpath's finding that excessive taxation inspires monopoly, about which we shall have more to say shortly.

Yet, in 1894, just four years after the embarrassing surpluses of which these authors speak, Congress gave us an income tax. If the reason wasn't money, what was the reason? The answer is that the income tax was the result of revolutionary agitation. Remember that in 1848, in the *Communist Manifesto*, Karl Marx had listed the income tax second in the steps he prescribed for Communism. The only thing he apparently thought was more important, was government control of all the land, which of course we already enjoy in this country, by way of zoning, property taxes, environmental laws and outright federal ownership.

A few immensely rich and powerful men had commissioned Marx to write the *Manifesto*—the young Marx was then totally unknown—and they wanted to use the income tax as a weapon to destroy the middle class, which they regarded as a threat. The tax would confiscate the middle class's money, and therefore cripple it, under the guise of a need to finance the government. They wanted to return to the static society of the Middle Ages, in which the middle class didn't yet exist, and you were either prince or peasant; there was nothing in between. The *Manifesto* of course fulminates on page after page against the *bourgeoisie*—the French word for middle class. It is a mistake to believe that the Communists oppose the super-rich. They don't. The super-rich of 1848, who hired Marx and financed the *Manifesto*, didn't do so to destroy themselves. Today, the monopolists who run the so-called "Soviet Union" are super-rich and live like it.

In other words, there *was* a thing called the Tax Rebellion, all right, but the income tax was not its target. The Tax Rebellion didn't oppose the income tax. On the contrary, the Tax Rebellion *was* the income tax. The target of the Tax Rebellion was the Middle Class.

In *Fabian Freeway* (Belmont, Massachusetts, Western Islands, 1966) Rose Martin wrote as follows: "As early as 1872 Karl Marx, speaking in Amsterdam, had intimated that social revolution might be accomplished by peaceful means in England and America—that is, by taking advantage of libertarian traditions and free institutions to subvert them. . . . While Marx never visited the United States, the weekly five dollars which he received as a special correspondent for the *New York Tribune* was for a time his chief source of income. He sent articles on the Crimean War to that newspaper, whose editor, Horace Greeley, likewise called himself a Socialist . . . ."

Marx believed that, in certain respects, the United States held the key to world revolution. Miss Martin points out that in the preface to Volume I of *Das Kapital*, he wrote: "As in the eighteenth century, the American War of Independence sounded the tocsin for the European middle class, the American Civil War sounded it for the European working class."

So, it was no surprise that, soon after his death, in 1883, his ideas and his followers were permeating and infiltrating the United States. The year 1886 saw the murderous Haymarket Square bombings in Chicago. Also in that year, in New York, Henry George, who advocated the Single Tax on land, drew 67,000 votes for mayor; seven thousand more than a robust, young politician named Theodore Roosevelt.

In 1888, Sidney Webb came to America to proselytize. Webb was the leader of the Fabian Society, which, more than any other group, deserves the discredit for turning Britain into a Socialist horror. Many years later, Webb would be regarded as a "god" in the satanic, Communist pantheon in Moscow. When he visited there, he was treated like royalty. His contribution to Communism was to advance it under a cloak of respectability. The Communists don't care how they get there, as long as they arrive.

Also in 1888, Edward Bellamy published his Socialist novel, *Looking Backward*. In one of the contradictions to which Socialism so often falls prey, *Looking Backward* preached the abolition of "wage slavery" by means of "the national organization of labor under a single direction." (Later, the Soviet Union did it.) In the perverted tradition of Sidney Webb, so-called Nationalist Clubs sprang up across the United States to spread Bellamy Socialism. Later, the People's Party absorbed the Nationalist Clubs.

Ridpath writes as follows of the political campaign of 1892: "The National Convention of the People's party assembled at Omaha on the 4th of July. The numbers in attendance and the enthusiasm showed conclusively a great increase in the following of this party, which now began to be designated as Populists. The platform declared in favor of the union of the labor forces of the United States in a common cause against corporate power; demanded governmental control of railroads, telegraph, and public corporations; demanded also the free coinage of silver at the existing ratio, and an increase in the circulating medium; *also an income tax* . . . ." (emphasis added)

Whether or not these people thought of themselves as Communists is not important. They had been infected by Communist ideas. They were at best political Typhoid Marys. In 1892, the Populists—who wanted the income tax—won more than a million votes and twenty two seats in the Electoral College.

On June 30, 1892, a few days before the Populists met, the managers of the iron works at Homestead, near Pittsburgh, locked out their workers, who had been planning to strike after a cut in pay. Workers made threats. Management sent secretly to Chicago for the Pinkertons. When they arrived, strikers fired on their boat. There was a battle. Ten strikers and four detectives were killed. The National Guard occupied Homestead for weeks. An anarchist tried to assassinate iron works Superintendent Frick.

In Coeur d'Alene, Idaho, union miners killed many non-union miners on their way to work. They destroyed railroad bridges and other property and established a reign of terror. On the 17th of July, military rule finally prevailed, and the chief terrorists were jailed. In Buffalo, New York, switchmen struck the Erie and Lehigh Valley Railway, burning hundreds of loaded freight cars. The governor summoned the entire National Guard of New York. Had Marx's feudal revolution finally arrived?

In 1893, there were bloody strikes. In 1894, Coxey's army of unemployed marched on Washington. President Cleveland sent federal troops to Chicago. There was violence. Eugene Debs, the Socialist leader, was arrested.

The fiscal manipulation that today is daily routine was already much in evidence. Starting on page 727, Mrs. Santmyer writes as follows of the situation in August, 1893: ". . . To Ludwig the cause of the prolongation of hard times was crystal clear: Congress brought under debate an act to lower tariffs; while it was in the air, any importer would hold his hand in the hope of lowering his costs, and in the meantime, since the country depended on the tariff for revenue, it could not meet its budget; it was running into debt; every citizen who questioned its solvency demanded gold for his silver and for his paper money.

"That the panic was fundamentally financial did not lessen its impact. Men were out of work; they saw no one to blame but their employers; they went on strike against large industries and small; there were criminal acts and even riots. . . ."

Since then, we have learned that the totalitarian Socialist billionaires routinely provoke a problem they can pretend to solve. Their "solution" always gives them more power and wealth, and they are praised in the process. So it was here. Mrs. Santmyer writes as follows on page 755: ". . . In January of 1895 the President called on Congress for remedial action, but met with no response. The President and his Secretary of the Treasury were forced into an alliance with Wall Street; after many emergency consultations, Morgan and Belmont in New York, along with Morgan and Rothschild in London, agreed to get the needed gold from abroad . . . ."

If you think all that happened by accident, please telex us immediately. For a limited time only we can make available to you a selected group of scenic vacation lots in the delightful town of Chernobyl, in the sunny Ukraine. But you must act quickly. This offer is going fast. (No checks, please.)

The income tax sprang from this ferment. Its purpose, again, was not to raise money, but to change society. As we have seen, the money panic was engineered. The 1894 law imposed a 2% tax on income.

However, in 1895, the Supreme Court threw the new income tax out. The Court said the tax was unconstitutional, and, therefore, illegal, null and void. Why? The name of the case is *Pollock v. Farmers' Loan and Trust*. The Supreme Court ruled on it twice. The number of the ruling we're going to look at is 158 U.S. 601. The lawyers call that number the "citation." They use the citation to look a case up. You can do it, too, and you should. The letters in the middle tell us which court made the decision. In this case, "U.S." tells us it is the U.S. Supreme Court. The first number tells us the volume in which the decision is printed; in this case, volume 158. The last number tells us the page; in this case, page 601. So, what did the Supreme Court say in the *Pollock* case?

The Court ruled that the 1894 income tax was defective because the tax was not imposed in a constitutional way. Early in his opinion, Chief Justice Fuller explained: "[T]he Constitution divided federal taxation into two great classes, the class of direct taxes, and the class of duties, imposts, and excises; and prescribed two rules which qualified the grant of power as to each class.

"The power to lay direct taxes apportioned among the several states in proportion to their representation in the popular branch in Congress, a representation based on population as ascertained by the census, was plenary and absolute; but to lay direct taxes without apportionment was forbidden. The power to lay duties, imposts and excises was subject to the qualification that the imposition must be uniform throughout the United States."

So, the Chief Justice of the United States explained that the Constitution authorizes the federal government to collect two kinds of taxes: direct and indirect. He mentions three kinds of indirect taxes: duties, imposts and excises. The Constitution requires the federal government to collect direct and indirect taxes in obedience to specific rules. Direct taxes are subject to the rule of apportionment, in which the taxes are collected from the states in proportion to the number of their members in the House of Representatives, as determined by the census. Indirect taxes are subject to the rule of uniformity: they must be the same everywhere.

What is a direct tax? What is an indirect tax? Keen, legal minds have argued about this since the beginning of our country, and still do. Even the courts of appeal disagree on the subject. A direct tax is a tax one cannot avoid; for instance, a head tax, also known as a capitation, or poll, tax. If the government puts a price on your head, you must pay it. There's no way around it. A tax on your land is a direct tax; again, there's no escape. Finally, a tax on your work is a direct tax. As we shall see, your work, or labor, is property, just as much as your land; just as much as your employer's business; and most of us must work in order to survive.

An indirect tax is a tax one can avoid. For instance, one can pay it, and then add it to the price of the product one sells, so that, in the end, one's customer pays it. In such a case, one is acting as a tax collector for the government. Generally, an indirect tax is a tax on an activity, on a situation, on a relationship; and one can avoid the tax legally by avoiding those things. That is why an indirect tax is voluntary. The dictionary says that "voluntary" means "without legal obligation." You are under no legal obligation to pay the bourbon whiskey tax, if you neither make nor buy bourbon whiskey. If you do make it, you do so voluntarily, and are liable for the tax.

No doubt there is still so much disagreement about the nature of the income tax because it can be both direct and indirect. When it is indirect, it can be either duty, excise or impost. For instance, the excise refers to the same thing the doctor does when he excises a wound. In the case of taxes, the excision, or cut, can be made just as surgically, and the theory is that the government deserves a cut of one's take if it does one a favor. An excise tax is a privilege tax. It allows one to do something that would be illegal without the privilege, in exchange for which one must pay the tax, the cut. In 1932, the Sixth Circuit Court of Appeal said as follows, in *American Airways v. Wallace*, 57 F.2d 877, 880: "The terms 'excise' tax and 'privilege' tax are synonymous, and the two are often used interchangeably. . . ."

What did the Founding Fathers think an income tax was? In *The Law That* Always *Was* (Tulsa, F.E.A. Books, 1987), Vern Holland, a former stockbroker with Paine Webber and Dean Witter, writes as follows at page nineteen: "Historical research shows that Massachusetts had taxed incomes for more than a hundred years prior to the assembling of the Constitutional Convention; other of the leading States were imposing like taxes at or about 1787, and the receipts therefrom were used to help pay the quotas demanded by the then Government of the Confederation for the maintenance of the Federal Government. The income tax so paid, and all the other internal taxes collected by the States, were known and collected as *direct* taxes and are so called today."

At page eighty four, Holland tells us this: "Adam Smith's *Wealth of Nations* was published in 1776. . . . It was mentioned by Judge Cooley as a book whose maxims had secured for them universal acceptance. It was recognized authority on both sides of the Atlantic. Smith made it clear that by 'direct taxes' he meant taxes on persons assessed according to property or income, and as opposed to 'indirect taxes' on expenses or consumption."

Another work in circulation at the time in America, had been published in 1764 by Turgot, the Frenchman. He wrote as follows about taxes: "There are only three possible: Direct upon the funds; direct upon the person, which becomes a tax upon labor; the indirect imposition, or that which is placed upon consumption."

In 1796, Albert Gallatin, later Secretary of the Treasury, wrote as follows, according to Vern Holland, at page 116: "The most generally received opinion, however, is that by direct taxes in the Constitution those are meant which are raised on the capital or revenue of the people . . . ." Finally, the fourth edition of the *Encyclopedia Britannica*, published in 1810, classified an income tax as direct.

The reason it is so important to determine the kind of tax one is dealing with is that, as we have seen, the law requires the federal government to levy the different kinds of taxes in obedience to different rules; and one must identify the tax in order to know which rule to invoke. For instance, the federal government has complete power to levy a direct tax on your labor—but it must do so in obedience to the rule of apportionment. In *Pollock*, the Supreme Court found that Congress had passed a direct tax *without* apportionment—which was illegal. So, the Court threw the tax out.

Pollock had complained about the effect of the illegal tax on his real estate and investments, and that was all the Court considered. On page 635, Mr. Chief Justice Fuller explained: "We have considered the act only in respect of the tax on income derived from real estate, and from invested personal property, and have not commented on so much of it as bears on gains or profits from business, privileges, or employments, in view of the instances in which taxation on business, privileges, or employments has assumed the guise of an excise tax and been sustained as such."

In other words, in this case the Court did not consider gains or profits—synonyms for income—derived from business, privileges, or employments, because taxation of those things was being treated and upheld as an excise; which, of course, is indirect, and governed by another rule, thereby avoiding apportionment. The Chief Justice explained that, were the Court to strike down only the effects Mr. Pollock had complained about, "this would leave the burden of the tax to be borne by professions, trades, employments, or vocations; and in that way what was intended as a tax on capital would remain, in substance, a tax on occupations and labor. We cannot believe that such was the intention of Congress. We do not mean to say that an act laying by apportionment a direct tax on all real estate and personal property, or the income thereof, might not also lay excise taxes on business, privileges, employments and vocations. But this is not such an act, and the scheme must be considered as a whole. . . ."

So, the Court struck down the entire would-be "law." Notice the Chief Justice's characterization of the "law" as a "scheme." He reaffirmed that federal taxes must be collected according to the Constitutional rules. Again, the government does have power to impose a tax directly on your pay—if it does so in obedience to the rule of apportionment. Or, it could perhaps impose an excise (that is, an indirect tax) on income (that is, gains or profits) derived from your pay. (We shall explain at length what that means.) What it was forbidden to do, said his honor, was to impose a direct tax without apportionment.

Why did the Founding Fathers construct such a system? We shall consider it in some detail later, when we see how the federal government would be financed today—adequately financed—without the income tax. For now, let's see how it was financed without the income tax for most of the existence of our country.

Remember that the Founding Fathers were what our friends at I.R.S. presumably would call "illegal tax protesters." That's why they went to war with George III. Consider that they rebelled against a tiny sliver of the tyranny we labor under now. If we had today what they went to war against, we would call it perfect freedom.

After victory, they wrote the Articles of Confederation to govern themselves. At the Philadelphia convention where they assembled to rewrite them, however, they decided instead to junk the Articles, so that the new federal government could more easily collect taxes. The states, which of course had been independent nations before the Articles—and, in effect, still were—had been derelict in payment of their tax bills, or "requisitions," to finance the war.

Yet, the Founders understandably were worried. They didn't want to impose upon themselves a new tax tyranny, as bad as, or worse than, the one imposed by George III. So, they made quite clear that, while the new nation would have full power to levy direct taxes, the states would have the chance to pay them—to pay their "apportionments"—before the federal government would intervene directly by sending agents to your home. On page 621 of *Pollock*, Mr. Chief Justice Fuller explained as follows: "The founders anticipated that the expenditures of the states, their counties, cities and towns would chiefly be met by direct taxation on accumulated property, while they expected that those of the Federal government would be for the most part met by indirect taxes. And in order that the power of direct taxation by the general government should not be exercised, except on necessity; and, when the necessity arose, should be so exercised as to leave the states at liberty to discharge their respective obligations . . . ."

So, from the beginning, the Fathers expected that the federal government would be routinely financed by indirect taxes; would rarely impose direct taxes; would do so only when the necessity arose. Indeed, in a letter dated January 29, 1789, James Madison —the father of the Constitution—wrote that the federal power of direct taxation would be exercised only in "extraordinary emergencies." Mr. Madison was of course talking about war. From the beginning, direct taxes have always been war taxes. If you oppose war, you will oppose routine, direct, federal taxes. Madison and the other Framers were immensely practical dreamers. They knew that in time of war we might need direct taxes to save the nation—but they expected us to dismantle them as soon as safely possible. They would be flabbergasted by permanent, direct taxes, and would rebel against them—again. Is not this a fertile field for peace lovers to sow? Why haven't they sown it, if they are really for peace?

Also in that letter, James Madison explained that federal intervention would rarely be necessary to collect direct taxes, because "every state which chooses to collect its own quota may always prevent a federal collection, by keeping a little beforehand in its finances, and making its payment at once into the federal treasury."

Remember, all of this comes to us from the Founding Fathers and the U.S. Supreme Court. In short, here's how they say our system is supposed to work, according to law:

Step One: Congress decides on a dollar figure it needs in direct taxes from the states—in an emergency—over and above what it has collected in indirect taxes;

Step Two: It sends each state a bill for part of that amount, an "apportionment," based upon its population and the number of its representatives in the federal House. New York's tax bill would obviously be considerably bigger than Wyoming's;

Step Three: The states collect the money for the special levy from their citizens, in the various ways mandated by their legislatures;

Step Four: If, for some reason, a state fails to pay up (which happened under the Articles of Confederation)—only then—the federal government steps in directly.

The Framers' purpose was to use the states as buffers to protect the citizens from the federal government. Today, we know what they were worried about. Again, when the states created the federal Union, they were independent nations—and still are, as we shall see. The Fathers created it, but at the same time they were afraid of it. For instance, historian William Archer Cocke wrote as follows in *The Constitutional History of the United States* (Philadelphia, J. B. Lippincott, 1858, v. 1, p. 56): "New powers were to be created. This occasioned the greatest apprehension on the minds of the people, recently from the thraldom of royalty. They knew the self-accretive tendency of power, and feared, in process of time, the evils they had overcome in overthrowing the English government would be revived on their own soil."

Cocke writes (p. 64) that Patrick Henry, of Virginia, objected to the Constitution, "because it gave too much strength to the federal government." Alexander Hamilton was the only New York delegate who signed. Lansing and Yates instead went home (p. 65): "These gentlemen feared the sovereignty of the States was absorbed by the enlarged capacity of the General Government." Now we know their fear was a prophecy.

Does the system they gave us work? From 1792 to 1802, there were direct, federal taxes, to pay for the war. President Tom Jefferson got nervous, because the federal tax take had skyrocketed to the confiscatory per capita sum of $2 a year. He abolished them. Direct, federal taxes were revived during the War of 1812, when the British, our traditional enemies, burned Washington, D.C. Unfortunately, they didn't get it all. It grew back.

Let's look at a couple of versions of what happened. *The American Way In Taxation, Internal Revenue, 1862-1963* (edited by Lillian Doris, Englewood Cliffs, New Jersey, Prentice-Hall, 1963) contains a foreword by Commissioner of Internal Revenue Mortimer M. Caplin, so it presumably is at least quasi-official. It says this (p. 17): "A special session of Congress in the summer of 1813 approved the tax recommendations of Treasury Secretary Albert A. Gallatin. Among the proposals was a direct tax, which under the Constitution had to be apportioned among the states according to population. The then 18 states were to pay their quotas into the federal treasury."

So, the tax was levied in obedience to the law—the Constitution—just as Mr. Chief Justice Fuller later explained it. The I.R.S.-approved book also says this (p. 18): ". . . Congress in 1817 abolished all internal revenue taxes. It was prompted to this action by the high customs receipts realized from imported goods. The Office of Commissioner of Revenue was abolished for the second time in less than a score of years. There was no need for internal revenue machinery again for more than forty years."

That's right! There were no internal, federal taxes at all. The I.R.S. of its time was abolished. As usual when the law was obeyed, there was more revenue than the government could handle.

In *Albert Gallatin: Fiscal Theories and Policies* (New Brunswick, New Jersey, Rutgers University Press, 1958), Alexander Balinky explains it as follows on page 199: "By August of 1813 Congress had approved the reimposition of the internal taxes. A direct tax was levied on slaves and dwellings and apportioned among the states to the amount of $3 million. Duties were laid on pleasure carriages, the refining of sugar and the distillation of spirits. A tax was placed on auctions and financial instruments. Retailers of wines and spirits were required to purchase a license. There was little difference between the items taxed this time and those which the Federalist administration had selected for taxation during its term in office. Congress called these war taxes and specifically provided for their repeal within one year after the end of the war."

So, not only did the 1813 Congress consider the direct tax (which was apportioned, pursuant to law) a war tax, and therefore temporary; Congress also regarded the duties and license requirements, et cetera, which of course were *in*direct, as temporary war taxes.

During the War Between the States, additional revenue again was needed. Taxes exploded. There was an income tax that expired in 1872. After the war, an attorney named Springer sued the United States and demanded the return of his property, arguing that the income tax was a direct tax, therefore requiring apportionment. Since it had not been apportioned, it was illegal, he said. In *Springer v. United States*, 102 U.S. 586, Mr. Justice Swayne, of the U.S. Supreme Court, concluded as follows: "Our conclusions are, that *direct* taxes, within the meaning of the Constitution, are only capitation taxes, as expressed in that instrument, and taxes on real estate; and that the tax of which the plaintiff in error complains is within the category of an excise or duty."

Notice that Justice Swayne defends the apportionment of direct taxes: "Was the tax here in question a *direct* tax? If it was, not having been laid according to the requirements of the Constitution, it must be admitted that the laws imposing it, and the proceedings taken under them by the assessor and collector for its imposition and collection, were all void."

So, William M. Springer lost only because he had mistakenly believed the tax was direct, said Justice Swayne. If it *had* been direct, said his honor, it would have been void without apportionment. Without apportionment, it never could have been a legal tax, despite the majestic trappings erected to maintain it, and a citizen would have been within his rights not to pay. *Springer* was no doubt one of the cases Chief Justice Fuller later had in mind when he talked about the income tax masquerading under "the guise of an excise tax." Congress called it indirect and the Court let them get away with it.

In *The Golden Egg: The Personal Income Tax, Where It Came From, How It Grew* (Boston, Houghton Mifflin, 1977), Gerald Carson writes at page seventeen that Charles Sumner, the Abolitionist, who was a member of Lincoln's Cabinet, started out as a defender of the tax, but by 1870 he was for repeal, on the ground that "an income tax is a war tax." Again, the tax died two years later.

Of course, the War Between the States inspired other taxes. Lillian Doris, editor of the Caplin-endorsed book, explains at page nineteen: "In addition to taxing incomes, the new law taxed estates, public utilities, occupations, liquors, beer, tobacco, banks, insurance companies, advertisements, slaughtered cattle, railroads, ferry boats, and other specified commodities. It provided stamp taxes on certain commercial papers, perfume, cosmetics, medicines and playing cards."

As you can see, there are echoes here of King George's hated Stamp Act. What happened to these oppressive taxes? Lillian Doris says this at page nineteen: "Collection of the various taxes, particularly those from the states, was carried on until 1868. Three years later Congress decided the money was no longer required and returned the funds on hand to the states.

"In mid-1868, taxation of distilled beverages and tobacco became the major source of internal revenue. From that year to 1913 nearly 90 per cent of all internal revenue collections came from taxes on those products."

Dwell a moment, if you would, on that last staggering paragraph. We're talking here about forty five years of American history—years of dynamic, economic expansion, when the United States became a world power. Yet, through all these years, almost 90% of internal revenue taxes came from alcohol and tobacco—and the government did not collapse. We can't find a year, not even a week, during which there was any genuine trouble. Of course, the government was still small, as the Founding Fathers had meant it to be. There was no so-called "need" for the billions it gives dictatorships around the world and wastes on inane studies about the sex life of the newt. As we have seen, throughout this entire period the big, federal, fiscal problem was what to do with all the money the government was collecting.

Indeed, remember that in 1898, when almost 90% of internal revenue taxes still came from alcohol and tobacco, the United States fought—and won—a war against Spain. This recalls the fact that the United States have been tricked into four major wars since the installation of the present income tax: World Wars I and II, Korea and Vietnam. We won the first two, but lost the peace in the subsequent negotiations. We lost the last two and lost the peace as well. It's getting worse. Does that tell you anything?

In the *Pollock* case, in which the Supreme Court threw the 1894 tax out, Chief Justice Fuller said of it as follows: "Being direct, and therefore to be laid by apportionment, is there any real difficulty in doing so? Cannot Congress, if the necessity exists of raising thirty, forty, or any other number of millions of dollars for the support of the government, in addition to the revenue from duties, imposts, and excises, apportion the quota of each state upon the basis of the census, and thus advise it of the payment which must be made, and proceed to assess that amount on all the real and personal property and the income of all persons in the state, and collect that same if the state does not in the meantime assume and pay its quota and collect the amount according to its own system and in its own way? . . ." (At the Constitutional Convention, it was suggested that the states themselves assume and pay the quota imposed upon their citizens. The suggestion was rejected, because of the unsatisfactory experience with that procedure under the Articles of Confederation. The Chief Justice here refers to the fact that Congress allowed the states to assume and pay the amounts apportioned them in the direct tax acts of 1813, 1815 and 1816; and, indeed, allowed each state a deduction of 15% for prompt payment.)

It was a good question, and the Socialist disciples of Marx, who wanted his income tax, had no answer. The Chief Justice explained that its advocates were asking the Court to affix its imprimatur to their violations of law: "The power to tax real and personal property and the income from both, there being an apportionment, is conceded; that such a tax is a direct tax in the meaning of the Constitution has not been, and, in our judgment, cannot be successfully denied; and yet we are thus invited to hesitate in the enforcement of the mandate of the Constitution, which prohibits Congress from laying a direct tax on the revenue from property of the citizen without regard to state lines, and in such manner that the states cannot intervene by payment in regulation of their own resources. . . ."

The Court struck down the income tax of 1894 because it authorized a federal invasion of the prerogatives of the states. Everyone who opposes dictatorship will want to preserve the powers of the states, because, without them, the power would be concentrated in Washington, where it would be easy for a potential dictator to grab. That is exactly what Socialist dictator Hitler did in Germany, which also has state governments. Hitler turned out the legislators and installed his own men, pretending all the while that nothing had changed. If you think you oppose dictatorship, but you also oppose "state's rights," you will get what you deserve, and it will not be liberty. Already, in our own country, the states have been reduced to mere lines on a map, to mere administrative appendages of the central government, which forces them into line by threatening to withhold funds. The denial of apportionment is another symptom of this dictatorial process. Apportionment is one of the keys that unlocks the mystery of the income tax.

A couple of important questions arise. We'll have more to say about them later, but, for now, let's look at them briefly. First, how could a government that governs a population as large as ours, survive on the revenue it raised legally, and indirectly, in the Nineteenth Century? The answer is: It couldn't. Remember, however, that today's much larger population is producing much more economic activity, which, in turn, produces much more revenue for government.

Second, isn't the apportionment system ponderous, unwieldy, inconvenient, troublesome, annoying, and a pain in the posterior? Yes, it is all those things, and probably a lot more that can't be mentioned with ladies present. However, that is not at all an accident. It's supposed to be all those nasty things, which is another manifestation of the genius of the Founding Fathers.

They made it that way to remind us that direct taxes are meant to be temporary—for use only in emergency—and then repealed. They did not design direct taxes—war taxes—to be the permanent, daily afflictions they are now.

3

WHAT THE LAW SAYS

After their defeat in 1895, the income tax advocates went back to the drawing board. Page 3138 of the *Congressional Record* of June 11, 1909, tells us that Nebraska Senator Norris Brown offered Senate Joint Resolution No. 39, which, according to page 3377, was introduced to the Senate six days later. It was referred to the Finance Committee, the Chairman of which was Rhode Island Senator Nelson Aldrich.

Senate Joint Resolution No. 39 read as follows: "The Congress shall have power to lay and collect direct taxes on incomes without apportionment among the several states according to population."

However, this apparently was too much like what the Supreme Court had forbidden in *Pollock*, just fourteen years earlier. So, the Senate Finance Committee went to work. Eleven days later, the proposal emerged—rewritten—as Senate Joint Resolution No. 40. Page 3900 of the *Congressional Record* of June 28, 1909, says that Senator Aldrich presented it to the Senate.

The *Record* of July 5, 1909 (page 4121) shows that the Senate passed it—unchanged—and we know it today as the Sixteenth Amendment: "The congress shall have power to lay and collect taxes on incomes, from whatever source derived, without apportionment among the several states and without regard to any Census or enumeration."

What's the difference between the two Resolutions? The difference lies in the deletion from Resolution No. 39 of the word "direct," and the addition to Resolution No. 40—and to the Sixteenth Amendment—of the phrase, "from whatever source derived." What do those words mean? If something is derived from something else, it is different from the thing it is derived from. The thing that is derived begins as part of the thing it is derived from; but, after the derivation has occurred, the two things are separate. The dictionary tells us that the word "from" implies separation. If something came from something else, the host it came from is different from the thing that comes. In the beginning, you were part of your mother. Now, you are derived from your mother; you are different, you are separate. The words "derived from" indicate relationship. They show where you started out; but they also show that you and the entity you started out as a part of are now divided.

The purpose of those words in the Sixteenth Amendment was to separate the *source* (the capital, the original investment) from the *income* (the profit or gain), so that the income—not the source—could be legally taxed without apportionment. According to some authorities, the authors of the legislation wrote it the way they did to protect the tax from the *Pollock* reaffirmation that a direct tax cannot be levied without apportionment; and protected it by turning the tax into an excise, an indirect tax, a privilege tax, which does not require apportionment. As we have seen, the terms "excise tax" and "privilege tax" mean the same thing. In this case, the "privilege" apparently was and is the so-called "privilege" of earning income, in return for which favor the government now was demanding a cut, an excise. Your obedient servant doesn't happen to agree that earning income is a privilege. We think it's an American right. However, our purpose here is just to tell you what the authors of the legislation meant.

So, the changes between Resolutions 39 and 40 were meant to underline the fact that, while the tax on the income may be direct, the tax is *only* on the income—not on the source from which it is "derived." With regard to the *source*, the income tax is indirect. With regard to the *income*, it's direct. Resolution 39 would have gone head-to-head with the Supreme Court, by discarding the "guise." Resolution 40 maintained it.

Why did the Congress go through all these contortions to avoid apportionment? If the Members wanted to impose a direct tax on the source, why didn't they just impose one—under the rules the Constitution had laid down? By now, 1909, that system had already proven its practicality for more than a hundred years. Remember, however, that the Founding Fathers had deliberately made the process cumbersome and painful. If you were apportioned, you would know it. No living American has ever survived an apportionment, but our guess is that it would be somewhat akin to a prostate examination conducted by Dr. Josef Mengele. However, if its advocates could slide this new system through the Supreme Court, it would be legal; and would have the advantage of plucking the goose with less pain and machinery.

A word should be said about "legislative history." No principle of our system of jurisprudence is better "settled," more accepted, than the fact that the intent of the authors of a piece of legislation is the law. What the man who wrote the law says he meant is decisive, and is known as the "legislative history." That is the main reason the *Federalist Papers* are studied today. They constitute part of the legislative history of the Constitution, because they show us what the men who wrote it thought.

When a question later arises about what a law means, investigators study the legislative history. In *Stewart v. Kahn*, 11 Wall. 493, 504, the Supreme Court said this: ". . . The intention of the lawmaker constitutes the law. . . ." In 1974, in *National Railroad Passenger Corp. et al. v. National Association of Railroad Passengers*, 414 U.S. 453, 458, the Supreme Court said again: ". . . But even the most basic general principles of statutory construction must yield to clean contrary evidence of legislative intent. . . ."

In other words, even if a law isn't written according to the rules, it still means what its authors said. There are endless such examples. In this case, once again, we have legislative intent written in stone, proving that the authors of the Sixteenth Amendment rejected a direct tax on the source (the investment) without apportionment; but approved instead a tax on the income, separated from the source. A tax on the source would be a direct tax.

Indeed, remember that the Founding Fathers said a tax on *income* is a direct tax.

Even some of the legislators who approved it were suspicious of the rewritten version of the proposed amendment. Sereno Payne was co-author of the Payne-Aldrich Tariff Act, which governed the nation's external revenue at the time. According to Gerald Carson (p. 80), he supported the proposed income tax, because he wanted the United States to have "the longest pocketbook" in time of war. However, he made abundantly clear his aversion to such a tax in time of peace: "I believe with Gladstone, that it tends to make a nation of liars. [It is] . . . a tax upon the income of honest men and an exemption, to a greater or lesser extent, of the income of rascals."

Doesn't that read as if Congressman Payne wrote it last week?

Also, did the government by now, 1909, truly need the additional revenue the proposed income tax would provide? According to page 3936 of the *Congressional Record* of June 29, 1909, California Senator Flint, a member of the Finance Committee, said this: "Prior to the receipt of the message of the President by the Congress of the United States the Finance Committee had considered the question of obtaining additional revenue. The committee were not altogether united on the question whether it was necessary to have revenue in addition to what would be produced by the pending bill." The bill he was talking about was the Payne-Aldrich tariff bill.

In other words, in 1909 some senators were maintaining that the government *still* had no need of more money. As we have seen, this had been the case since soon after the War Between the States; indeed, for most of the history of our country, when the government obeyed the law. Remember that now, in 1909, almost 90% of the federal government's internal revenue collections still came from taxes on tobacco and alcohol. Our country still had never lost a war. The National Debt was next to nothing.

The proposed Amendment left the Congress and went to the states. Our friends at I.R.S. say that, by 1913, enough state legislatures had endorsed it to win ratification. The trouble is that the records were falsified. For years, Bill Benson was the Illinois Department of Revenue's counterpart of a Special Agent of the Internal Revenue Service, and carried a gun for the purpose. Martin "Red" Beckman is a Montana historian. In 1983, they launched an incredible odyssey that took Bill Benson to the archives of every one of the forty eight states that had considered the proposed Amendment. They found that all thirty six of the endorsements of the state legislatures were defective, for reasons ranging from mistakes in transcription, to rewording of the Amendment, which is forbidden; to, perhaps, outright fraud.

For instance, California was listed as a state whose legislature had passed the Amendment, but no record of that putative action could be found. The Kentucky Senate did vote—twenty two to nine—*against* the Amendment. When we went to school, twenty two was a larger number than nine, and, as far as we know, still is, but that Kentucky vote nevertheless was listed as a vote for passage. In Washington, Secretary of State Philander Knox knew about all this, but he exercised his prerogative to certify that the Amendment had been ratified. Did Knox commit that fraud because he was a close associate of the Socialist billionaires who were slyly pushing the income tax?

Bill Benson and Red Beckman assembled the proof of all this, which consists of thousands of pages of certified documents from the forty eight state archives. Some of those certified pages cost a dollar a piece. They have published their findings in an authoritative volume entitled *The Law That Never Was* (South Holland, Illinois, Constitutional Research Associates, 1985), which we strongly recommend. In our opinion, it irrefutably supports their thesis that the Sixteenth Amendment was never ratified, and, indeed, came about as close to genuine ratification as Ollie North is to winning a Man of the Year award from the Communist government of Nicaragua. Needless to say, the courts so far have rebuffed them, because a) it happened "so long ago," and b) it's a "political question," both of which arguments hold no legal water. Indeed, as your reporter sets this down our friends at I.R.S. have arranged Mr. Benson's indictment in this land of alleged freedom of speech.

Be all that as it may, the book you are reading now is not based even a little bit on *The Law That Never Was*. The thesis of *this* book is that even if the Sixteenth Amendment was ratified perfectly, and *The Law That Never Was* consequently never was; the glaring fact remains that, while the tax authorized by the Amendment is legal, the administration of the tax today is illegal. Again, that is why we refer in this book to the "so-called 'income tax.'" When we do so, we refer to the perverted and illegal version of the tax that our friends at I.R.S. administer by usurpation.

So, let's assume the Amendment was ratified. We know it wasn't, but let's assume, *arguendo*, as the attorneys say, that it was, in 1913. A tax was shortly enacted under its authority. Gerald Carson says this at page 83: ". . . The income tax measure, *as usual*, was not set forth in a separate bill but tucked into a new tariff act, known as the Underwood-Simmons Tariff Act, officially entitled 'An Act to Reduce Tariff Duties and Provide Revenue for the Government, and for Other Purposes.' Section II, which assessed the new income tax, was buried among bauxite, gloves, false teeth, wool, beads and spangles, human hair, sheep dip, statuary for bona fide orphan asylums, and wild animals not for sale." (emphasis added)

Notice that, *as usual*, the income tax was written into a tariff act. The tariff, of course, is an indirect tax. It's voluntary, in the sense that if avoiding it is more important to you than enjoying the things it taxes, you can thumb your nose at it—legally—by staying out of its path; by avoiding those things. In other words, if you don't want to pay the tax, stay out of the sheep dip.

Question: Would a direct tax be written into an *in*direct tax? The presence of the income tax in the tariff was just another indication that it was indirect—or, so its authors wanted us to think, in order to escape apportionment. Meanwhile, page 3839 of the *Congressional Record* of August 28, 1913, quoted Senator Henry Cabot Lodge as telling his colleagues this: ". . . But this tax which we are now imposing for the first time is a direct tax; and this country has hardly known direct taxes except in times of war." Which is just another indication of the fact that the tax is both direct and indirect, depending upon whether you are talking about the income or the source.

In 1915, the tax went to the Supreme Court for the usual constitutional test. Today, if you ask an Internal Revenue Service official for the source of his authority, the chances are that he will point with immense satisfaction to the 1915 case of *Brushaber v. Union Pacific*, 240 U.S. 1. You will be told that the *Brushaber* Court upheld the constitutionality of the tax.

Did it? Yes. The trouble is that our friends at I.R.S. carefully avoid telling you what *kind* of tax the Court upheld. As we have seen, the *nature* of a tax is basic to America's revenue system, because each tax is governed by a different rule. To learn whether you are subject to a tax, and, if so, how to pay—which we strongly recommend, if you are subject—you first must know *what kind* of tax it is.

So, what *did* the United States Supreme Court say? Remember, this is one of the rulings under which I.R.S. operates.

By now, 1915, there was a new Chief Justice, Edward Douglass White, appointed by President Taft, who had proposed the Sixteenth Amendment to the Congress, in 1909. Taft would later be appointed Chief Justice himself by President Harding.

White delivered the opinion in *Brushaber*. He says the idea that the new income tax is unconstitutional—in conflict with the Sixteenth Amendment—is the result of confusion (Pp. 10-11): ". . . We are of opinion, however, that the confusion is not inherent, but rather arises from the conclusion that the Sixteenth Amendment provides for a hitherto unknown power of taxation; that is, a power to levy an income tax which, although direct, should not be subject to the regulation of apportionment applicable to all other direct taxes. . . ." Chief Justice White calls this "an erroneous assumption."

In other words, he says, it's erroneous to believe that the new income tax is a direct tax which the government is now allowed to impose without apportionment. It's erroneous to believe that the Sixteenth Amendment creates a new power of taxation. The Chief Justice says that the same constitutional principles apply now—in 1915—in *Brushaber*, that applied in 1895, in *Pollock*, when the Court found the income tax illegal. Nothing basic has changed.

White says that the arguments against the new income tax are defective, not because the tax gives the government new power, but precisely because it *doesn't*; because the arguments are fighting a straw man, fighting a tax that doesn't exist.

Here's what the Chief Justice says about those arguments (pp. 11-12): "But it clearly results that the proposition and the contentions under it, if acceded to, would cause one provision of the Constitution to destroy another; that is, they would result in bringing the provisions of the Amendment exempting a direct tax from apportionment into irreconcilable conflict with the general requirement that all direct taxes be apportioned. Moreover, the tax authorized by the Amendment, being direct, would not come under the rule of uniformity applicable under the Constitution to other than direct taxes, and thus it would come to pass that the result of the Amendment would be to authorize a particular direct tax not subject either to apportionment or to the rule of geographical uniformity, thus giving power to impose a different tax in one state or states than was levied in another state or states. This result, instead of simplifying the situation and making clear *the limitations on the taxing power, which obviously the Amendment must have been intended to accomplish*, would create radical and destructive changes in our constitutional system and multiply confusion." (emphasis added)

In other words, says the Chief Justice, the income tax isn't what you may think it is. There's nothing to protest. Our friends at I.R.S. have assiduously created the impression that the Sixteenth Amendment abolished apportionment; as you see, however, the Chief Justice says it's still the law that a direct tax must be apportioned. Indeed, a moment ago we saw that the Sixteenth Amendment created no new power of taxation. Not only that, now Chief Justice White says the Amendment was intended to make clear "the limitations on the taxing power." Far from granting new taxing power, the purpose of the Amendment is to make clear what the government *cannot* tax, not what it can.

Again and again, White makes the same point. For instance (p. 19): ". . . [T]he Amendment contains nothing repudiating or challenging the ruling in the Pollock Case that the word 'direct' had a broader significance, since it embraced also taxes levied directly on personal property because of its ownership, and therefore the Amendment at least impliedly makes such wider significance a part of the Constitution—a condition which clearly demonstrates that *the purpose was not to change the existing interpretation except to the extent necessary to accomplish the result intended; that is, the prevention of the resort to the sources from which a taxed income was derived in order to cause a direct tax on the income to be a direct tax on the source itself, and thereby to take an income tax out of the class of excises, duties, and imposts, and place it in the class of direct taxes.*" (emphasis added)

So, *Brushaber* did not destroy the rule of apportionment. All it did—by judicial definition—was to reconvert the income tax from the direct tax *Pollock* had said it was, into the indirect tax *Springer* had said it was, thereby avoiding apportionment.

A moment ago, we saw that the Amendment was intended to make clear "the limitations on the taxing power." Now, Chief Justice White tells us exactly what those limitations are. For one, he says, the purpose of the Amendment was precisely to prevent a direct tax on the source (without apportionment). He concedes that a tax on the income may be direct, but, if it is, it's the only direct tax without apportionment the Amendment allows. Indeed, the Chief Justice indicates that, since the new tax will be levied exclusively on the income, not on the source, that strict separation will maintain its status as indirect, as an excise (indirect) tax on the government-granted "privilege" of making income. Were there two kinds of direct taxes, one requiring apportionment, one not requiring it? Such a construction was unknown to the Founding Fathers and White did not explain. As you see, he turned himself into a pretzel trying to justify the new tax without totally junking the Constitution.

Our friends at I.R.S. today try to create the impression that the *Brushaber* ruling reversed *Pollock*. However, as we see here from the mouth of the man who wrote *Brushaber*, the Chief Justice of the United States, that is not the case at all. Indeed, it is fair to say that *Brushaber* not only sustained *Pollock*, but also expanded it. The Founding Fathers, as we have seen, considered a tax on receipts or property to be a direct tax. *Springer* drastically narrowed the definition of a direct tax, so that apportionment would only rarely be required. *Pollock* again expanded the definition, in substantial agreement with the Founding Fathers, saying that a direct tax could also be a tax on personal property. A direct tax must be apportioned, so the more direct taxes there are, the more apportionment there must be.

White says the Sixteenth Amendment supports this. He agrees that a tax on personal property is a direct tax. Your automobile, for instance, is personal property. So is your labor, as we shall see. The federal government can tax it, but only with apportionment. The people who gave us the income tax knew that free Americans would never tolerate a direct, federal tax on their labor—without apportionment—especially in peacetime. Would they?

In 1939, Henry Rottschaefer was Professor of Law at the University of Minnesota, and the West Company, in St. Paul, published his *Handbook of American Constitutional Law*. He said this: ". . . It was undoubtedly such considerations as these that led the Supreme Court to hold that the Sixteenth Amendment transformed the taxes, which the Pollock cases had held to be direct, into excises, and thus subject to the uniformity requirement. All federal income taxes levied since the adoption of the Sixteenth Amendment are thus excise taxes."

What does a tax on the source mean, as opposed to a tax on income derived from the source? For instance, suppose a man performs a service from carpentry to lawyering, and is paid for that service. The money he is paid is "the source." The federal government can't tax it—without apportionment. So, it isn't subject to the income tax. Now, suppose that carpenter invests some of that compensation in stock, or in an interest-bearing account. The dividend he realizes, or the interest he earns, is income *derived from* the source, to use the language of the Sixteenth Amendment, and therefore *is* subject to the tax. The source itself—the compensation—is not.

This is a good place to make an apology. The reader has seen that your Intrepid Correspondent has been repeating the same thing, over and over, in as many different ways as he can think of. We have been doing that because our friends at I.R.S. have buried the truth for so long, under so much propaganda, today it seems novel. Your reporter, who may be slow, needed several years to understand. You may be faster, and have already understood. The trouble is that we don't know how much repetition is required to turn on each reader's light; so, we have opted for overkill to avert the possibility that you won't understand because we have not explained enough.

The question arises: *Why* has the truth been hidden, and by whom? Why isn't it generally understood? If the *Brushaber* ruling was so beneficial, why are we in such a mess today? This brings us to The Plan. Remember that, in the beginning, the tax was sold to us as a scheme to "soak the rich." That is why the people mistakenly endorsed it in 1909 and thereafter. Its backers said it wouldn't hit the working man. No, it would hit the allegedly nasty people who clip coupons and draw dividends. The working woman had nothing to fear. Indeed, the advocates of the tax made that so clear—by means of the usual propaganda blitzkrieg—that it has become a prominent part of the tax's legislative history.

The trouble is that the billionaires the income tax was supposed to soak, were the very people behind it. For instance, in the years the income tax was working its way through Congress and the states, Nelson Aldrich was one of the most powerful members of the Senate. Indeed, you can make a convincing case that he was the *most* powerful member of the U.S. Senate at the time. You will remember that Senator Aldrich was Chairman of the Finance Committee. It is fair to say that the Sixteenth Amendment could not have passed in the Senate without his support. In earlier years, Senator Aldrich had dramatically denounced the proposed income tax as "Communist and Socialistic," which of course it was, as we have seen. Imagine the Chairman of the Senate Finance Committee saying such a thing today.

Now, in 1909, Senator Aldrich suddenly did a 180. The *Dictionary of American Biography* (New York, Scribner's, 1964) says this: ". . . Just when the opposition had become formidable, he took the wind out of its sails by bringing forward, with the support of the President, a proposed amendment to the Constitution, empowering Congress to lay income taxes. . . ." In other words, he started out as the leader of the opposition, and wound up cutting off the opposition's legs. When Aldrich did that 180, the opposition collapsed. Apparently, we're talking about a switch as flabbergasting as it would have been if John Wayne had suddenly become Chairwoman of the Gay Liberation Front. So, who and what was Senator Nelson Aldrich?

He was the maternal grandfather of Nelson Aldrich Rockefeller, of Standard Oil and the Chase Manhattan Bank. The Senator's daughter, Abby Greene Aldrich, married John D. Rockefeller, Jr., in 1901. At the time, it was widely understood that Nelson Aldrich was Rockefeller's mouthpiece in the Senate.

Remember, the alleged purpose of the income tax was to "soak the rich." Why on earth would Rockefeller and other Insiders at the top want it? Wouldn't such a communistic device—so labelled by Senator Aldrich himself—destroy them? No, it wouldn't. Aldrich changed his mind about it publicly—if it was a genuine change, rather than a stunt designed to steamroll support—because his conspiratorial associates had arranged to use the proposed income tax to protect themselves while it crippled the enemy. Who was the enemy?

Remember that Communism is an ideological weapon concealing a conspiracy, devised by totalitarians among the super-rich, for the specific purpose of destroying the middle class; with the result that the favored few can rule without fear they will be challenged. The middle class is halfway up the hill, and is a threat to the *king* of the hill at the top. With the middle class eliminated, there are only the king at the top and the peasants at the bottom. Again, this was the system of the so-called Dark Ages, before the Middle Class emerged, and that is what today's billionaire Socialists want.

The original John D. Rockefeller was the author of the statement: "Competition is a sin." Yes, that is what the man said. He wasn't a Free Enterpriser. As you see, he was just the opposite. A Free Enterpriser believes that competition is a blessing. Rockefeller and his flunkies believed in squelching competition by means of government. Don't the Communists believe the same thing? In the United States, we call it monopoly. In the Soviet Union, they call it a "dictatorship of the proletariat." In practice, don't they amount to the same thing?: government control of the economy, creating monopoly for the benefit of a small group of totalitarians at the top.

That is why the address of the Chase Manhattan Bank in Moscow is One Karl Marx Plaza. The Rockefellers always get the most prestigious address in town. That is why Chase Chairman David Rockefeller liberally financed construction of the Kama River truck factory, six hundred miles east of Moscow, the biggest such factory in the world—indeed, bigger than the combined capacity of all U.S. truck-makers—where, in violation of their signed agreement, the Soviets make the heavy, military trucks, the tank engines and the armored personnel carriers they have been using in their genocide in Afghanistan. That is why David Rockefeller has publicly praised Mao Tse-tung, whose "experiment" in Red China has murdered as many as sixty million Chinese.

American monopolists and Communist monopolists can collaborate so closely, because they both want the same thing: monopoly, or call it what you will. Communism isn't made and can't be made by poor, sick, hungry, illiterate peasants, as the biggest lie the Communists have ever told tells it; because such peasants are too poor to print the necessary propaganda, too sick to riot, too hungry to think, and too illiterate to read Marx—which is the only blessing of illiteracy we are aware of. No one rises up from the bottom for Communism. Communism always is imposed from the top down, by the healthiest, wealthiest, best fed and best educated individuals in any country; by wealthy intellectuals like Fidel Castro and Harvard lawyer Alger Hiss. In short, many of the so-called sins of Free Enterprise have been committed by the

Monopolists who hate it—like Rockefeller. Please understand that by no means are we condemning wealth. Get as rich as you can, in this greatest of all countries, with our blessing, but do it without using the government as a weapon.

So, how did the Monopolists plan to use the income tax? It is important to note that, around the turn of the century, competition—the thing Rockefeller hated—was spreading, despite everything "Big John" had done. Exploding Free Enterprise was making it possible for more and more Americans to own property, to go into business, to make profit, to accumulate wealth. In other words, Insider control over the economy was being diluted. If the Mob had done nothing, it could have been overthrown.

In *The Triumph of Conservatism: A Reinterpretation of American History, 1900-1916* (New York, the Free Press, a division of Macmillan, 1963), Professor Gabriel Kolko writes as follows on page four: "Despite the large number of mergers, and the growth in the absolute size of many corporations, the dominant tendency in the American economy at the beginning of this century was toward growing competition. Competition was unacceptable to many key business and financial interests, and the merger movement was to a large extent a reflection of voluntary, unsuccessful business efforts to bring irresistible competitive trends under control. . . . As new competitors sprang up, and as economic power was diffused throughout an expanding nation, it became apparent to many important businessmen that only the national government could rationalize the economy. . . . Ironically, contrary to the consensus of historians, it was not the existence of monopoly that caused the federal government to intervene in the economy, but the lack of it."

Today, we see the latest phase of that process, known to the headlines as "Merger Mania."

On page thirteen of the Kolko book, S. C. T. Dodd, Standard Oil's lawyer, calls industrial cooperation and concentration part of the "march of civilization." (This recalls Marx's dictum of "the inevitability of history.") Kolko comments: ". . . Although there was a formal commitment to varieties of laissez faire economic theory in most of the academic world, big businessmen developed their own functional doctrine very much opposed to competition as either a desirable mechanism or as a goal. . . ."

Indeed, since there was no so-called "right wing" at the time that could raise the alarm, the Socialists were quite bold in their praise of such businessmen. Starting on page sixteen, Kolko says this: "But the resignation of the socialists to inevitable monopoly was not merely a passive commitment to an article of faith. It stimulated many of them to a personal admiration of big businessmen unequalled by most paid eulogists. Indeed, big businessmen were the vehicles of progress and the guarantors of socialism, and worth defending from personal attacks for the parts they played in an impersonal industrial process. . . ." In April, 1901, *The Worker* said that the Socialists "are not making the Revolution. It would be nearer the truth to say that Morgan and Rockefeller are making it."

Along these lines, Professor Kolko says as follows, starting on page sixty three: ". . . John D. Rockefeller, John D. Archbold, and H.H. Rogers of Standard called for a national incorporation law . . . . There should be, Rockefeller suggested, 'First. Federal legislation under which corporations may be created and regulated, if that be possible.'. . ." Many years later, "corporate gadfly" Ralph Nader, who says he is fighting the Establishment, but whose every "solution" would give the government more power, proposed exactly the same thing. Shouldn't that tell us something? Either Rockefeller was the Socialist *The Worker* said he was, or Ralph Nader is an undercover Capitalist spy. Pick one.

The trouble for the imperialists was that the turn of the century's Merger Mania was unsuccessful. Competition, which to them was chaos, kept breaking out. Professor Kolko writes as follows on page fifty seven: "All of the efforts of Morgan and the corporate promoters to introduce economic stability and control over various industries, and to end the bane of destructive and unprofitable competition, were heading toward failure. . . . Laissez faire provided the businessman with an ideological rationale on an intellectual plane, but it also created instability and insecurity in the economy. The dominant fact of American political life at the beginning of this century was that big business led the struggle for the federal regulation of the economy."

By means of the income tax, the billionaire Socialist imperialists planned to cripple the competition—prohibit "instability" and "insecurity"—while making themselves immune. This was imperative, because in August, 1907, Judge Kenesaw Mountain Landis fined Standard Oil $29,240,000 for 1,462 counts of taking rebates; and in May, 1911, the U.S. Supreme Court ordered the Standard Oil monopoly to divest itself of its holdings in thirty seven other companies.

The imperialist solution was admittedly brilliant. By now, because of Rockefeller's crimes, his name was mud. For an unbought, good word, he could turn to his fellow Socialists, the Reds, but to not many others. With the assistance of Ivy Lee, the nation's foremost advertising genius of his day, Big John started handing out dimes to children when he condescended to appear in public. He also created and controlled a system of tax-exempt foundations. He gave them money—getting credit for humanitarianism and philanthropy—and they used it to generate even more power and profits for John D. If Al Capone had had the prescience to hire some Harvard professors instead of more headbusters, who knows but that he could have been elected to high office. So, almost with one blow, the billionaire Socialist imperialists arranged to impose the income tax on the competition; and, at the same time, they created the tax-exempt foundations to protect themselves.

When the Sixteenth Amendment took effect, the Rockefeller Foundation was already in operation. The lesson we need to learn from this is that the name of the game these days isn't ownership; it's control. Not enough Americans realize it yet, but the fact is that ownership, the American Dream—"Someday, my son, all this will be yours."—is as old-fashioned and dangerous as "sexual liberation." What counts these days isn't who "owns" something, but who gets to enjoy it. The Socialist Monopolists can dump substantial wealth in such foundations, pay no tax on it; but control it as surely as they would if their names were on it. Indeed, in the case of the Rockefeller Foundation, their name *is* on it. Not only did Big John thereby avoid taxes; when the Supreme Court ordered him to divest himself of Standard Oil assets, he gave them to his own foundations—in effect transferring them from one pocket to the other—thereby also protecting them from the estate and gift taxes everyone else had to pay. Again, the present system makes ownership a disadvantage. At the end of this book, we'll show you how everyone can take advantage of that fact.

In his fascinating book, entitled, *The Rockefeller File* (Seal Beach, California, '76 Press, 1976), Gary Allen, the late, great historian, says this: ". . . The careful orchestration of both parts of the campaign represents one of the most successful financial coups in history. The money the Rockefellers have made by it is incalculable. By exempting themselves from the burden they forced on their competitors, the Rockefellers were able to operate in a world of near *laissez-faire* capitalism while foisting the weight of more and more Socialism on their competitors. It is the equivalent of a sprinter forcing every other runner in a race to carry a sixteen-pound shot."

Along these lines, notice that the income tax has made it increasingly difficult for the newcomer to challenge the powers-that-be. In order to do that, the newcomer must accumulate capital; but, when he does so, the Internal Revenue Service takes it away. That's why the Monopolists are happy to pay income tax. Income tax is their insurance against competition, and they can pass it along to you. Indeed, in 1970, while working people were filing 1040s and paying income tax, Nelson Rockefeller's financial managers were arranging for him legally to pay nothing. That fact came out during the hearing on his appointment as Vice President.

Ferdinand Lundberg, author of many works on America's super-rich, says as follows of the income tax (*The Rich and the Super-Rich: A Study in the Power of Money Today*, New York, Lyle Stuart, 1968, p. 350): "What it became, finally, was a siphon gradually inserted into the pocketbooks of the general public. Imposed to popular huzzas as a class tax, the income tax was gradually turned into a mass tax in a jujitsu turnaround. . . ." At page 410, Lundberg adds this: "As to the cause of it all, the socialist will murmur 'capitalism.' Yet the American tax structure has no intrinsic relationship to capitalism and can, indeed, be shown as functionally inimical to it. . . ."

Remember that the Rockefeller Foundation and outfits like it make such outrages possible. In fact, the various Rockefeller foundations are doubly outrageous, because they not only were founded to shield the family whose name they bear from taxation; they also have literally been financing subversive activity. In the famous Occasional Letter No. 1, published by the Rockefeller General Education Board in 1904, a man named Fred Gates, who ran it for John D. Rockefeller, said this: "In our dreams we have limitless resources and the people yield themselves with perfect docility to our moulding hands. The present educational conventions fade from our minds, and, unhampered by tradition, we work our own good will upon a grateful and responsive rural folk. . . ."

The conventions and traditions Gates wanted to get rid of were, among other things, true patriotism; limited, Constitutional government and genuine Free Enterprise. They would be replaced by internationalism leading to world government, totalitarianism and Socialism. In case you farmers are wondering, the answer is yes, you are the "grateful and responsive rural folk" Gates is talking about. Years later, a committee of the U.S. House of Representatives investigated the influence of the biggest tax-exempt foundations in American education. The Chairman of that committee was Congressman Eugene Cox, a Democrat. Cox said that the funds of the Rockefeller Foundation and others "have been used to finance individuals and organizations whose business it has been to get Communism into the private and public schools of the country, to talk down America and play up Russia . . . ." (Special Committee to Investigate Tax-Exempt Foundations and Comparable Organizations, House of Reps., *Tax-Exempt Foundations*, Hearings, 83rd Cong., second sess., Wash. D.C., U.S. Gov't. Print. Off., 1954, p. 43)

Later, Congressman Carroll Reece, a Republican, conducted another investigation, that was sandbagged by the White House. Reece Committee Counsel René Wormser wrote (*Foundations: Their Power and Influence*, New York, Devin-Adair, 1958) that the evidence compiled about foundations "leads one to the conclusion that there was, indeed something in the nature of an actual conspiracy among certain leading educators in the United States to bring about Socialism through the use of our school systems. . . ."

Today, we see the effects of that subversion all around us: in the students who say they don't believe in profit; in the poor victims who have never seen the Declaration of Independence and don't know what it is; in the simpletons who truly believe we can entrust the existence of our nation to a Soviet signature on a treaty.

You now have the tools to begin unravelling the mystery. You now know—from the mouths of the legislators who enacted it and the Supreme Court that sustained it—what the income tax is under law. You know who was behind it and who perverted it. The supremely important question arises: Did the courts back us up?

4

WHAT IS INCOME?

There is a foolproof way to test what we have told you so far. Remember that *Brushaber* is the main Supreme Court ruling on which I.R.S. says it depends. If what we've said so far has been mistaken, then we should logically expect to find dramatic changes in federal court rulings and expert opinion on the subject immediately *after Brushaber*. For instance, the courts and the experts should then have been saying that the federal government—under the Sixteenth Amendment—now has the power to tax the wages of the working woman (the source) directly, without apportionment. On the other hand, if we are correct, we should expect to find no change. The Supreme Court issued the *Brushaber* ruling in 1915. What did the courts and the experts say immediately thereafter?

In the very next year, 1916, the case of *Stanton v. Baltic Mining*, 240 U.S. 103, came before the Supreme Court. Chief Justice White again delivered the opinion, in which he said as follows, referring to *Brushaber* (pp. 112-13): ". . . [B]y the previous ruling it was settled that the provisions of the 16th Amendment conferred no new power of taxation but simply prohibited the previous complete and plenary power of income taxation possessed by Congress from the beginning from being taken out of the category of indirect taxation to which it inherently belonged and being placed in the category of direct taxation subject to apportionment by a consideration of the sources from which the income was derived . . . ."

Again, the Sixteenth Amendment created no new power of taxation. Indeed, it restricted, rather than expanded, the government's power to tax. Chief Justice White reminds us that the income tax authorized by the Sixteenth Amendment is an indirect tax. While it is a direct tax on the income, it is an indirect tax on the source. Of course, the Supreme Court had said all this the previous year, in *Brushaber*. Now, in *Stanton*, White was saying it again.

As we have seen, there was constant disagreement among the experts about the exact meanings of "direct" and "indirect" with regard to taxes. There still is. Even today, the courts of appeal disagree. In *Brushaber*, the Supreme Court said an income tax is an excise, an indirect tax. As we have seen, however, long before the founding of our nation, the colonies agreed that an income tax is direct.

Remember that Congress had the power to impose an excise without apportionment from the beginning. An excise, being indirect, is subject rather to the rule of uniformity; so, if the income tax is an excise, the Amendment would have been unnecessary. Why would Congress invoke the deliberately cumbersome amendment process just to restate the law? Isn't it more sensible to expect that the Sixteenth Amendment was meant to *make some change*—in this case the exception of income alone from the rule of apportionment—and that if a change was necessary the tax must be direct? As we have seen, one can construct a tortuous interpretation, in which the separation of the income from the source makes the tax indirect; but its treatment of the income—once separated—makes it also direct. Along these lines, *Pollock* said the income tax had "assumed the guise of an income tax." Was the Sixteenth Amendment necessary to turn that guise into law; to turn the tax from direct into indirect, as Professor Rottschaefer, for one, said?

This argument is important. However, we don't have to solve it. We leave the solution to brains more devious than ours. Indeed, the good news is that, for the purpose of our present discussion, the argument is largely irrelevant.

Cordell Hull is probably best known for his service as Franklin Roosevelt's Secretary of State during World War II. As a Congressman from Tennessee, in 1913, Hull was also one of the House's leading advocates of the income tax. His views on the subject can be found in Senate Document No. 171 (63rd Congress, 1st Sess., Washington, D.C., 1913), entitled, "The Income Tax." It is interesting to note that the subtitle of the Document is, "On The Proposed Income-Tax Provision Of The Pending Tariff Bill." There is no disagreement about the fact that the tariff is an indirect tax. Again, would the authors of the new income tax write a direct tax into an indirect tax?

It's an interesting question, but, again, we don't have to answer it. Cordell Hull explains why more than once: ". . . The recent amendment, however, provided that Congress might impose a tax on incomes without apportionment, whether considered as direct or indirect taxes. It is evident, therefore, that in so doing the rule of uniformity must govern. . . ." ". . . The inquiry is not whether profits from any source are *property*, but are they *income*. If so, they are taxable."

If the rule of uniformity must govern, then the tax must be indirect; but, in this case, it doesn't matter.

Hull nails it down as follows: "The constitutional amendment simply exempts the entire tax to which it relates from the rule of apportionment. It then becomes utterly immaterial to inquire whether the tax is direct or indirect or as to the origin or source of the income or its disposition—the only inquiry pertinent and necessary is, What amount of net income accrued to an individual during a given taxing period? The tax is thereupon measured by the same and collected out of *his general property*."

In other words, says Hull, it makes no difference—and we don't need to know—whether the tax is direct or indirect. The only thing we need to know is: Did the individual accrue income? Notice that the tax is collected out of, not levied on, his general property. It is levied on and measured by his income, if there is any. Apportionment isn't necessary, because the income and the property have been separated. A tax on the property would still require apportionment.

So, it becomes obvious that one of the keys to the income tax is the definition of "income." What is it? You must know the answer to determine whether or not you are subject to the tax, and words in law don't necessarily mean what they mean in common usage. Well, what did Cordell Hull say income is? He was a father of the tax, so his opinion constitutes legislative history; and time after time he makes it clear: ". . . It must follow that the account of annual income required of a citizen is for the purpose solely of ascertaining what amount of tax ought to be imposed upon him in consequence of his having made *profits* . . . ." (emphasis added)

"The proposed measure would require no act of the citizen until the 1st of January next. It would assess and collect a tax off the individual during next year. Until the 1st day of January the citizen could not balance off against his gross profits his losses, expenses, etc., and ascertain his net income for the preceding year. Until the close of the year the citizen could not know whether his income would be absorbed by losses, expenses, etc., or otherwise disposed of without even being received, nor in fact could he know whether he would have any net income until he had balanced his receipts and expenditures *after* the end of the year. Within the meaning of the proposed tax the cumulating items of profit must necessarily *remain in abeyance* until the expenditures for the year are deducted therefrom at the end of the year . . . ."

Also in that Senate Document, Cordell Hull quotes the Supreme Court with approval in *Maxwell v. Dow*, 176 U.S. 581: "The language of a constitutional amendment should be read in connection with the known condition of affairs out of which the occasion for its adoption may have arisen, and then construed if there be therein any doubtful expressions, in a way, so far as is reasonably possible, to forward the known purpose or object for which the amendment was adopted."

In short, the Supreme Court says the legislative history is decisive—and Cordell Hull's views *are* the legislative history.

According to Volume 50 of the *Congressional Record*, Mr. Hull also said as follows at page 506: ". . . Income as thus defined does not embrace capital or principal, but only such gains or profits as may be realized from rent, interest, salaries, trade, commerce, or sales of any kind of property . . . ."

So, "income" is profit/gain. Profit/gain is income. Profit/gain is the thing being taxed. That is why the tax can't be paid, or even known, during the year being taxed: because you can't know your profit/gain until the year is over. The things taxed are not mere receipts, which may turn out not to be profits at all. Income does not embrace capital or principal—the source—only the income derived from the source.

It is also crucial to establish that, while Hull's views do constitute part of the legislative history of the income tax, they by no means originated with him. All Hull was doing was repeating the same definition of income the government had applied from the beginning.

During the War Between the States, there was an income tax that expired in 1872. The 1862 Act explained that the tax would hit "annual gains, profits, or income." The official record of the Congress then was known as the *Congressional Globe*, and in that publication for the 37th Congress, second session, a Congressman Stevens said as follows at page 1531: ". . . The words 'gain' and 'income' mean the same thing. They are equivalent terms. They mean the net profits. You cannot have any gains until you pay the expenses. What it costs to produce is to be deducted, and then there will be left only the net profits."

The 1864 Act spoke of "the annual gains, profits, or income." The 1865 Act spoke of "the annual gains, profits, and income," and "the annual gains, profits, *or* income." The 1866 Act spoke of "the gains, profits, and income." The 1867 Act spoke of "the gains, profits, and income." The 1870 Act spoke of "the gains, profits, and income." Finally, the 1894 Act spoke of "gains, profits, and income," and "gains, profits, or income." The 1894 Act also spoke of "net profits or income." In your reporter's opinion, this constitutes a trend.

So, what did the 1913 Act—the one sustained by *Brushaber*—say? Like all the others, it said income is "gains, profits, and income." So, for instance, did the 1918 Act, the 1921 Act, the 1924

Act, the 1928 Act and the 1932 Act. Indeed, in the entire history of our nation, Congress has never said income is anything else but profit/gain.

On January 5, 1914, the Commissioner of Internal Revenue issued regulations concerning the new income tax. Article three of those regulations said this: "The NET INCOME shall consist of the total gains, profits, and income derived from all sources (designated as gross income) less deductions . . . ."

So, your profit/gain is your "gross income." You arrive at your profit, of course, by deducting your cost from your receipts. From your gross income, your profit/gain, you further subtract your deductions, thereby producing your "net income."

What did Congressman Hull's colleagues say? Turn with your reporter now to the *Congressional Record* of August 26, 1913. On page 3775, there is a colloquy between Mississippi Senator John Sharp Williams and Iowa Senator Albert B. Cummins. Senator Williams says this: "The Senator seems to attach to the word 'income' a meaning that is not attachable to it in this connection. 'Income' means the net gains or profits. . . ." Senator Cummins asks: "What is it used for?" Senator Williams responds: "A man's taxable income means his gains and profits during the year. Those gains and profits or income derived from any business of any description are taxed. If a man is engaged in dealing in horses, if he buys horses and sells horses and makes a profit or an income out of that dealing, he must pay a tax upon the income.

"I do not know that I exactly catch the Senator's point. But if I do catch it, he seems to have in mind the idea that the word 'income' means receipts of every sort. The income within the contemplation of a tax law does not mean that. It means net income, and is so defined in the bill. That means profits or gains."

Two days later, at page 3843, Illinois Senator Lawrence Y. Sherman said this: ". . . If by professional effort any person should earn a given sum annually and he spends half of it, he saves the other half. The half so saved in turn becomes principal. That principal is property. The savings from the income by professional effort or by any form of skilled labor or unskilled by hand becomes property. At the end of any given period that saving is a principal, and any income derived from it is an income from property, not an income from the earning capacity or the personal ability of the taxpayer in question. . . ." Senator Sherman spoke of a need "to distinguish between those who have incomes from fixed investments of property and those who have incomes from earning capacity. . . . Those investments that produce an income from a property source I think are properly to be distinguished from those arising from the earning capacity of the individual. A public officer, an employee, one who earns by professional ability, an architect, a musician, a lawyer, a doctor of divinity, a doctor of medicine, all are earning because of their personal ability."

Also at page 3843, and page 3844, Senator Cummins, the Senator with whom Senator Williams had conducted that colloquy two days prior, made some edifying comments as follows (to make for easy reading, we have omitted the usual elisions): "I want to make a lawyer's argument that the authority of the Congress of the United States with regard to this subject is not unlimited. Our authority is to levy a tax upon incomes. I take it that every lawyer will agree with me in the conclusion that we can not levy under this amendment a tax upon anything but an income. I assume that every lawyer will agree with me that we can not legislatively interpret the meaning of the word 'income.' That is purely a judicial matter. We can not enlarge the meaning of the word 'income.' The word 'income' had a well-defined meaning before the amendment of the Constitution was adopted. It has been defined in all the courts of this country. When the people of the country granted to Congress the right to levy a tax on incomes, that right was granted with reference to the legal meaning and interpretation of the word 'income' as it was then or as it might thereafter be defined or understood in legal procedure. If we could call anything income that we pleased, we could obliterate all the distinction between income and principal. [T]he Congress can not affect the meaning of the word 'income' by any legislation whatsoever. If it were within the power of Congress to enlarge the meaning of the word 'income,' it could, as I suggested a moment ago, obliterate all difference between income and principal, and *obviously the people of this country did not intend to give to Congress the power to levy a direct tax upon all the property of this country without apportionment.*" (emphasis added)

Could it be said any clearer? Your reporter can't imagine how. The source still cannot be taxed without apportionment.

Finally, at page 3845 of the *Congressional Record* of August 28, 1913, South Dakota Senator Thomas Sterling asks this: "If in the definition of the word 'income' as given in a standard dictionary the words 'gains and profits' are also given as synonymous with the term 'income' would there be anything wrong in the use of those words in the section to which the Senator refers?" Senator Cummins replies: "I do not think there would be, although they would be wholly unnecessary. . . ."

In short, whenever the word "income" appears in the income tax law, it means gains/profits—even if those words do *not* appear.

Now, what did the courts say immediately after the Sixteenth Amendment was "ratified" and the new tax became "law"? On December 1, 1913, the Supreme Court ruled in *Stratton's Independence v. Howbert*, 231 U.S. 399, at page 415, that "'income' may be defined as the gain derived from capital, from labor, or from both combined, and here we have combined operations of capital and labor. . . ." Labor here refers to the work of employees a taxpayer hires to make profit.

In 1917, a federal court heard the case of *Southern Pacific v. Lowe.* This was only a couple of years after the Supreme Court had found the tax constitutional, so the matter was still fresh. According to volume 238 of the Federal Reporter, at page 850, New York District Judge Manton said this: "I do not think that 'income,' as used in the statute, should be given a meaning so as to include everything that comes in. The true function of the words 'gains' and 'profits' is to limit the meaning of the word 'income' and to show its use only in the sense of receipts which constituted an accretion to capital. So the function of the word 'income' should be to limit the meaning of the words 'gains' and 'profits.' The increased value of capital as such constitutes in one sense a gain or profit, but not income. Hence such gain or profit is not taxable, but only such profits and gains as constitute income are taxable. . . ."

In other words, said his honor, income does not at all mean everything that comes in. "Income" and "comes in" are so similar, there is a natural tendency to believe they are the same. However, as you see, his honor says they aren't. Income, of course, does not occur in nature. It doesn't grow on trees, which you knew. Income is an invention of law, and his honor says it doesn't mean receipts. In order for there to be income, there must be gains or profits. Indeed, notice that even if you do have gains or profits, you still may have no income.

This same case then went to the Supreme Court (247 U.S. 330), where, on June 3, 1918, Mr. Justice Pitney made it even clearer, if that was possible, at page 335: "We must reject in this case, as we have rejected in cases arising under the Corporation Excise Tax Act of 1909 (*Doyle v. Mitchell Brothers Co., ante*, 179, and *Hays v. Gauley Mountain Coal Co., ante*, 189) the broad contention submitted in behalf of the Government that all receipts—everything that comes in—are income within the proper definition of the term 'gross income'. . . ."

Again, receipts and income are two different things. Yes, everything that comes in may be income. On the other hand, none of it may be. The fact that it comes in means nothing by itself.

As you see, the Court mentioned *Doyle v. Mitchell Brothers Co.*, 247 U.S. 179, which the Court decided on May 20, 1918. At page 185 of that case, the Court said as follows, again by Mr. Justice Pitney: ". . . Whatever difficulty there may be about a precise and scientific definition of 'income,' it imports, as used here, something entirely distinct from principal or capital either as a subject of taxation or as a measure of the tax; conveying rather the idea of gain or increase arising from corporate activities. . . ." His honor then quoted *Stratton's Independence* with approval. He also said this: ". . . In order to determine whether there has been gain or loss, and the amount of the gain, if any, we must withdraw from the gross proceeds an amount sufficient to restore the capital value that existed at the commencement of the period under consideration.

"This has been recognized from the beginning by the administrative officers of the Government. . . ."

Of course, this is Elementary Accounting 101. The price at which you sell your doohickey is not your profit. To determine your profit, you must subtract your cost from that price. What was the value of your investment, the cost of your labor, your advertising and rent, etc.? Notice his honor's statement that the people who run the government were aware of this from the beginning.

On March 8, 1920, the Supreme Court ruled in the famous case of *Eisner v. Macomber*, 252 U.S. 189. Again Mr. Justice Pitney delivered the opinion of the Court. Starting at page 198, he said this: "Income is the gain, come to fruition, from capital, from labor, or from both combined. This is sound doctrine both in law and in economics. . . ." Gain and profit of course are synonymous. Next, his honor quotes with approval from another Supreme Court ruling (*Towne v. Eisner*, 242 Fed.Rep. at 704): "It is manifest that the stock dividend in question cannot be reached by the Income Tax Act, and could not, even though Congress expressly declared it to be taxable as income, unless it is in fact income."

In other words, if it isn't income, *it isn't income*, even if Congress says it is. Congress can't buck the Constitution. Notice that all of this even applies to a stock dividend.

Then his honor turned to the meaning of the Sixteenth Amendment: ". . . As repeatedly held, this did not extend the taxing power to new subjects, but merely removed the necessity which otherwise might exist for an apportionment among the States of taxes laid on income. . . .

"A proper regard for its genesis, as well as its very clear language, requires also that this Amendment shall not be extended by loose construction, so as to repeal or modify, except as applied to income, those provisions of the Constitution that require an apportionment according to population for direct taxes upon property, real and personal. This limitation still has an appropriate and important function, and is not to be overridden by Congress or disregarded by the courts."

From a distance of almost seven decades, we find the importance of these remarks staggering. We have said before that today, no doubt because of disinformation engendered by our friends at I.R.S., many Americans believe that the Sixteenth Amendment totally repealed apportionment. Here, however, the Supreme Court says that, while the Sixteenth Amendment did exempt *income* from apportionment, no other tax enjoys that exemption. *Apportionment is still the law for direct taxes on property, real and personal. A direct tax on the source must still be apportioned.* Notice the Court's warning to Congress and the lower courts not to disregard this, or even to modify it; not to extend it by "loose construction."

Next Justice Pitney considered the term "income": "In order, therefore, that the clauses cited from Article I of the Constitution may have proper force and effect, save only as modified by the Amendment, and that the latter also may have proper effect, it becomes essential to distinguish between what is and what is not 'income,' as the term is there used; and to apply the distinction, as cases arise, according to truth and substance, without regard to form. *Congress cannot by any definition it may adopt conclude the matter, since it cannot by legislation alter the Constitution*, from which alone it derives its power to legislate, and within whose limitations alone that power can be lawfully exercised." (emphasis added)

The reader will recall that Senator Cummins said the same thing. Here, again, we see that income and receipts are not necessarily the same. The mere fact that somebody pays you money—the mere fact that something comes in—does not automatically mean you have income for income tax purposes. Yes, all the money you are paid may be subject to income tax. On the other hand, none of it may be. Notice, especially, the language we have placed in italics. You will see the supreme importance of it later. In it, the Supreme Court warns Congress that it is forbidden to define the term 'income' by legislation. This means that Congress may pass all the laws it likes, that say income is something it isn't, but those laws will be dead the moment they are born, as if never written. 'Income' is only what the Sixteenth Amendment says it is.

And what is that? In *Eisner v. Macomber*, the High Court said this: "After examining dictionaries in common use (Bouv. L.D.;

Standard Dict.; Webster's Internat. Dict.; Century Dict.), we find little to add to the succinct definition adopted in two cases arising under the Corporation Tax Act of 1909 *(Stratton's Independence v. Howbert*, 231 U.S. 399, 415; *Doyle v. Mitchell Bros. Co.*, 247 U.S. 179, 185)—'Income may be defined as the gain derived from capital, from labor, or from both combined,' provided it be understood to include profit gained through a sale or conversion of capital assets, to which it was applied in the *Doyle* Case (pp. 183, 185)."

The reader will recall that we have already examined *Stratton's Independence* and *Doyle*. Here, in *Eisner*, Mr. Justice Pitney added the requirement that "income" includes "profit gained through a sale or conversion of capital assets." If whatever you are doing does not include those things, *you don't have income*. Income equals profit. Income equals gain.

So, where has the government gone wrong? Mr. Justice Pitney explains: ". . . The Government, although basing its argument upon the definition as quoted, placed chief emphasis upon the word 'gain,' which was extended to include a variety of meanings; while the significance of the next three words was either overlooked or misconceived. *'Derived—from—capital'; —'the gain—derived—from—capital,'* etc. Here we have the essential matter: not a gain accruing to capital, not a *growth* or *increment* of value *in* the investment; but a gain, a profit, something of exchangeable value *proceeding from* the property, *severed from* the capital however invested or employed, and *coming in*, being *'derived,'* that is, *received* or *drawn by* the recipient (the taxpayer) for his *separate* use, benefit and disposal; —*that* is income derived from the property. Nothing else answers the description."

All the italics are Justice Pitney's. Again, income is not just an increase in value of the investment, of the capital. Income does not just arise from the fact that a seller's market has made your land more valuable, or that additional training has made *you* more valuable. Income means gain, means profit, separated from, severed from, the source; from the investment, from the capital. The High Court says here that the government is ignoring the requirement of that separation, expressed in the two words, "derived from." Today, our friends at I.R.S. are still trying to ignore them, in defiance of the Court. The difference is: Today's lower courts have been letting them get away with it—so far.

Question: How can a working woman's wages be separated from her? Many humorous answers instantly spring up. Our friends at I.R.S. have proven themselves adept at such surgery, but not in a legal, constitutional way. We shall explore the issue a bit further down. For now, let it fester.

Meanwhile, let's establish that none of this was a fluke. In 1921, in *Merchants' Loan & Trust Co. v. Smietanka*, 255 U.S. at page 517, the Supreme Court again repeated the definition of income from *Stratton's Independence*, and now from the *Eisner* ruling of the previous year. Mr. Justice Clarke, speaking for the Court, concluded at page 519 that "there would seem to be no room to doubt that the word must be given the same meaning in all of the Income Tax Acts of Congress that was given to it in the Corporation Excise Tax Act and that what that meaning is has now become definitely settled by decisions of this court."

Five years later, in *Bowers v. Kerbaugh-Empire Co.*, in 271 U.S. at 174, Justice Butler, writing for the Court, said it again: ". . .'Income' has been taken to mean the same thing as used in the Corporation Excise Tax Act of 1909, in the Sixteenth Amendment and in the various revenue acts subsequently passed. . . ."

These are just a few examples. It is important to note that, in these early, definitive cases, the issues were whether certain activities involving corporations were taxable. The idea of allowing the federal government to tax wages directly—without apportionment—didn't even come up. Workers were not being thrown into prison. Their cars were not being stolen by the government. Their children were not being kidnapped by our friends at I.R.S. Remember that our source is not some "tax protest" group. Just about everything we are telling you comes from the U.S. Supreme Court. It would be difficult, and perhaps impossible, in our system of jurisprudence, to find a principle better settled than the one we have been citing.

Along these lines, here is an example of a state ruling: *Sims v. Ahrens*, 271 Southwest 720, dated May 18, 1925, when the income tax was still relatively fresh. At page 730, the Arkansas Supreme Court quoted a Mississippi case as follows with approval: "Income is necessarily the product of the joint efforts of the state and the recipient of the income, the state furnishing the protection necessary to enable the recipient to produce, receive, and enjoy it, and a tax thereon in the last analysis is simply a portion cut from the income and appropriated by the state as its share thereof, and, while a tax on income includes some of the elements both of a tax on property and of a tax on persons, it cannot be classified as strictly a tax on either, for it is generally and necessarily an excise, and should be enforced as such . . . ."

In other words, an essential element of income is a favor from the state, from the government. If you take such a favor, if you enjoy such a privilege, then your profit, your gain, is income, and is taxable. If you choose to make bourbon whiskey, the government will protect you, in return for which it demands a cut. You become liable for the tax when you volunteer to make bourbon, but you are not required to volunteer.

Finally, on February 8, 1952, in Maryland, U.S. District Judge Chesnut ruled in *Anderson Oldsmobile, Inc. v. Hofferbert, Collector of Internal Revenue*, 102 Federal Supplement 902. The case concerned an automobile dealer who, during World War II, paid more for some automobiles than permitted by the Office of Price Administration. At page 902, his honor quoted from an Oklahoma case as follows: ". . . Money actually paid, although in excess of the prevailing ceiling price, for the purchase price of an article cannot be classified as a gain, profit or income."

Judge Chesnut also said this, at page 905: ". . . Constitutionally the only thing that can be taxed by Congress is 'income.' And the tax actually imposed by Congress has been on net income as distinct from gross income. The tax is not, never has been and could not constitutionally be upon 'gross receipts.' . . .

"It is to be noted that it is only profits and income from business which constitutes gross income. It is only after such profit has so been determined (constituting gross income) that further deductions are to be made therefrom, as authorized by section 23, in order to arrive at the net income which is taxable. And it is also to be noted that, as an economic and mathematical truism, gain or profit which constitutes gross income cannot be determined without deducting the cost of the goods sold from the gross selling price. The deduction so made in the computation is a necessary one under section 22 to determine gross income and is definitely different and distinct from the deduction authorized by section 23 to be made from gross income to determine net income. . . ."

This is so clear, we don't need to explain it. Although it was just a district court case, *Anderson* was never overruled.

How does all this apply to the working woman?

5

SOAK THE POOR!

What is labor? Labor is property, just as much as capital is property. When the working woman goes to work, she is selling her property, just as much as her employer is selling his product. This principle has a long history in our system of jurisprudence. For instance, on May 5, 1884, the Supreme Court ruled in *Butchers' Union Co. v. Crescent City Co.*, 111 U.S. 746. Mr. Justice Miller delivered the opinion of the Court, and, at page 757, he quoted with approval from economist Adam Smith's classic, *Wealth of Nations*: "The property which every man has in his own labor, as it is the original foundation of all other property, so it is the most sacred and inviolable. The patrimony of the poor man lies in the strength and dexterity of his own hands, and to hinder his employing this strength and dexterity in what manner he thinks proper, without injury to his neighbor, is a plain violation of this most sacred property. . . ."

So, according to Adam Smith and the Supreme Court, labor is the supreme property.

In 1907, the Supreme Court considered the case of *Adair v. United States*. Mr. Justice Harlan delivered the opinion of the Court, and in 208 U.S. at page 172, he refers to the Fifth Amendment of the Constitution, and says the Court finds "an invasion of the personal liberty, as well as of the right of property, guaranteed by that Amendment. Such liberty and right embraces the right to make contracts for the purchase of the labor of others and equally *the right to make contracts for the sale of one's own labor* . . . ." (emphasis added)

So, labor is the supreme property, and selling it is a right.

Now, let's move along to January 25, 1915, the year of the *Brushaber* ruling. The case was *Coppage v. State of Kansas*, 236 U.S. 1. Mr. Justice Pitney delivered the opinion of the Court, and at page ten he explained as follows: ". . . The right of a person to sell his labor upon such terms as he deems proper is, in its essence, the same as the right of the purchaser of labor to prescribe the conditions upon which he will accept such labor from the person offering to sell it. . . ."

At page fourteen, his honor says this: ". . . Included in the right of personal liberty and the right of private property—partaking of the nature of each—is the right to make contracts for the acquisition of property. Chief among such contracts is that of personal employment, by which labor and other services are exchanged for money or other forms of property. If this right be struck down or arbitrarily interfered with, there is a substantial impairment of liberty in the long-established constitutional sense. The right is as essential to the laborer as to the capitalist, to the poor as to the rich; for the vast majority of persons have no other honest way to begin to acquire property, save by working for money."

There is also *Adkins v. Children's Hospital*, where, in 261 U.S. at 558, Mr. Justice Sutherland wrote in 1923 about what the Supreme Court called a "moral requirement implicit in every contract of employment, viz., that the amount to be paid and the service to be rendered shall bear to each other some relation of just equivalence . . . . In principle, there can be no difference between the case of selling labor and the case of selling goods. . . ."

So, according to the U.S. Supreme Court, the worker in effect is exchanging property with his boss. The kinds of property they are exchanging are different—labor and Federal Reserve Notes—but they are both property. The difference is that labor is the superior property.

Now, what did the authors of the income tax intend to tax? Let's look again into the legislative history, to determine whether they intended to tax labor. On January 24, 1894, during the second session of the 53rd Congress, the House Committee on Ways and Means submitted Report No 276. In it, the Committee proposed the income tax that the Supreme Court would strike down in 1895. On page seven of that report, the Committee said this: "The committee think that too large a portion of the taxes are collected from the necessaries of life, and consequently too small a part from the wealth of the people, which has been accumulated and is held in excess of what is necessary for their comfort. . . ." Further down the same page, the Committee asked: ". . . Why tax clothing and necessaries of life to pay all instead of letting a small part of the burden rest on incomes?"

Indeed, on March 14, 1912, during the second session of the 62nd Congress, the House Committee on Ways and Means submitted another report (No. 416) to the House. In it, the Committee proposed that the then recent corporation tax be extended to private business and individuals. The report explains on page two that "when he purchases for himself and family the necessities of life, the man of meager earnings contributes out of his daily wage to the support of the Government. When a citizen pays taxes according to his earnings, from whatever source, he gives support to his Government, and receives protection from it in a more equitable manner than under any other plan of taxation yet devised. If his earnings increase his taxes increase, and justly so, for he is better able to pay increased taxes. If his *gains* decrease, so do his taxes, and fortunately for him, because he is less able to pay them. . . ." (emphasis added)

Notice that the Committee here was using "earnings" as a synonym for "gains," and was proposing that the tax burden be shifted away from wages and instead imposed upon earnings. So the Committee understood perfectly in 1912, the year before the Sixteenth Amendment was "ratified," that wages and earnings, also known as profit/gain/income, are two different things.

On the next page, the Committee argues that "if the act of 1894 had been drawn in the form of the law now proposed, and had levied an *excise tax upon business* measured by income, it would have been sustained . . . ." (emphasis added) The Committee also says this: "The proposed tax is not a direct tax upon the property, real or personal, of the copartnerships or individuals, but a special excise upon the carrying on or doing business by such copartnerships or individuals . . . ."

As we have seen, an excise tax is a privilege tax. The two terms are identical. So, the Committee considered doing business a privilege. Again, we disagree. We think doing business is a right. Be that as it may, however, notice that it *was business* the Committee meant to tax; again, by shifting the burden *away from wages*. Remember that the battle cry at the time was, "Soak the Rich!"

Indeed, since every legal authority, from the Supreme Court on down, says that income means profit, and that income means gain, the obvious question arises: Are the working woman's wages profit or gain? The reader will recall what Senator Lawrence Sherman said on the subject, quoted in the previous chapter. Noah Webster himself couldn't make it any clearer. The reader will recall that what the worker saves from his pay becomes capital/principal he can invest. If he invests it in stock, any dividend paid thereon would be income. It would be gain, profit, derived from—separated from—the source, the wages, the salary or compensation. The gain, the profit, the income, would be taxable; the source, the wages, the salary or compensation would not.

Let's look at a couple of state cases. On May 27, 1946, the Supreme Court of Pennsylvania ruled in *Laureldale Cemetery Association v. Matthews*, 47 Atlantic 2d. 277. At page 280, Justice Patterson said as follows for the Court: ". . . Reasonable compensation for labor or services rendered is not profit. . . ." On April 25, 1955, the Virginia Supreme Court of Appeal ruled in *Oliver v. Halstead*, 86 S.E. Rep. 2d. 858. Justice Smith delivered the opinion of the Court, and at page 859 he said this: ". . . There is a clear distinction between 'profit' and 'wages' or compensation for labor. 'Compensation for labor can not be regarded as profit within the meaning of the law. The word "profit," as ordinarily used, means the gain made upon any business or investment—a different thing altogether from mere compensation for labor.' *Commer-*

cial League Association of America v. People ex rel. Needles, Auditor, 90 Ill. 166. . . ." In short, profit and gain—synonyms for income—are one thing. Wages and compensation are another.

Again, we realize we are belaboring this point to exhaustion, for which we again apologize. We do so because our friends at I.R.S. have deliberately concealed the truth for so long.

How is profit calculated? Is there a formula for doing so in the law? Yes, there is. Turn with your reporter now to Section 1001 of the Internal Revenue Code, headed: "Determination of amount of and recognition of gain or loss." Paragraph (a) is headed: "Computation of gain or loss," and it tells us as follows: "The gain from the sale or other disposition of property shall be the excess of the amount realized therefrom over the adjusted basis provided in section 1011 for determining gain, and the loss shall be the excess of the adjusted basis provided in such section for determining loss over the amount realized." In other words, your gain (profit, income) is not your receipts. Your gain (profit, income) is the amount you receive over the adjusted basis. What is the adjusted basis?

Section 1011 prescribes this general rule: "The adjusted basis for determining the gain or loss from the sale or other disposition of property, whenever acquired, shall be the basis . . . ." What, then, is the basis? Section 1012 of the Code tells us this: "The basis of property shall be the cost of such property . . . ." In short, the adjusted basis is the cost.

Of course, all this boils down to the obvious fact that, to establish one's income (profit, gain), one must subtract one's cost from one's receipts. How much did the property you eventually sold cost you in the first place? Did you spend anything to improve, or to assemble, it? Did you hire anyone to work on it? Did you pay rent and utilities for it? Did you advertise it? Nothing in business could be more routine. Only after you answer these questions—and a lot more like them—are you able to answer the question of how much income you made.

For instance, in *Jack Daniel Distillery v. United States*, 379 F.2d 569, Judge Nichols wrote as follows for the U.S. Court of Claims, on June 9, 1967, at page 579: "From all the foregoing, it is concluded that plaintiff's valuation of the unbottled inventory constitutes the fair market value as of September 17, 1956, and was properly used by it as a basis for computing its cost of goods sold and income for the years in question."

Court records are full of such cases. The government will dispute the numbers; but we are not aware of any case in which the government told a business that it would not be permitted to deduct the cost from the receipts, for income tax purposes. Were our friends at I.R.S. to try such a thing, you would see a revolution in the boardrooms that would collapse the government.

Yet, our friends at I.R.S. are doing exactly that to the working woman. What is *her* income (profit, gain)? For ease in calculation, suppose that her wages—let's call them "labor receipts"—are $100. According to our friends at I.R.S., her gain is $100, the entire amount. They demand that she enter the entire amount as gain on her return.

Remember that the law says her gain (income) is the difference between the amount she received and the adjusted basis of the labor property she sold. Question: If the entire amount of her wages is gain, then what was the value, or cost, or basis, of that property? Answer: Nothing. According to our friends at I.R.S., her labor was worthless. It sounds crazy—and it is—but that is what I.R.S. says, in effect. If your receipts are $100, and the entire $100 is profit, doesn't that mean you started out with zero? It means you started with no investment. It means your employer paid you for nothing.

Again, if our friends at I.R.S. said that to an employer about his own investments, they would be laughed out of town. They say it to the working woman, because she cannot afford to pay expensive lawyers to do the laughing. (Indeed, her standard of living is falling fast, because of the machinations of the multinational swindlers who control our economy.) Our friends at I.R.S. are saying that capital property has value; that real property has value; that factories and machinery have value—but that labor property is worthless. Remember, we proved from the mouth of the Supreme Court that labor is the supreme property, the basis of all other property.

Is the working woman's labor worthless? Her boss obviously doesn't think so. If he did, he wouldn't hire her. He hires her precisely *because* he believes her labor has value. How much? Isn't it worth $100, the amount he pays? Again, if it were not worth $100, he wouldn't pay it. If it were worth less, naturally he would pay less. If it were worthless, obviously he wouldn't hire her at all. Notice that whenever Congress increases the federal minimum wage, unemployment, especially among young people, increases along with it. One can just about chart such expectations on a graph; which proves that employers pay very close attention to the cost of their labor.

All right, we have $100 worth of labor, for which $100 has been paid. How much gain is there? Answer: None. There is an exchange. There is a wash. There is no gain and no profit. What happens between employer and employee is an equivalent exchange for mutual advantage; a trade of different kinds of property of the same value. Remember, that's what the Supreme Court said; and if there is no gain, there is no income for the income tax to tax.

So, here we have the most outrageous case of discrimination—for business, against workers—since the nightmares of Nat Turner; the victims of which are working Americans of all colors. Why have the people let it happen? Why have the *unions* let it happen?

Indeed, in *Grosjean v. American Press Co.*, 297 U.S. 233 (1936); and *Murdock v. Penn.*, 319 U.S. 105 (1943), the Supreme Court ruled that a state is forbidden to impose an excise tax upon a right secured by the Constitution. Ours is a system of delegated powers, in which the federal government gets *all* its powers from the people and the states. Therefore, it can't have a power that the people and the states didn't and don't have. So, the federal government can't impose an excise tax, such as the income tax, on a right secured by the Constitution, either. And it doesn't. Remember that the law allows the government to tax income, not labor, which is one of those rights.

The reader may be somewhat incredulous about your obedient servant's assertion that our friends in government really believe your labor is worthless. Surely they would never dare put such a thing in print. Or would they?

Your reporter is now looking at a document published by the Congressional Research Service of the Library of Congress. The title is, "Some Constitutional Questions Regarding the Federal Income Tax Laws." The author is Howard Zaritsky, Legislative Attorney, American Law Division. John R. Luckey, a Legislative Research Assistant in that Division, updated it on September 26, 1984. On the cover, it says, "Report No. 84-168 A," and "HJ 4625 U.S.A." The obvious purpose of the authors is to provide "legal" support to our beleaguered friends at I.R.S.

Here's what they say on page eleven: "Wages to be taxable income must pass the same type of examination. For example, if John Doe works 5 hours for $5.00 an hour, is the $25.00 he receives taxable income to him? As we have seen in the above analysis, the question as to whether there has been a gain is not answered by looking only at the fair market value of Doe's labor, but rather by determining the difference between that fair market value and his basis (cost) in that labor. *Generally one has a zero basis in his labor*. Therefore Doe's gain is $25.00 minus 0 or $25.00." (emphasis added)

We warned you that reading this book could be dangerous to people with heart conditions. Now that you have gotten off the floor, you may want to read that paragraph again. Yes, it does really say what you thought it says, doesn't it? It says that generally (not specifically?) you have a zero basis in your labor. In other words, it says your labor is worthless. Now you know. Why does your employer, who is presumably intelligent, buy something that is worthless? Notice that these government authors do admit you must have gain in order to have income, even if wages are your only receipts.

Among the reasons they believe there is no basis (cost) in your labor, is no doubt the fact that you didn't pay for it. Where then did it come from? Your labor is a gift from God, and our friends at I.R.S. themselves say that gifts over a certain amount are taxed to the donor. In recent years, the people who run our government have extruded growing hostility toward God, a losing enterprise. Could that be why they demean His gift?

The question arises: What do the courts say about all this today? How do our friends at I.R.S. respond? As we shall see, the reign of terror they conduct even includes the intimidation of federal judges. Whether or not the reason is that intimidation, we don't know, but the fact is that I.R.S.has managed to orchestrate a string of victories in court—lower court. As you will see now, however, those "victories" only prove our point and buttress our argument.

6

CONFUSION IN THE COURTS

One of the cases the government likes to cite in its desperate claim that wages constitute gain, is *Lonsdale v. C.I.R.*, 661 F.2d 71 (1981). The petitioners-appellants were Eugene M. Lonsdale, Sr. and Patsy R. Lonsdale, who represented themselves. The Fifth Circuit Court of Appeal heard the case, and on November 12, 1981 Judges Gee, Garza and Tate ruled as follows: "As nearly as we can tell from their pro se brief, these arguments are two, or possibly three, in number. The first category of contentions may be summarized as that the United States Constitution forbids taxation of compensation received for personal services. This is so, appellants first argue, because the exchange of services for money is a zero-sum transaction, the value of the wages being exactly that of the labor exchanged for them and hence containing no element of *profit*. This contention is meritless. The Constitution grants Congress power to tax 'incomes, from whatever source derived . . . .' U.S. Const. amend XVI. Exercising this power, *Congress has defined income* as including compensation for services. 26 U.S.C. §61(a)(1). Broadly speaking, that definition covers all 'accessions to wealth.' See Commissioner v. Glenshaw Glass Co., 348 U.S. 426, 431, 75 S.Ct. 473, 477, 99 L.Ed. 483 (1955). This definition is clearly within the power to tax 'incomes' granted by the sixteenth amendment." (emphasis added)

Did their honors Gee, Garza and Tate sniff something illegal that day? Notice that they begin with the typical condescension such legal monopolists usually direct at private citizens who dare to enter their lucrative preserve. Then, they write that the citizens' argument is meritless, because the Sixteenth Amendment gave Congress power to tax incomes "from whatever source derived." As we have seen, that is perfectly true (always assuming, *arguendo*, that the Amendment was actually ratified). We don't argue about it. However, the court here totally ashcans the avalanche of legislative history that tells us for sure what "income" is. The court totally disregards the phrase "from whatever source derived," which the court quotes itself. The court quotes it for support and then rejects it.

Then their honors write that Congress "has defined income" in Section 61(a)(1) of the Internal Revenue Code. Later, we shall see that Congress didn't do that at all; that, in fact, Congress defines "gross income" in that Section. Indeed, nowhere in the vast Internal Revenue Code is there any definition—not one—of "income." Is this an oversight? No, the reason "income" is not defined in the Internal Revenue Code is that the Supreme Court forbade Congress to define it. Remember? In *Eisner*, the Court explained: ". . . Congress cannot by any definition it may adopt conclude the matter, since it cannot by legislation alter the Constitution . . . ." In other words, "income" is only what the Sixteenth Amendment says it is; not at all what Congress says it is. Remember also that, in *Eisner*, the Court specifically nailed the government for disregarding the language of the Amendment. Now, in *Lonsdale*, the fifth circuit does the same thing. Indeed, the fifth circuit says the authority for its own ruling is the "fact" that Congress has done something the Supreme Court says it has no power to do (which, in fact, Congress hasn't done).

Finally, the fifth circuit says that Congress's "definition" covers all "accessions to wealth." In other words, the circuit says that "income" is whatever comes in; that income = receipts. Again, all the legislative history—which is decisive—gives this absurdity the lie.

Now, let's move along to *Ficalora v. C.I.R.*, 751 F.2d 85. Alfred Ficalora was the appellant. Judges Oakes, Winter and Clarie ruled on it in the second circuit, on December 13, 1984. On page eighty seven, they say this: ". . . While ruling that a tax upon income from real and personal property is invalid in the absence of apportionment, the Supreme Court explicitly states that taxes on income from one's employment are not direct taxes and are not subject to the necessity of apportionment. Pollock v. Farmers' Loan and Trust Co., 158 U.S. at 635, 15 S.Ct. at 919. . . ." Again, we don't argue about that. The court is typically pecking at a scarecrow. Notice, however, that the court totally ignores the crucial language of the Sixteenth Amendment: "derived from." The Amendment does not authorize a tax "on" the wages, but on the income "derived from" the wages.

On the same page, the court said this: "Finally, in the case of New York ex rel. Cohn v. Graves, 300 U.S. 308, 57 S.Ct. 466, 81 L.Ed. 666 (1937), the Supreme Court in effect overruled Pollock, and in so doing *rendered the Sixteenth Amendment unnecessary*, when it sustained New York's income tax on income derived from real property in New Jersey. Id. at 314-315, 57 S.Ct. at 468-69. . . ." (emphasis added)

Pardon us for repeating ourselves. We must, because today's courts keep repeating these perversions. Again, the issue here is not a perfectly proper tax on income derived from real property. The issue is whether Congress can impose a direct tax on the property itself without apportionment. It can't. Notice also here the second circuit's novel idea that the Supreme Court can unilaterally amend the Constitution. Were that really the case, we wouldn't need a Congress. The simpering peacocks in that body could go home. The laws would be enacted by the Court.

There is also the typical fact that *New York ex rel. Cohn v. Graves* doesn't say what *Ficalora* says it does. It doesn't "overrule" *Pollock*. All it does is affirm the power of a state to tax income derived by one of its citizens from property in *another* state, which is hardly controversial. Mr. Justice Stone writes at page 315 of *Cohn*, "Nothing which was said or decided in *Pollock v. Farmers Loan & Trust Co.*, 157 U.S. 429, calls for a different conclusion. . . ." Does that sound like a "reversal" of *Pollock*?

Indeed, the *real* blockbuster in *Cohn* is found at page 313, where Mr. Justice Stone, speaking for the Court, says that "income is not necessarily clothed with the tax immunity enjoyed by its source. . . ." Which means—surprise—that the income and the source are different, separate, and the source is *immune*. The fact that the taxpayer was a citizen of New York, while her property was in New Jersey, *underlines* the separation.

On page 88 of *Ficalora*, the judges say this: "Lastly, the appellant asserts that the term 'income,' as used in the taxing statutes, has no defined meaning and is unconstitutionally vague and indefinite. As discussed above, Section 61 of the Code defines gross income as 'all income from whatever source derived.' Even if we were to assume, *arguendo*, that this phrase is somehow vague or indefinite, Section 61 of the Code specifically cites '(c)ompensation for services . . .' as a concrete example of what is meant by the term income. . . . The appellant's argument that the term is unconstitutionally vague and indefinite, is totally without merit."

Probably the first rule of lexicography is that you can't use the thing you are defining in its definition. As you see, however, the second circuit can. It has the guns. Indeed, notice that the court here does not even pretend to present a definition of "income." Instead, it presents a defective definition of "gross income," as a putative equal of "income." This somewhat akin to defining an archeopteryx as a robin redbreast. Again, we shall look at Section 61 soon.

Meanwhile, let's look at *Funk v. Commissioner of Internal Revenue*, 687 F.2d 264, in which the eighth circuit takes us on a tour of cases on the subject. Gerald C. Funk and Judith M. Funk were the appellants, and on September 1, 1982, Circuit Judges Bright, McMillian and Gibson ruled as follows on page 265: "It is not disputed that Taxpayers failed to report as income wages received during the 1976 and 1977 taxable years. They argue that compensation for labor is not constitutionally subject to the federal income tax, that an individual's labor is capital in which he or she possesses a property right, that an individual has the right to exchange that property for other property, i.e. money, and that such a transaction is an equal exchange which does not give rise to any profit. We reject Taxpayers' sixteenth amendment claim because *the constitutionality of the sixteenth amendment was upheld by the Supreme Court in Brushaber v. Union Pacific R.R.*, 240 U.S. 1, 18, 36 S.Ct. 236, 241, 60 L.Ed. 493 (1916). *See generally: Eisner v. Macomber*, 252 U.S. 189, 205-06, 40 S.Ct. 189, 192-93, 64 L.Ed. 521 (1920). . . ." (emphasis added)

Did the Supreme Court uphold the constitutionality of the Sixteenth Amendment in *Brushaber*? No, in fact the Supreme Court has no power to do anything like that. Once an amendment is ratified, it is as much a part of the Constitution as any other part, and the Supreme Court is stuck with it; is bound to uphold it. If the Supreme Court has the power to strike down a constitutional amendment, it has the power to strike down the entire Constitution, by a 5-4 vote. But, it has no such power. It *does* have power to rule on whether a *law* enacted under the Constitution is in conflict with it; in which case, of course, it rules the *law* unconstitutional. That's what it did in *Brushaber.* The Court found the *tax law* constitutional, because its provisions were in obedience to the Sixteenth Amendment.

There are only two possibilities here. Either the judges in *Funk* understood this, or they didn't. If they did understand it, but said the opposite, the question arises of whether they lied, and, if so, why. If they didn't understand it, the question arises of how men as consummately ignorant of the Constitution as these became circuit court judges. We don't know, and leave it to the reader to figure out. Suffice it to say here that something is fatally wrong.

Also in *Funk* on the same page (265), the court says this: ". . . In sum, the sixteenth amendment authorizes the imposition of a tax upon income without apportionment among the states . . . ." Yes, it does (assuming it was ratified and assuming the pretense that it is not a direct tax), and we don't argue about it. What it doesn't authorize is a tax on the *source* of the income without apportionment, because a tax on the source is direct without question.

There is a third possibility, which is that on the day they wrote all this—if they did write it—the judges in *Funk* were in a funk, blue or otherwise. Again, we don't know. Notice, however, that the court cites *Eisner*, and that on one of the very pages it cites, the Supreme Court explains why Congress has no power whatsoever to define 'income'; and that on the next page the Supreme Court says income is profit (gain), and chastises the government for ignoring the words "derived from" in the Sixteenth Amendment.

In support of their revolutionary, subversive doctrine, their honors in *Funk* cite still another case: *United States v. Francisco*, 614 F.2d 617, 619 (8th Cir.), *cert. denied*, 446 U.S. 922, 100 S.Ct. 1861, 64 L.Ed.2d 278. Harold Francisco was the appellant. The judges were Floyd R. Gibson, chief judge of the eighth circuit, McMillian and Lay. On February 6, 1980, Lay wrote as follows for the court, at page 618: ". . . Gross income for merchants is the amount representing gross receipts less the cost of goods sold. See *United States v. Ballard*, 535 F.2d 400, 404-05 (8th Cir.), *cert denied*, 429 U.S. 918, 97 S.Ct. 310, 50 L.Ed.2d 283 (1976) . . . ."

As we have seen, the Supreme Court has ruled time after time that labor is property; and that there is no difference between selling one's labor property by going to work, and selling doohickeys door to door. For tax purposes, the working woman is a labor merchant, in the same sense that General Motors sells cars. As we have also seen, however, today's lower courts spit in the Supreme Court's face, and discriminate against the working woman, by ruling that her labor is worthless; by denying her the right to subtract the cost of her labor from the property sold.

On the next page (619), Judge Lay says this: "The cases cited by Francisco clearly establish that the income tax is a direct tax, thus refuting the argument based upon his first theory. See *Brushaber v. Union Pacific Railroad Co.*, 240 U.S. 1, 19, 36 S.Ct. 236, 242, 60 L.Ed. 493 (1916) (the purpose of the Sixteenth Amendment was to take the income tax 'out of the class of excises, duties and imposts and place it in the class of direct taxes')."

Again, the experts disagree about what kind of tax this is. The trouble is that in the *Brushaber* case, from which Judge Lay quotes, the Supreme Court said *exactly the opposite* of what he says it did. In that ruling, the Supreme Court said, as you will recall, that the income tax is an indirect tax. To save you the trouble of finding it earlier in this book, here again we offer what the Supreme Court actually did say, in 36 S.Ct. 239: ". . . We are of opinion, however, that the confusion is not inherent, but rather arises from the conclusion that the 16th Amendment provides for a hitherto unknown power of taxation; that is, a power to levy an income tax which, although direct, should not be subject to the regulation of apportionment applicable to all other direct taxes. And the far-reaching effect of this erroneous assumption will be made clear . . . ."

Brushaber had argued that the tax was defective because it was a direct tax without apportionment. On the same page of the *Brushaber* ruling (239), the Supreme Court responded as follows to his argument: "But it clearly results that the proposition and the contentions under it, if acceded to, would cause one provision of the Constitution to destroy another; that is, they would result in bringing the provisions of the Amendment exempting a direct tax from apportionment into irreconcilable conflict with the general requirement that all direct taxes be apportioned. Moreover, the tax authorized by the Amendment, being direct, would not come under the rule of uniformity applicable under the Constitution to other than direct taxes, and thus it would come to pass that the result of the Amendment would be to authorize a particular direct tax not subject either to apportionment or to the rule of geographical uniformity, thus giving power to impose a different tax in one state or states than was levied in another state or states. This result, instead of simplifying the situation and making clear the limitations on the taxing power, which obviously the Amendment must have been intended to accomplish, would create radical and destructive changes in our constitutional system and multiply confusion."

So apportionment still lives, says the Supreme Court, but it doesn't apply to this tax, because it isn't a direct tax. Notice again that the purpose of the Amendment was to make clear "the limitations on the taxing power." Remember that we're quoting this passage again, not to resurrect the direct/indirect controversy, but merely to recollect what the Supreme Court actually did say.

Indeed, here is what the Supreme Court said in *Brushaber* in 1916, earlier in the same paragraph from which Judge Lay quotes sixty four years later, on February 6, 1980, in *Francisco*: ". . . [T]he contention that the Amendment treats a tax on income as a direct tax although it is relieved from apportionment and is necessarily therefore not subject to the rule of uniformity as such rule only applies to taxes which are not direct, thus destroying the two great classifications which have been recognized and enforced from the beginning, is also wholly without foundation . . . . [T]he purpose was not to change the existing interpretation except to the extent necessary to accomplish the result intended; that is, the prevention of the resort to the sources from which a taxed income was derived in order to cause a direct tax on the income to be a direct tax on the source itself, and thereby to take an income tax *out of the class of excises, duties, and imposts, and place it in the class of direct taxes*." (emphasis added)

The words in italics are of course the ones Judge Lay quoted. The key word, however, which precedes them by a few lines, is "prevention." The Supreme Court was telling us here that the Amendment *prevents* the government from doing the things Judge Lay now cites. In other words, the Supreme Court says it's forbidden; but Judge Lay, who is bound thereby, tells us the Court says it's perfectly okay.

Is this deliberate falsification, or something else? Your intrepid correspondent leaves it to the reader to characterize. Whatever the cause, be it conspiracy or ignorance or incompetence—or funk—suffice it to say here that the proof of corruption is there on the page to see.

Indeed, remember that Judge Lay says the cases Francisco cites "clearly establish that the income tax is a direct tax." If that is true, then the income tax is illegal without apportionment—because, according to the Supreme Court in *Brushaber*, all direct taxes must still be apportioned.

Judge Lay says "it is clear Congress intended to tax income from whatever source derived," which we don't contest; and he concludes as follows: "Francisco stipulated to receiving amounts representing gross proceeds less costs, which constitute gains. . . . Thus, by his own admission Francisco received taxable income.

"We find this appeal frivolous."

Where are the working woman's gains? Why have the women's "liberation" groups and unions not bitten into this? In recent years, they have lost many members to irrelevance. Imagine the possible effect on recruitment, were the unions to join the battle to secure the working woman's unalienable right to enjoy her *entire* paycheck.

Remember that Judge Lay also quoted from *Ballard*, another eighth circuit case. What did the court say there? Jack Ballard was the appellant. Henley, Stephenson and Bright were the circuit judges, and, on April 28, 1976, at page 404, the latter wrote as follows for the court: ". . . The Government here contends that all gross receipts represent income which must be reported.

"But gross receipts may or may not represent income, depending on the circumstances. . . ." Of course, that is what the Supreme Court said in *Eisner*, for instance. Judge Bright quotes the then late Circuit Judge Johnsen, in *Clark v. United States*, 211 F.2d 100 (8th Cir., 1954): "Of course, gross income and not gross receipts is the foundation of income-tax liability, for it is only earnings, profits and gains which the statute subjects to tax. . . ." Again, Judge Johnsen said it in 1954; Judge Bright quotes it with approval in 1976. The fact that somebody pays you—no matter how much—does not necessarily mean that that money is subject to the tax. Only "earnings" (profits and gains) are subject to the tax. If your receipts constitute gross income (profits or gains), they are subject to the tax. If your receipts do not constitute those things, *they are not subject to the tax.* This is true whether you make $5,000 a year as a dishwasher, or $5,000,000 as a rock star.

Judge Bright also cites our old friend, *Doyle v. Mitchell Bros. Co.*, 247 U.S. 179, 38 S.Ct. 467, 62 L.Ed. 1054 (1918): "Whatever difficulty there may be about a precise and scientific definition of 'income,' it imports, as used here, something entirely distinct from principal or capital either as a subject of taxation or as a measure of the tax, conveying rather the idea of gain or increase arising from corporate activities. . . ." The court also quoted *Stratton's Independence*, another case we have examined. Then, Judge Bright said: "Understanding the term in this natural and obvious sense, it cannot be said that a conversion of capital assets invariably produces income. . . ." When you exchange your labor for wages or compensation, you are converting a capital asset. According to Judge Bright, that doesn't necessarily mean you have income.

Remember that we got the *Ballard* case from Judge Lay. *Ballard* Judge Bright tells us this, on page 404, one of the pages Judge Lay cites: "The general term 'income' is not defined in the Internal Revenue Code. . . ." This of course is perfectly true, and the reader knows why. Remember, however, that, in *Ficalora*, the second circuit said the Code does define it; and in *Lonsdale* the fifth circuit said the Code defines it. Our friends at I.R.S. expect you and your reporter to be experts, while the various courts of appeal don't know for sure what they are talking about.

Finally, Judge Bright tells us this at page 405: "Applying these definitions to the respective contentions made by the parties, it appears that the Government makes too broad a claim in asserting that gross receipts invariably measure income or gross income. . . ."

Again, gross receipts and "gross income" are not the same thing. Remember that these cases are the ones the *government* uses to "prove" its point. As we have seen, they either misquote the law and the legislative history; or, they quote it, and then boldly tell us it says the opposite of what it really says. Notice that while we have one Supreme Court ruling after another to support the premise of this book, our friends at I.R.S. have *not one*—not one—to support theirs. How do they get away with it?

They get away with it by judicial, but injudicious, use of the weapon of *stare decisis*. This of course is Latin for, "to stand by things decided." In stare decisis, the judge relies for authority not on the Constitution, but on rulings by other judges. By means of such "judicial precedent," so-called "case law" has been developed, in which opinion and sociology replace justice and law. *Stare decisis* has thereby stolen the law from the people, making it difficult to understand without the very expensive assistance of a licensed member of the Bar Association monopoly. It has facilitated the perversion of our limited, constitutional system into something it was never intended to be.

Here is an example of *stare decisis* at work (Floyd R. Gibson, Senior Circuit Judge, 9th Cir., in *U.S. v. Romero*, 640 F.2d 1014, 1016) in 1981: ". . . Compensation for labor or services, paid in the form of wages or salary, has been universally held by the courts of this republic to be income, subject to the income tax laws currently applicable. . . ."

As we have seen, this isn't true at all (with one minor exception to which we are coming), which raises the usual question of whether Judge Gibson is lying or just ignorant. However, even if it were true, it would be irrelevant. The only relevant question is: What does the *Constitution* say income is?

Suppose we want to argue that the moon is made of green cheese. The idea will be difficult to sell, because it is so patently absurd, and we have no scintilla of scientific backup. Indeed, Neil Armstrong has been there, and knows what it is. Suppose further, however, in this scenario, that we have a brother-in-law who has a government-granted monopoly on observatories, and that his sister, our wife, is nagging us to do something for him—so your intrepid correspondent writes a piece entitled, "The Moon," in which we put forth the assertion that the moon is indeed made of green cheese. Of course the article will be derided; but now *you* write an article in which you put forth the same assertion, after which there now appears a footnote, which looks like this: [1]—and at the bottom of the page it says: 1. See Alan Stang, "The Moon," *American Journal of Applied Something Or Other*, volume XVI, number 5, June, 1992, pp. 16-19.

Indeed, suppose after a while we are able to accumulate fifty such footnotes, so that whenever we make the assertion we are able to cite each other. Now, we have impressive support. We have half a page of squiggles. There's no conspiracy, you understand. There is just a small group of immensely powerful and influential people who breathe together (conspire). As sure as Marx didn't make green apples, Americans trained for slavery in our government schools will start parroting our assertion, even arguing about what kind of cheese it is. Panic will erupt in the dairy industry. Now, Neil Armstrong will be derided. Armstrong will be accused of lying for the Reagan Administration to help the Contras. There would be Congressional hearings.

Things as crazy as this—and probably crazier—have been accomplished, which is why we are in so much trouble today. If we accomplished it, no matter how many footnotes we had, it still wouldn't be true. This is the reality of *stare decisis*, applied to the income tax. There are I.R.S. attorneys making claims completely unsupported by constitutional or Supreme Court authority; there are judges repeating them; and there are other judges quoting those judge as "proof."

Indeed, we arrive at last at the man who doth bestride the issue like a colossus. He is Easterbrook, a seventh circuit judge, the brazen panache of whose fulsome prevarication would have been the envy of P. T. Barnum. As we have seen, the ordinary judicial charlatan quotes other judges. Easterbrook actually has the temerity to quote *himself*.

In the seventh circuit case of *Coleman v. C.I.R.*, 791 F.2d 68, Easterbrook wrote as follows of petitioner-appellant Norman Coleman at page 70, on May 7, 1986: ". . . Coleman thinks that only net income may be taxed under the Sixteenth Amendment—net income as Coleman defines it, rather than as Congress does. . . ." As we have seen, Congress doesn't define it, and is forbidden to define it, by the U.S. Supreme Court, which Easterbrook chooses to disobey.

On the same page, Easterbrook says this: ". . . These are tired arguments. The code imposes a tax on all income. See 26 U.S.C. §61. Wages are income, and the tax on wages is constitutional. See, among hundreds of other cases, United States v. Thomas, 788 F.2d 1250, 1253 (7th Cir. 1986) . . . ."

Guess who wrote that ruling. Easterbrook himself. And it gets worse. As you see, Easterbrook says we should consult page 1253 of *Thomas*, but there is nothing at all on that page about wages being income. On page 1254, Easterbrook speaks of Thomas's "belief that wages are not income . . . ." There is not another word on the issue. In short, Tax Rebel Easterbrook quotes himself for authority, and then doesn't say anything, at least not here.

Also in *Coleman*, Tax Rebel Easterbrook cites *U.S. v. Koliboski*, 732 F.2d 1328 (1984), in which a footnote at page 1329 tells us this: "Although not raised in his brief on appeal, the defendant's entire case at trial rested on his claim that he in good faith believed that wages are not income for taxation purposes. Whatever his mental state, he, of course, was wrong, as all of us already are aware. Nonetheless, the defendant still insists that no case holds that wages are income. Let us now put that to rest: WAGES ARE INCOME. Any reading of tax cases by would-be tax protesters now should preclude a claim of good-faith belief that wages—or salaries—are not taxable."

The Tax Rebels who wrote this put the key statement entirely in capitals, but methinks they doth protest too much. They put it in capitals precisely because they know they have no authority. They put it in capitals because they either didn't know what an American judge is on the bench to do, or they knew it and betrayed it. In this country, a judge is forbidden to make law, even if he types his tantrum in capital letters. As Chief Justice John Marshall explained in *McCulloch v. Maryland*, 4 U.S. (Wheat.) 316, 407, "[W]e must never forget that it is a constitution we are expounding." In our system, the judge is bound to apply the Constitution to each particular case. Again, if the judge just rules according to what he thinks is "right," why would we need a Constitution and Congress? Question: How likely is it that the judges don't know all this?

As we shall see, wages *are* income—in just one place in the law that probably doesn't apply to you—but not at all in the way Easterbrook says they are. The typical defendant doesn't know that, and therefore cannot distinguish between wages that are income and wages that aren't—and Tax Rebel Easterbrook doesn't explain which is which because he is "impartial." Typically, Easterbrook doesn't lie, but he doesn't tell the truth either.

To complete this judicial daisy chain, Easterbrook finally cites *Granzow v. C.I.R.*, 739 F.2d 265, 267 (7th Cir., 1984): ". . . It is well settled that wages received by taxpayers constitute gross income . . . and that such gross income is subject to taxation. See *United States v. Koliboske* (sic), 732 F.2d 1328, 1329, n.1 (7th Cir., 1984); *Lonsdale v. Commissioner*, 661 F.2d 71, 72 (5th Cir., 1981) . . . ."

Which brings us back to where we started. The entire, increasingly rickety, structure is designed to preserve the secret of the "income tax"; which is that—as presently applied to working people—it has been perverted into a direct tax on the source without apportionment. Such a tax is as illegal today as it was when the Founding Fathers wrote the Constitution. That is the secret our friends at I.R.S. are trying to hide.

7

HOW IT WAS PERVERTED

On March 1, 1914, the present income tax took effect. On that day, 357,598 people filed returns. That number was less than ½ of 1% of the American population at the time, which, according to the 1910 census, was 91,972,000. More than 99.5% of the population filed no returns and paid no tax. Most Americans probably had heard of the income tax, but it had no direct effect on them. Many Americans probably didn't know there was one.

This shouldn't surprise us. Remember that the income tax was supposed to "soak the rich." Whether or not you think that's a good idea—we don't—"soak the rich" *was* the slogan its backers used to sell the tax to American workers.

Indeed, as late as 1939, during World War II, after the income tax had been in business for a quarter-of-a-century, only four million people reported taxable incomes. Our population at the time was 131,669,000. In other words, after all this time, the income tax affected only 3% of our people; so, it was still soaking the rich. A full 97% of our people had never filed and never paid. This remained true until America entered the war, when the income tax was perverted into an even bigger perversion than it had been from the beginning; perverted from a perversion that was legal to one that is illegal. Remember that in the beginning the Socialist billionaires designed the income tax to crush their competitors. That was "legal." Now, during World War II, they perverted the perversion, so as to crush Rosie the Riveter illegally. The tax that was and is legal (assuming as always the ratification of the Sixteenth Amendment) remained, but they hid it, deeper every year.

By means of what sinister magic was the income tax transformed into an outrage in which the super-rich have been paying little or no income tax, while the Internal Revenue Service is literally shaking down waitresses? That's right; Congressman George Hansen reports that I.R.S. agents went to a neighborhood restaurant in a small town in Idaho, and actually asked the teenaged waitresses to empty their pockets. "Soak the rich" has degenerated into "Rob the working girl."

In 1941, the Tenth Circuit again affirmed the principle that wages do not constitute gain, and therefore cannot be income subject to the income tax. In *Champlin Refining Co. v. C.I.R.*, 123 F.2d at 203, the court said this: "Where property is given in exchange for other property, the cost of the property acquired is the value of the property given in exchange therefor. . . ." In other words, the value of your week's work is the amount your employer pays for it. Again, you have gained nothing. You have swapped, traded, exchanged a certain amount of work for a certain amount of cash. To be subject to the tax, you must have gain.

Like Woodrow Wilson before him, President Franklin Roosevelt had been talking peace, while he plotted war. To trick us into World War I, Wilson and his Machiavellian manager, Edward House, along with Winston Churchill, had arranged for the Germans to torpedo the munitions ship *Lusitania*, aboard which American civilians had been gulled into sailing, despite German warnings. Now, on December 7, 1941, Roosevelt finally succeeded in provoking the Japanese to attack, meanwhile denying our Pearl Harbor commanders the available intelligence they could perhaps have used to turn the disaster into victory. For many years, Roosevelt's disciples bitterly denied that their idol had done any such thing. By now, however, so much of the smelly truth has oozed out that they admit it; but, typically, they transform it into yet another demonstration of their idol's genius. You see, Roosevelt *had* to trick us into the war; because at the time we the people were just too stupid and ignorant to know we should be in it.

Washington typically used the war to pull a sneak attack on the American worker, thereby adding substantially to its power. There is substantial precedent for this. History reeks of governments that used war as the justification for totalitarian purposes at home. The career of the late Roman Empire will suffice to prove the point. Shakespeare had Henry IV advise his son: "Be it thy course to busy giddy minds with foreign quarrels." Such minds are thereby prevented from realizing what is being done to them at home. War gives a government with a mind to grab power, the ready-made excuse that anyone who objects to its power grab is hindering the war effort and is therefore unpatriotic. Of course the Nazis and Communists were and are masters at this.

So it has always been everywhere, because of the sinful nature of man, and so it was in Washington because of the war. In 1942, Congress passed the Victory Tax—that's what they called it—to raise money for the prosecution of the war. The reason the levy was called the Victory Tax was precisely because it was a temporary exaction to fight an emergency. Section 476 of this temporary, emergency law said as follows: "The taxes imposed by this subchapter shall not apply with respect to any taxable year commencing after the date of cessation of hostilities in the present war."

The Victory Tax introduced the new concept of withholding on wages. The tax was 5%; yes, 5%! That's how small it was, even in the face of the emergency. The bill of which it was a part was expected to reap about $24 billion. Senator Walter George, of Georgia, Chairman of the Senate Finance Committee, said this: "The bill approaches the maximum direct tax which can be levied on the taxpayers during war." What percentage of the worker's earnings would you guess government at all levels was taking at the time? State and local taxes brought the total to something more than $26 billion, which meant that the answer was in the neighborhood of 33.3%, the height of the government's take during this battle for survival. Today, taxes take more than *50%*!

The Victory Tax was a direct tax. We can be sure of that, because, as we have seen, Senator George said so. Indeed, according to the *Congressional Record* of October 20 1942, a Congressman Doughton said as follows on page 8468: "The Victory tax will greatly increase the number of persons who will pay a direct tax to the Government—a direct contribution to the war effort. It is estimated that under the regular income tax there will be 27,500,000 taxpayers, and with the Victory tax there will be approximately 46,000,000 taxpayers." Our population at the time was about 131,000,000, so, even in the middle of the war, only a tad more than 20% of our people were paying income tax. The Victory Tax was designed to hit workers who had never been liable for income tax and still were not liable.

The trouble was that the Victory Tax was a direct tax levied without apportionment, and was therefore illegal. Remember that, while a tax on a source is unarguably direct, the courts themselves don't agree on whether or not the tax on income is direct. If it is, it must be apportioned. Certainly all other direct taxes must be apportioned. Remember that *Brushaber* didn't cancel apportionment. It merely reclassified the income tax as indirect. However, the Victory Tax was not an income tax—its authors said it wasn't— which means it was illegal without the application of the constitutional rule that still governs the collection of all direct taxes. The Victory Tax had nothing to do with the Sixteenth Amendment. The Sixteenth Amendment did not control it. In view of the illegality—the criminality—of our entry into the war, our guess is that there would have been a Victory Tax had the Sixteenth Amendment never existed.

Why didn't someone stand up and complain? Why didn't someone in government—or out of it—demand that the illegal tax be struck down? Why didn't someone demand that it be apportioned?

Would *you* have done it? Would you have done it just after the Japanese had attacked Pearl Harbor "without warning"; when the West Coast awaited a Japanese invasion before Midway; when our beloved nation was "fighting for its very survival?" Would you have done it in the grim knowledge that other Americans who had challenged our nation's policy of war, were tried for sedition in 1944? Would you have done it had you known at the time what our own government did to Tyler Kent, a U.S. Embassy code clerk in London, who discovered from the cable traffic that our leaders were plotting war?

Later, the same world-government conspirators who had plotted war for the purpose—calling Americans who organized for peace "isolationists" and "Nazi sympathizers"—called themselves "liberals" and "peace lovers." The record shows that they are for shooting peace when the Soviets want peace; and they are for shooting war when the Soviets want *that.*

So, the Victory Tax sailed into law. Meanwhile, on March 27, 1943, starting at page 2579, the *Congressional Record* printed a study of the income tax by F. Morse Hubbard, who was there identified as "formerly of the legislative drafting research fund of Columbia University, and a former legislative draftsman in the Treasury Department."

On page 2580, Mr. Hubbard wrote as follows of the Sixteenth Amendment: ". . . So the Amendment made it possible to bring investment income within the scope of a general income-tax law, but did not change the character of the tax. It is still fundamentally an excise or duty with respect to the privilege of carrying on any activity or owning any property which produces income.

"The income tax is, therefore, not a tax on income as such. It is an excise tax with respect to certain activities and privileges which is measured by reference to the income which they produce. The income is not the subject of the tax; it is the basis for determining the amount of the tax."

Again, the purpose of the Amendment was to tax *investment* income, a different thing entirely from working for a living. The tax, according to Hubbard, is an excise, which is the same thing as a privilege tax, the theory being that, if you take a privilege from the government—in this case, the "privilege" of making a profit—then you owe the government a cut. The thing being taxed is the privilege. The amount of income (profit) gained from the privilege, determines the *amount* of the tax. Working for a living is not a privilege, but a right, an unalienable right that existed long before the Constitution that guarantees it. So, according to legislative draftsman Hubbard at least, thirty years after "ratification" of the Sixteenth Amendment nothing had changed.

Also in 1943, Congress passed the Current Tax Payment Act, which replaced the withholding features of the Victory Tax of 1942. This 1943 substitution enabled an individual who anticipated a tax liability to pay the tax by installments withheld from his wages. The wages constituted the fund from which the tax could be paid. At page 2501 of the *Congressional Record* of March 25, 1943, a Congressman Cooper explained: ". . . We now have a withholding tax of 5% at the source. It is commonly confused as being a Victory tax. That is not correct. We have a Victory tax of 5 percent gross, but, as I pointed out a moment ago, it only amounts to about 3.2 percent net. But we have withheld a tax of 5 percent at the source. That withholding tax is first applied to the discharge of the victory tax, but any amount that may be over the Victory tax liability is applied to the income tax. . . ."

Again, the Victory Tax and the income tax were two different taxes. Since the Victory Tax was direct, it was illegal without apportionment; just as a direct income tax would be.

In 1944, Congress passed another tax law, which expressly repealed the Victory Tax. All these wartime withholding measures were supposed to be *temporary*; were supposed to expire automatically at the end of the war, or within two years. This was just as well, because they were illegal; which was appropriate because our leaders had illegally tricked us into the war. They did not call them "income taxes," and they were not income taxes. They were related to the income tax by means of the new science of withholding, which, for the first time, directly attacked the wages of the people.

It was Beardsley Ruml who concocted the idea of withholding. Ruml was Chairman of the Federal Reserve Bank of New York. You will see how revealing that is later, when we look at the true purposes of the present perversion of the income tax. The Federal Reserve is the engine of inflation in our country. It was conceived by the same people who gave us the tax. The Fed conducts the boom-and-bust cycles that regularly take our people to the cleaners. The Fed is one big reason—perhaps the biggest—that our currency, or, rather, *their* currency, is now headed for the tubes. The booms and busts have been far worse since the advent of the Fed, than they ever were before.

It now becomes clear that, with the end of the war, the federal leviathan, having feasted on the people's wages by means of those temporary, emergency laws, refused to let go. The Socialist billionaires decided to use those laws as spurious justification to usurp the illegal power to impose a permanent, direct tax on wages without apportionment.

We have seen what the courts said immediately after the "ratification" of the Sixteenth Amendment and the imposition of the tax. The important question now arises of what the three branches of government said about wages and the income tax after the war. For instance, in 1953, Dwight E. Avis testified before a House Ways and Means subcommittee. Dwight Avis was then Head of the Alcohol and Tobacco Tax Division of the Bureau of Internal Revenue, as it was then still known. Later, it molted and became the Internal Revenue Service. Notice that the more "service" it provides, the more the situation degenerates. That is because the Internal Revenue Service "services" you the way a bull services a cow.

According to a report on the proceedings entitled, "Internal Revenue Investigation," printed for the Committee on Ways and Means (83rd Congress, first session), Mr. Avis testified as follows on page thirteen: "Let me point this out now: Your income tax is 100 percent voluntary tax, and your liquor tax is 100 percent enforced tax. Now, the situation is as different as day and night. Consequently, your same rules just will not apply . . . ."

Whether or not Mr. Avis was the first to say this, we don't know. We do know that, down through the ages since Dwight Avis, one Commissioner of Internal Revenue after another has said the same thing, in the annual 1040 instruction manuals. Why? What are they referring to? They are referring to the fact that if the income tax is indirect, as *Brushaber* said it is; then it is (in part) an excise tax, a privilege tax, in which the "privilege" is making profit. The tax is voluntary in the sense that, if you find it intolerable, there is a legal way not to pay it. You don't have to pay it if you don't exercise the "privilege"; if you decline to make profit. There are many ways to live, and live in luxury, without profit. You could work for wages or compensation, for instance. You could make a million Federal Reserve Notes a year as a C.P.A. or a comedian. If that's what your clients or fans pay you, then that's what your services are worth.

In the same sense, the liquor tax, also being an excise, is also "100 percent voluntary." The law only requires you to pay it if you make liquor. If you don't want to pay it, don't make it and you're free. Remember that in the great system the Founding Fathers gave us, all taxes are supposed to be voluntary; except, if necessary, in case of war.

In recent years, some Americans have made much of the fact that the I.R.S. Commissioners have said the income tax is voluntary; so, our friends at I.R.S. have concocted a remarkable explanation, according to which the income tax is "voluntary" because the taxpayer completes the form. Your obedient servant has actually heard an assistant U.S. attorney tell a jury in court that I.R.S. constantly uses the word *voluntary* because a taxpayer fills out his return himself; and that to insist on any other definition is to play semantic games. Unfortunately, this amounts to what you run the risk of stepping in when you walk across a bull field. In law, "voluntary" means *without legal obligation*. If it's voluntary, the law does not require you to do it.

There is another crucial reason the income tax is "voluntary," and we shall look at it later. For now, what did the courts say about wages and the income tax after the war? If the thesis of this book is haywire, if our friends at I.R.S. are right, then we should reasonably expect to find that the courts began supporting them. We should expect a dramatic change; a change we looked for and did not find after the landmark *Brushaber* case in 1915. We did finally find such a change in the 1970s and '80s, when, no doubt for reasons we shall examine, the mendacious daisy chain that included such corrupt links as *Funk* and *Francisco* was forged; but, immediately after World War II, did the courts begin to say there could be a direct, federal tax on the source without apportionment? No, the courts continued to say exactly what they had said on these subjects since the Supreme Court had thrown out the income tax in 1895.

For instance, in 1959, the Tax Court of the United States made a remarkable admission. In *Penn Mutual Indemnity Co. v. Commissioner*, 32 Tax Court at page 660, Judge Raum said this: "[T]he authority of Congress to impose a tax is plenary, except that direct taxes must be apportioned among the States according to population . . . .

". . . If the tax is a duty, impost, or excise, the rule of apportionment does not apply; only if it is a 'direct' tax does that rule come into play."

In other words, the language of the Constitution to which Judge Raum refers still stands as the Founding Fathers wrote it, despite propaganda to the contrary extruded by our friends at I.R.S. A direct tax must still be apportioned, and there is no tax more direct than a tax on one's wages. The Sixteenth Amendment authorizes a tax without apportionment not on wages, but on income (if that tax is indirect). In the same case, at page 681, Tax Court Judge Train nailed it down like this: "The rule of *Eisner v. Macomber* has been reaffirmed on so many occasions that citation of the cases to this effect would be unnecessarily burdensome. To depart from the rule at this late date would ignore the sound principles upon which that case was decided and would throw into confusion the fundamental income tax structure and law as it has developed in the almost half century which has elapsed since adoption of the 16th amendment. That *there cannot be 'income' without a 'gain'* accords with the common understanding of the term, a test of construction which is particularly appropriate in our system of a *self-assessed Federal income tax. . . . Moreover, that which is not income in fact manifestly cannot be made such by the legislative expedient of calling it income. . . .*" (emphasis added)

So, here we are in 1959, exactly fifty years from the passage by Congress of the Sixteenth Amendment, and the Tax Court itself says income is still gain (profit). What does the term "self-assessed" mean? In this context, it refers to the fact that the accumulation of income (profit, gain) is voluntary, so it is appropriate for someone with income to assess himself.

Notice also Judge Train's remark that if something isn't income, it isn't income—even if Congress passes a law that says it is. It certainly can't be income just because the Internal Revenue Service says it is. Of course, Judge Train was just repeating here what the Supreme Court had said forty years earlier in *Eisner*; namely, the Sixteenth Amendment, not Congress, defines income. The power to define income, in the hands of Congress, would constitute usurpation, because Congress could use such power to change something allegedly "ratified" by the people pursuant to the Constitution, through their legislatures. Yet, as we have seen, today's lower courts, besmirched by the daisy chain of corruption, say Congress can do just that.

It is also worth mentioning that Tax Court judges, unlike other federal judges, are often income tax specialists, who have risen through the ranks of income tax administration. They have lived off the income tax for years; it is close to their hearts. So, the Tax Court's opinion in *Penn Mutual* is especially telling.

Along these lines, in the next year, 1960, Supreme Court Chief Justice Earl Warren said as follows, in *Flora v. United States*, 362 U.S. 179: ". . . Our system of taxation is based upon voluntary assessment and payment, not upon distraint. . . ." Roget's *Thesaurus* says that synonyms of distraint include execution, confiscation and eviction. An unabridged *Funk & Wagnall* says the verb distrain means to take and detain, to rend asunder, to compel, to restrain, to torment and to seize. As you can see, there's nothing voluntary about distraint. Distraint means force. Again, the Chief Justice of the United States says our system of taxation is *not* based upon these things, not based on force, but on voluntary assessment and payment. This means that the individual, not the government, decides voluntarily whether or not he is subject to the tax and must pay. He decides to do that either by making profit, or by not making profit—by taking a government "favor," or by not taking it. Remember, this comes from the Chief Justice of the high court.

Finally, on September 18, 1969, U.S. District Judge Singleton ruled in Houston in *Conner v. United States*, 303 F.Supp. 1187. George and Dorothy Conner were the plaintiffs, and the case involved receipts, so his honor conducted an exhaustive search for the meaning of "income." At page 1191, Judge Singleton explained that "the meaning of income in its everyday sense is 'a *gain* or recurrent benefit usually measured in money that derives from capital or labor; also: the *amount of such gain* recovered by an individual in a given period of time.' Webster's Seventh New Collegiate Dictionary, p. 425 (1965—Emphasis Added). Income is nothing more nor less than realized gain. Shuster v. Helvering, 121 F.2d 643 (2nd Cir. 1941). It is not synonymous with receipts. 47 C.J.S. Internal Revenue §98, p. 226.

"Whatever may constitute income, therefore, must have the essential feature of gain to the recipient. This was true when the sixteenth amendment became effective, it was true at the time of the decision in Eisner v. McComber (sic) *supra*, it was true under section 22(a) of the Internal Revenue Code of 1939, and it is likewise true under section 61(a) of the Internal Revenue Code of 1954. If there is no gain, there is no income."

Again, income and receipts do not mean the same thing. If there is no gain (profit), there is no income. How on earth could this be said any clearer? It couldn't. *Conner* was just a lowly district court ruling, but the government appealed it all the way to the top without success, so it still stands.

All right, we've looked at what the Executive Branch says. We've looked at what the courts have said. Now, let's see what the Congress says. The first Internal Revenue Code was the version of 1939, section 22(a) of which said this: "'Gross income' includes gains, profits, and income derived from salaries, wages, or compensation for personal service . . . of whatever kind and in whatever form paid, or from professions, vocations, trades, businesses, commerce, or sales, or dealings in property, whether real or personal, growing out of the ownership or use of or interest in such property; also from interest, rent, dividends, securities, or the transaction of any business carried on for gain or profit, or gains or profits from any source whatever."

We don't have to rival Noah Webster to realize that if gross income means gains, profits, and income *derived from* salaries, wages, or compensation; then the gains, etc., must be different from the salaries, etc. Again, the thing that is derived is not the same as the thing it is derived from. You are derived from your mother, but you are not your mother. If Congress had meant to say that gross income includes salaries, rather than gain derived from salaries, it could and would have said so.

Now, let's move along to 1954, when Congress rewrote the Internal Revenue Code, replacing section 22(a) of the 1939 Code with section 61(a), the one we use now: "Except as otherwise provided in this subtitle, gross income means all income from whatever source derived, including (but not limited to), the following items . . . ." Then follows a list of fifteen items, starting with "Compensation for services, including fees, commissions, and similar items"; which is as close as the list comes to wages and salaries. If Congress meant to include those things, why didn't it?

Indeed, whose compensation for services is the list talking about? Only human beings receive wages and salaries. They also receive compensation for services, but so do corporations. Is corporate compensation what Congress meant here? Remember that in *Doyle v. Mitchell*, the Supreme Court defined income as the "gain or increase arising from corporate activities. . . ." On the other hand, notice that, while §61(a) retains the words, "from whatever source derived," the concept of gain has been eliminated, except for item (3): "Gains derived from dealing in property . . . ." Did the Congress thereby intend to make some dramatic change?

Judge Singleton has the answer in *Conner*: "The language of section 61(a) of the Internal Revenue Code of 1954, set forth above, might at first glance appear to have broadened the definition of gross income by the omission of any reference to gain. This, however, is not so, because the Supreme Court had before it the then recently enacted 1954 Code of Internal Revenue when it decided Commissioner v. Glenshaw Glass Co., *supra*. It noted that, *although the definition of gross income had been simplified, 'no effect on its present broad scope was intended.'* 348 U.S. 432, 75 S.Ct. 477. . . ." (emphasis added)

Remember that *Glenshaw Glass* is a link in the I.R.S. daisy chain. As usual, it proves exactly the opposite of what the courts of corruption say it does.

Judge Singleton adds that in *General American Investors Co., v. C.I.R.*, 348 U.S. 434, 75 S.Ct. 478, 99 L.Ed. 504 (1955)—decided the same day as *Glenshaw*—the Supreme Court spoke at pages 436 and 479 of "the legislative design to reach all *gain* constitutionally taxable." (emphasis added)

Indeed, his honor also says this: "The opinion in *Glenshaw Glass Company, supra*, regardless of what it said about Eisner v. McComber (sic), *supra*, did not repudiate the concept that there must be gain before there is income within the meaning of the sixteenth amendment. 1 Mertens, section 5.02, p. 4. This is verified by the fact that in Commissioner of Internal Revenue v. Lo Bue, 351 U.S. 243, 76 S.Ct. 800, 100 L.Ed. 1142 (1956), a year after the decisions in *Glenshaw Glass Company, supra*, and General American Investors v. Commissioner, *supra*, it was said:

" 'We have repeatedly held that in defining "gross income" as broadly as it did in §22(a) Congress intended to "tax all *gains* except those specifically exempted." ' . . ." (emphasis added)

Indeed, would you agree that the best authority on the intent of Congress is Congress itself? A footnote on page 1190 of the Singleton ruling refers to a Senate Finance Committee Report. That Report is No. 1622, 83rd Congress, 2nd Session, 168 (1954); which you can find in *U.S. Code Congressional & Administrative News 1954*, p. 4802. Entitled, "Internal Revenue Code of 1954," it says as follows on that page: "Section 61(a) provides that gross income includes 'all income from whatever source derived.' This definition is based upon the sixteenth amendment and the word 'income' is used as in section 22(a) in its constitutional sense. *It is not intended to change the concept of income that obtains under section 22(a). . . .*" (emphasis added)

In other words, "income" is still what it was in the revenue law of 1862; still what it was in *Pollock*; still what it is in the Sixteenth Amendment; still what it was in *Brushaber*—and still what it was in the Internal Revenue Code of 1939. Income is profit or gain. As you see, our source now is the United States Senate. The trouble is that our Socialist billionaires have been making the meaning of income more and more difficult to see. Our friends at I.R.S. have turned the law and the regulations into a masterpiece of deception; by omitting the truth entirely, or by distorting it to such an extent that it becomes unrecognizable.

8

ALICE IN REVENUELAND

Everyone agrees that I.R.S. language is just one step this side of incomprehensible and maybe worse. For instance, on February 13, 1979, the Internal Revenue Service published some proposed regulations in the *Federal Register*, on page 9452. Our friends at I.R.S. said this: "If a school engages in any acts or practices that are racially nondiscriminatory as to students, the school is not entitled to tax exemption . . . ." How's that again? Our friends at I.R.S. seem to be saying here that if a school is racially *non*discriminatory, it is guilty of discrimination and will lose its tax exemption. The reader may be thinking that this madness was a misprint; but, on the same page, the Internal Revenue Service also said this: "A school 'adjudicated to be discriminatory' means any school found to be racially *non*discriminatory as to students . . . ." (emphasis added) In fact, on the next page, 9453, I.R.S. listed several conditions a school must meet in order to keep the tax men off its neck. One condition is satisfied if "there is no evidence that the school system operates on a racially *non*discriminatory basis." (emphasis added) Again, if there is such evidence that the school does not discriminate, it could lose its tax-exemption for discrimination.

Was all this a George Orwell joke, or just stupidity? We don't pretend to know. It does appear that our friends at I.R.S. are promoting racism, for which they should clearly lose their tax-exemption. Along these lines, on May 30, 1985, at the Capitol Building in Williamsburg, Virginia, President Reagan said as follows in support of his latest tax proposal: "Well, it's a system so utterly complex and ultimately inexplicable that half the time the tax professionals themselves aren't sure what the rules are—a system that even Albert Einstein is said to have admitted he couldn't begin to fathom. You know, it's said that his hair didn't look that way until after he experienced his first tax form. (laughter)"

Even the people who, in one way or another, run the system agree. William E. Simon, who, as Secretary of the Treasury, was the Commissioner of Internal Revenue's boss, told an audience at a National Conference of the Tax Foundation as follows, all the way back on December 3, 1975: "I'm not even sure the I.R.S. experts fully understand the system anymore. How can they when they are dealing with a tax code and regulations that now exceed 6,000 pages of fine print?"

Yet, they expect you and your reporter to be experts. Indeed, the President's tax "simplification" law does not simplify the law. Its byzantine pages were *added* to the already metastasizing mess, which presumably means, according to William E. Simon, that the "I.R.S. experts" understand less than they did before.

Caryl Conner, a speechwriter in the Jimmy Carter White House, wrote as follows of the Internal Revenue Code in *The Wall Street Journal*, on May 13, 1983: "Nobody understands it. . . . [P]eople won't obey laws they can't understand. . . . From a practical standpoint the code is virtually unenforceable. . . . Ten years—eight major tax bills—ago, the New York bar's 'complexity report' said it was already impossible to teach 'largely unlearnable law' to revenue agents. . . . [L]ike wonder drugs that create new disease while curing the one for which they were prescribed, the code creates tax evasion."

There is also Bill Archer, the Congressman from Texas, who is a member of the House Ways and Means Committee. A while back, he wrote as follows in a column for *The Houston Post*: "Perhaps it is significant to note that I have now come to the point myself where I need outside help in filing my own tax return—and I serve on the Committee which writes the laws and ought to be in a better position than most to figure out a 1040 Form."

Indeed, according to *The Wall Street Journal* of January 30, 1985, Mortimer Caplin says the tax code has grown "horrendously complex." He uses Arthur Andersen & Company to prepare his return. Caplin is a Washington tax lawyer, and was I.R.S. Commissioner himself from 1961 to 1964. Remember that after Reagan the horror is as byzantine as it was, and maybe more so; an example of which was the new, "simplified" W-4. Along these lines, the *Journal* of August 12, 1987 discussed new I.R.S. Form 8598, which comes with a four-page instruction booklet, and concerns mortgage deductions. Peter K. Scott, deputy chief counsel of I.R.S., concedes that for many taxpayers the new process will "ferociously complicate calculations."

Did you know that it is dangerous to rely on what I.R.S. tells you officially—because our friends at I.R.S. could change their minds after you rely on it? Kenneth Culp Davis is Professor of Law at the University of San Diego, and John P. Wilson Professor Emeritus at the University of Chicago. You will find his massive, four-volume study entitled, *Administrative Law Treatise* (San Diego, University of San Diego, 1978-83) in law libraries across the United States. Professor Davis says this (v. 2, p. 103): "When the Internal Revenue Service's interpretative rules favor a taxpayer, the I.R.S. may retroactively change its position and impose a tax, even when the taxpayer has relied to his detriment. The I.R.S. thus is not bound by its own rules. . . ."

What do the courts say about this? In *Carpenter v. United States*, 495 F.2d 175, the Treasury Department issued a "Tax Guide for U.S. Citizens Abroad." The Fifth Circuit held that I.R.S. was free to depart from it after the taxpayer had followed it: "We . . . sympathize with the taxpayer who in fact relies upon what he accepts as an authoritative interpretation of the laws and of the Treasury publications. But nonetheless it is for the Congress and the courts and not the Treasury to declare the law applicable to a given situation."

This of course makes sense. The Court is here alluding to the principle of Separation of Powers. In our great system, no branch of government is permitted to exercise the powers of the other two. The Executive branch is forbidden to make law, a power reserved strictly to the Congress. When the executive in a government does make law, you have a prescription for dictatorship. That is why totalitarians have always hated our Separation of Powers. Whenever you hear proposals to "modernize" our system and make it more "efficient," remember Socialist dictator Mussolini, who "made the trains run on time."

So, I.R.S., which is found in the Treasury Department, which is found in the Executive branch, is forbidden to make law. For the same reason, our friends at I.R.S. are also forbidden to collect taxes. Article I, Section eight, paragraph one of the law—the Constitution—says this: "The Congress shall have Power To lay and collect Taxes, Duties, Imposts and Excises . . . ." But, again, I.R.S. is not an agency of Congress, and Congress has no power to delegate its power. In short, our friends at I.R.S. have no power to collect taxes, but they do it anyway.

As we just saw, the Fifth Circuit practically tells us to disregard whatever I.R.S. says. Indeed, in the 1978 case of *Caterpillar Tractor Co. v. United States*, 589 F.2d 1040, 1043, the U.S. Court of Claims said this: "It is hornbook law that informal publications all the way up to revenue rulings are simply guides to taxpayers, and a taxpayer relies on them at his peril."

Professor Davis says this (v. 2, p. 104): "The idea that a taxpayer relies on an I.R.S. publication at his peril is strongly supported by *Dixon v. United States*, 381 U.S. 68 (1965)."

Why is the tax language so satanically confusing? The answer is that, on one hand, our friends at I.R.S. won't tell you the truth, which you have been reading here, for fear you would see it; and, on the other, they won't exactly lie, for fear they would run afoul of the accidental judge who still supports the Constitution. So, they do neither. They don't exactly lie, but they don't tell the truth, either. The most important thing to understand about I.R.S. language is that its purpose is to trick you into doing voluntarily something the law does not require; which points irrevocably to the conclusion that our friends at I.R.S. know perfectly well what they are doing.

The trouble with all this is that all by itself it renders the present income tax system invalid, under a long-standing, well-settled principle of American law. According to that principle, a law must be clear to be a law. If the average man—you and your reporter—can't understand it, it's null and void. It doesn't exist and never did. It's a legislative abortion. Notice that when a defendant is arraigned—when he is accused in court of specific, criminal acts—he is routinely asked whether he understands the charges. A rapist is asked whether he understands the charges. An arsonist is asked whether he understands the charges. If he doesn't understand the charges—however serious the crimes—he can't be guilty. John Hinckley didn't understand, so the man who shot our President was not guilty of the crime.

The courts are quite clear about this. For instance, in *State v. Phillips*, 540 Pacific 2d 940, Justice Crockett wrote as follows for the Utah Supreme Court on September 15, 1975, about law in general: ". . . What it does require is that a statute be sufficiently clear that persons of ordinary intelligence, who desire to know what the law is and to abide by it, can understand what is required of them."

The U.S. Supreme Court has said the same thing time after time. In the well-known case of *Spreckels Sugar Refining Co., v. McClain*, 192 U.S. 397 (1904), the Court spoke at page 416 of "the well-settled rule that the citizen is exempt from taxation unless the same is imposed by clear and unequivocal language, and that where the construction of a tax law is doubtful, the doubt is to be resolved in favor of those upon whom the tax is sought to be laid. . . ."

In 1939, the Supreme Court ruled in *Lanzetta v. New Jersey*, 306 U.S. 451. Headnote three tells us this: "Persons may not be required at peril of life, liberty or property to speculate concerning meaning of penal statute . . . ." As we shall see, however, that is exactly what our friends at I.R.S. demand that you do. Indeed, remember that the courts of appeal can't even agree on what kind of tax the income tax is.

Headnote four of the same case says this: "A penal statute creating a new offense must be sufficiently explicit to inform those subject to it what conduct will render them liable to its penalties, and a statute forbidding or requiring doing of an act in terms so vague that men of common intelligence must necessarily guess at its meaning and differ as to its application is repugnant to due process clause."

Again, in 1972, in *Papachristou v. City of Jacksonville*, 405 U.S. 156, the U.S. Supreme Court said a law "is void for vagueness because it fails to give person of ordinary intelligence fair notice that his contemplated conduct is forbidden. . . ."

All of this fits the so-called "income tax" perfectly. The term *void for vagueness* is a routine item in a lawyer's vocabulary. If a legal instrument is vague, it is void. So, on this ground alone, the "income tax" convicts itself. How can Mr. Average American comply, if he genuinely doesn't understand?

Let's look through some I.R.S. publications, keeping all this in mind. On March 11, 1981, Robert J. Brann, Chief, Technical Services Branch, Internal Revenue Service, Washington, D.C., sent a letter to a gentleman in New York. Mr. Brann said this: ". . . In carrying out its responsibilities for administering the federal income tax laws, the Service encourages voluntary compliance by taxpayers. Voluntary compliance places on taxpayers the initial responsibility for deciding whether under the law they are required to file returns, and the responsibility for paying any tax that may be due. . . ."

Remember, this is not somebody our friends at I.R.S. have labelled an "illegal tax protester" talking. It's I.R.S. itself. Under the law, says our friend at I.R.S., you decide whether you are required to file. You decide whether you are required to pay. If you are, then you are. If you're not, then, presumably, you're not. This is somewhat akin to former Senator Barry Goldwater's description of Richard Nixon's so-called "full employment" budget: "If we had some ham, we could have some ham and eggs, if we had some eggs."

Our friends at I.R.S. use Publication 21 to indoctrinate high school students. Yes, did you know that your government school teacher is told to use valuable classroom time training your children to file tax returns? Could that be just one reason so many of today's graduates are not familiar with the Declaration of Independence? Can we realistically expect our civilization to continue, when millions of children are denied its basic principles?

Publication 21 tells them this: "The Internal Revenue Service relies on all taxpayers to know their tax responsibilities and to meet them. This is our system of voluntary compliance." "This system of voluntary compliance places the responsibility for filing a tax return upon you. . . ." "If you meet the minimum requirements for filing a return, you must do so by the date it is due."

Our friends at I.R.S. thereby try to create the impression that there is some universal, automatic, inescapable requirement to file. However, an impression is all it is. Look at the actual words. The actual words convey the true meaning. Notice that I.R.S. uses the word *voluntary* twice. Again, this means just what you think it does. As we have seen, *voluntary* means without legal obligation. In other words, says I.R.S., *you* decide whether or not to become subject to the tax. If you decide to become subject, you are subject. If you are required, then you are required. Is this true? Sure it is. Our friends at I.R.S. are telling you the truth—and the truth will make you free, if only you will heed it. If you are required—if, for instance, you have corporate income—then you are required; a statement you just can't argue with. On the other hand, if you are *not* required, then you are not required, a possibility our friends at I.R.S. don't like to mention.

Publication 21 was revised in October, 1982. The previous version had made all this even clearer: "'Voluntary compliance' places on the taxpayer the responsibility for filing an income tax return. You must decide whether the law requires you to file a return. If it does, you must file a return by the date it is due."

Again, if you are required—because you have voluntarily become subject in exchange for government "rewards"—then you are required, and must obey I.R.S. rules.

As we have seen, the Internal Revenue Code—a compendium of laws passed by Congress—does not define the key word *income.* It is forbidden to do so by the Sixteenth Amendment and the

Supreme Court. Our friends at I.R.S. reply that the Code *does* define *gross income* as follows, in Section 61(a): "Gross income means all income . . . ."

Again, the Code uses the word *income*—which it is forbidden to define—in its definition of gross income; which is somewhat akin to defining "mass hysteria" as "a lot of hysteria"; or like saying "a rose is a rose is a rose." It may sound pretty or profound, but it isn't a definition. You can't define a word by using the word. So, the Code's definition of *gross income* falls flat—because our friends at I.R.S. would really rather you don't know what *income* is.

As we have seen, Section 61(a) lists fifteen items, the first one of which is compensation. Neither wages nor salaries are mentioned, but compensation is. What is compensation? Our unabridged *Funk & Wagnalls* says compensation is "whatever makes good loss or lack." Compensation is also *amends; especially, an equivalent* in value. In other words, compensation makes amends for a loss, by replacing it with something of equal value. Compensation restores the *status quo ante*: the condition you enjoyed before you suffered the loss. So, compensation does not mean gain. It just puts you back where you were when you started. Our working woman has suffered the loss of time and labor on behalf of her boss, who makes amends for that loss by compensating her with a different kind of property.

How, then, can the Code tax it? We have seen that the Sixteenth Amendment, the law and the Supreme Court all forbid such a tax *without apportionment*. If compensation just restores a loss without gain, how can the Code tax the working woman's compensation?

It doesn't. Look again at the exact language: "[G]ross income means all income *from whatever source derived* . . . ." (emphasis added) Of course that is the language of the Sixteenth Amendment. Compensation then is listed in Section 61(a) as an example of a source from which income could be derived. Remember, however, that the tax is forbidden to hit the source itself (without apportionment). The tax hits the income *derived from* the source. If you are not aware of this—as you may not have been before you read this book—you could fall, innocently and ignorantly, into the trap set by our good friends at I.R.S., in which you would think that the tax hits the source directly.

That is exactly what they want you to think, and they are not going to tell you differently. In short, they haven't lied, but they haven't really told the truth. If you mistakenly conclude that your compensation is taxable, they can smile like the cat who ate the canary, and say it isn't their fault.

Section 61(a) is found in Part I of Subchapter B. Now, let's go to Part II of the same Subchapter, entitled, "Items Specifically Included In Gross Income." Here is I.R.S.'s chance to sock it specifically to the wage earner. Yet, again, there is no mention whatsoever of wages or salaries. Compensation isn't mentioned either. In other words, our friends at I.R.S. had the chance to nail your wages specifically to the wall, but they totally failed to do so!

You will find some remarkable examples of the deliberate confusion we are talking about, in the Internal Revenue Service's successive Privacy Act Notices. The Privacy Act of 1974 says that when a federal agency asks you for information, it must tell you whether the law requires you to give it; why the agency wants it; and what could happen to you if you refuse it. If you could be thrown into jail, the agency must say so.

Here's the last paragraph of the Privacy Act Statement issued by the Selective Service System: "Your failure to provide the required information may violate the Military Selective Service Act. Conviction of such violation may result in imprisonment for not more than five years or a fine of not more than $250,000, or both imprisonment and fine."

There's not much mystery here, is there? The information is required. If you refuse it, you could spend five years in the crowbar motel. (Here too, of course, the law must, and does, state clearly whom it covers. It doesn't cover females. It doesn't cover males above and below certain ages.) Now, let's look at the I.R.S. Privacy Act Notice in the 1040 instruction booklet for the year 1980. The I.R.S. is required to include it, as we have seen, but it usually does so deep in the entrails of the booklet, hoping you don't find it. In 1980, for instance, it was on page forty five. Shouldn't a statement so important be printed at or near the front page?

The Privacy Act Notice for 1980 said that "you must file a return or statement with us for any tax you are liable for. . . ." By now you know that this means just what it says. If you are liable—required to pay the tax—then you are liable, and you must file. Notice also what I.R.S. may do with the information you provide: "We may give the information to the Department of Justice . . . ." Our friends at I.R.S. are telling you here that the information you provide may be used against you in a criminal trial; that, by providing it, you are testifying against yourself, surrendering your rights. This is the Internal Revenue Service's version of the Miranda warning the rapist is supposed to get. Indeed, the same paragraph concludes as follows: ". . . And we may give it to foreign governments because of tax treaties they have with the United States."

Communist-occupied Russia has such a treaty with the United States. Information from your tax return could wind up in Moscow, if, for instance, you do business in that Socialist dictatorship. So, how can the government force you to testify against yourself? Section 6103(h) of the Code confirms that return information, and even complete returns, may be given to the Justice Department for criminal prosecution.

The answer is that the government is *not* forcing you to file. You do so voluntarily. Remember?

Finally, said I.R.S. in 1980: "If a return is not filed, or if we don't receive the information we ask for, the law provides that a penalty may be charged. . . ." Not a word was said about prison. Not a word was said about *criminal* penalties. Many people called attention to this, so, in 1981, our friends at I.R.S. rewrote their Notice. The new I.R.S. Privacy Act Notice contained this sentence: "Your response is mandatory under these sections." This certainly sounds as if everyone had better file forthwith, doesn't it? But it doesn't say that. All it says is that you are required to respond! This apparently means that if our friends at I.R.S. ask whether you are liable for any tax, you are required to tell them whether or not you are liable. According to this sentence and its context, if you are not liable, you are required to tell them that. Nothing is said about providing information. Again, all you are told to do is respond.

But, now here comes 1983. Our friends at I.R.S. apparently still were not satisfied. Now, the Notice says that "in certain cases, you may be subject to criminal prosecution." Doesn't this finally imply you could be sent to prison? Yes, it does, but notice what I.R.S. is talking about. Immediately before the warning about criminal prosecution, the 1983 Notice said this: "If you do not file a return, do not provide the information we ask for, *or provide fraudulent information*, the law provides that you may be charged penalties." (emphasis added)

In other words, if you voluntarily make and file a 1040 under penalty of perjury—and then commit perjury on it—you could wind up in prison, which is easy to understand. However, you are going to prison for perjury, not because you didn't file. You are going because you volunteered into the system and then broke the rules. Our friends at I.R.S. nevertheless create the threatening impression—without actually saying so—that you could lawfully go to prison for not filing, even if you have no reason to file; even if you have not volunteered into their system by making bourbon or profit. Again, the I.R.S. art consists of creating a spurious and oblique impression. Their theory is that if they say nothing directly, they can't be pinned down.

Now, let's look at the matter of liability. "Liability" means obligation or requirement. In the context of taxes, it means the person who is required to pay a certain tax. As you know, the Internal Revenue Code contains many taxes, and in all of them—except one—liability is clear. For instance, Internal Revenue Code Section 2002, headed, "Liability for payment," says as follows of the tax on estates: "The tax imposed by this chapter shall be paid by the executor." Are you the executor? If so, you must pay. If you are not the executor, you can forget the whole thing.

Section 4071(a) imposes a tax upon tires; Section 4071(b) says that the manufacturer, producer, or importer of those tires is liable for the tax. If you are one of those people, we recommend you pay.

Section 4161(a) imposes a tax upon sport fishing equipment, and Section 4162(c) makes the retailer of that equipment liable. If you retail sport fishing equipment, please pay that tax. The Communist dictators around the world who enjoy your "foreign aid" are waiting for their checks. If you find this intolerable, stop retailing sport fishing equipment.

Chapter 34 of the Code is entitled, "Policies Issued By Foreign Insurers." Section 4374 of that Chapter, headed "Liability for tax," explains as follows: "The tax imposed by this chapter shall be paid, on the basis of a return, by any person who makes, signs, issues, or sells any of the documents and instruments subject to the tax, or for whose use or benefit the same are made, signed, issued, or sold. The United States or any agency or instrumentality thereof shall not be liable for the tax."

So, if you are doing any of those things, the law requires you to pay that tax. If you aren't, it doesn't.

The Code of course contains several taxes on alcohol. Section 5005, for instance, headed, "Persons liable for tax," tells us this: "The distiller or importer of distilled spirits shall be liable for the taxes imposed thereon by section 5001(a)(1)."

Section 5043 clearly explains who is required to pay taxes on wines: "The taxes on wine provided for in this subpart shall be paid . . . . In the case of wines removed from any bonded wine cellar, by the proprietor of such bonded wine cellar . . . ."

Alcohol of course has also been the subject of two constitutional amendments, and is still controversial, but the alcohol tax is not confusing. As with the income tax, *you* decide whether to become subject to it. You become subject to it by making bourbon whiskey, for instance. If you become subject to it, you do so voluntarily. No one forces you to make bourbon. If you become subject to it—voluntarily—the law requires you to obey certain rules.

If you later decide that the rules are so intolerable that you no longer wish to obey them, you don't have to. You can legally stop paying alcohol taxes, and the way to do it is to stop making bourbon. If you never make bourbon, you will never be subject to the bourbon tax. If you never make income, you will never be subject to the income tax.

There is also Section 5703(a)(1), which says this: "The manufacturer or importer of tobacco products and cigarette papers and tubes shall be liable for the taxes imposed thereon by section 5701." Did you know there is a tax on cigarette tubes? We sure didn't. We still don't know what a cigarette tube is. Whatever it is, the law requires you to pay a tax on it, if you make or import it; and we strongly encourage you to pay it, if you are doing those things.

We said a few paragraphs ago that liability for only one tax in the Code is unclear. Which tax would you guess that is? The right answer wins you a scenic vacation lot in the *Better Homes & Gardens* neighborhood of Addis Ababa, in sunny Ethiopia; or an all-expense paid trip to the next Congressional hearings on the personal, financial activities of Speaker Jim Wright.

The answer of course is that the Code nowhere specifies liability for income tax. Nowhere with one exception. Yes, Section 1 of the Code does impose a tax on taxable income of individuals; and yes, Section 11 imposes a tax on taxable income of corporations, but there is no provision in Subtitle A or anywhere else in the Code that makes anyone liable to *pay* either tax. There are no liability sections like the ones you have just read about alcohol, tobacco, etc.

It is important to establish that the thing taxed and the liability for the tax are two different things. The thing taxed may be done, received or imported by one entity; but the law may require a different entity to pay the tax. For instance, the gift tax is not paid by the person who receives the gift, but by the person who gives it (26 U.S.C. 2502(d)). So, again, it isn't enough for the Code to lay a tax. The Code must also establish liability: name the entity that is required to file and pay. However, the Code doesn't do that for income tax, with one shattering exception that we shall examine in the next chapter.

Our friends at I.R.S. do refer to section 6001 in their Privacy Act Notice, which, as you will recall, is routinely buried in the 1040 instructions. There, they say that section 6001 is their legal authority to ask for information. What does that section say?: "Every person liable for any tax imposed by this title, or for the collection thereof, shall keep such records, render such statements, make such returns, and comply with such rules and regulations as the Secretary may from time to time prescribe. . . ."

Notice that Section 6001 is quite different from the other, genuine liability sections we have examined. It does not apply specifically to income tax, but to all the taxes in the title (Code). Indeed, it tells what you must do if you are liable—but it doesn't tell whether you are. Unlike those other sections, it doesn't say who must do those things. So, Section 6001 does not establish any liability for income tax.

Also in its Privacy Act Notice, the I.R.S. refers to Section 6011(a), as another legal basis for its questions. That section says this: "When required by regulations prescribed by the Secretary any person made liable for any tax imposed by this title, or for the collection thereof, shall make a return or statement according to the forms and regulations prescribed the Secretary. . . ."

Again, who is the "person made liable?" Your Aunt Letitia? Your boss? The President? Section 6011 does not say a word.

There is also Section 6012, which used to say that income tax returns "shall be made" by "Every individual having for the taxable year a gross income of $1,000 or more . . . ." A 1986 revision says those returns "shall be made" by "Every individual having for the taxable year gross income which equals or exceeds the exemption amount . . . ."

Aside from the trouble with "gross income," which there is no need to repeat, notice that, as usual, Section 6012 says not a word about who is required to pay the tax. Making the return is not at all the same thing as paying the tax.

Believe it or not—and you will have to—the Internal Revenue Code nowhere establishes liability to pay the income tax, with the one staggering exception we are coming to. Yet, as we have seen, its authors are perfectly capable of writing liability for alcohol and tobacco, et cetera. Could it be that somebody up there doesn't want you to know who is liable, because of the fatal defect we have set forth in this book?

Many Americans have been convicted of and imprisoned for alleged violations of I.R.C. Section 7203, entitled, "Willful

Failure to File Return," and so on. Section 7203 says in pertinent part as follows: "*Any person required* under this title to pay any . . . tax, or required by this title . . . to make a return . . . , who willfully fails to pay such . . . tax, make such return, . . . shall, in addition to other penalties provided by law, be guilty of a misdemeanor . . . ." (emphasis added)

Section 7203 typically applies to *all* the taxes in the Code, not specifically to the income tax. Notice that the key language does not say every individual is required to pay. It doesn't say every American is required to make a return. It says *any person required* must do so. Who, then, is the "person required?" The alcohol and tobacco sections are very specific, but, as you see, Section 7203 typically stands mute.

Indeed, the Internal Revenue Code defines certain key terms in Chapter 79. Those definitions govern those terms, unless a Code subtitle or chapter contains its own definitions. Section 7203 is located in Chapter 75, headed, "Crimes, Other Offenses, and Forfeitures." Also in Chapter 75 is Section 7343, which defines "person" as follows: "The term 'person' as used in this chapter includes an officer or employee of a corporation, or a member or employee of a partnership, who as such officer, employee, or member is under a duty to perform the act in respect of which the violation occurs."

Now apply the definition in Section 7343 to Section 7203, and we find that it pertains only to the people mentioned in Section 7343: officers or employees of corporations, or members or employees of partnerships.

The question arises: How can we be sure that 7343 applies only to those people? Could it be that 7343 just lists them as *examples* of many others to whom it applies? Is its language meant to be inclusive, rather than exclusive?

Compare Section 7343 to our old friend, Section 61, which, as you will recall, pretends to "define" gross income as follows: "Except as otherwise provided in this subtitle, gross income means all income from whatever source derived, including (*but not limited to*) the following items . . . ." (emphasis added)

So, our friends at I.R.S. know perfectly well how to use the phrase, "but not limited to." Yet, they didn't use it in Section 7343. They neglected to add any other language that would have extended the section's reach. So, the "person" mentioned in Section 7203 is the same "person" defined in Section 7343—*and no one else*. If the Code does establish liability for the income tax, those are the "persons" liable for it: officers or employees of corporations, or members or employees of partnerships.

What do the words "includes" or "including" mean? In *Montello Salt Company v. Utah*, 221 U.S. 452, 31 S.Ct. 706 (1911), the U.S. Supreme Court considered that question regarding an act of Congress and held that the word "including" means "to confine within." The State of Utah argued against such a limited meaning, but the Supreme Court disagreed. So, the word "includes" means only the things specified, not things that are not specified. The things that are specified are not just examples of what is included; they are the *only* things that are included.

Along these lines, what does the word "employee" mean? As we have seen, words in law often mean something entirely different from what they mean in conversation. So it is here. Internal Revenue Code Section 3401(c) defines the word "employee" as follows: "For purposes of this chapter, the term 'employee' includes an officer, employee, or elected official of the United States, a State, or any political subdivision thereof, or the District of Columbia, or any agency or instrumentality of any one or more of the foregoing. The term 'employee' also includes an officer of a corporation."

So, an employee for income tax purposes is either a government official or a corporate officer. Notice again the absence of the phrase, "but not limited to," or any other inclusive language. Therefore, if you are a government official or a corporate officer, you are the "employee" the law means. If you are not, you are not.

According to Section 31.3401(c)-1(c) of the *Federal Tax Regulations*: "Generally, physicians, lawyers, dentists, veterinarians, contractors, subcontractors, public stenographers, auctioneers, and others who follow an independent trade, business, or profession, in which they offer their services to the public, are not employees."

If you are not an employee, you are not subject to withholding from wages.

After the so-called Tax Equity and Fiscal Responsibility Act of 1982 took effect, waitresses launched angry demonstrations, in the (spurious) belief that, under the new law, the Internal Revenue Code requires them even more rigorously to report their tips. Does it? Remember that the income tax is supposed to soak the rich, not the waitress. Internal Revenue Code Section 6053(a), headed, "Reports by Employees," tells us this: "Every employee who, in the course of his employment by an employer, receives in any calendar month tips which are wages . . . or which are compensation . . . shall report all such tips . . . ."

Are tips wages or compensation? In some establishments, the employer adds a "service charge" to the bill, and then pays a portion of that "service charge" to the waitress. Such a payment presumably would constitute wages or compensation. Notice, however, that in speaking of tips which are wages or compensation, Section 6053(a) implicitly admits that there are tips which are *not* wages or compensation.

Wages or compensation are one end of a contractual agreement between employer and employee or client and businesswoman. When the employee delivers his labor, the employer is required to pay his wage. If the employer refuses to do that—which sometimes happens—the judge orders him to choose between payment and prison. On the contrary, when the restaurant patron pays the tip directly to the waitress, he alone controls it. He alone decides the amount. Indeed, if he decides not to tip at all, he doesn't have to. There is no contractual relationship. The poor waitress has no recourse—except that such a diner would be wise not to eat there again. A tip is a gift. So, there's no reason for our waitress to get upset, because the Code does not require her to report her tips. If the Code really did require waitresses to report their tips, Section 6053(a) would say so. It doesn't. Yet, as usual, our friends at I.R.S. pretend that it does.

Time after time, to steer clear of the law, I.R.S. language is designed to trick you into accepting liability, when in fact you are not liable. Confronted later with the outrage, our friends at I.R.S. say blithely that you "volunteered." In their own uniquely perverse way, the authors of I.R.S. language are minor literary geniuses. Former Oklahoma Senator Henry Bellmon said as follows in 1969: "[I]n a recent conversation with an official at the Internal Revenue Service, I was amazed when he told me that, 'If the taxpayers of this country ever discover that the Internal Revenue Service operates on 90% bluff, the entire system will collapse.'"

As far as we know, the late Czech author Franz Kafka is the only writer who could do total justice to I.R.S. His works dramatize the fact that dictatorship encourages arbitrary and confusing law. Law that is clear is easy to obey. Law that is arbitrary and confusing is law one can fall afoul of by accident. A dictator uses such law to turn the target population into "criminals" who can be jailed if they step out of line. That's exactly what is happening now. The bureaucrats and martinets are using such "law" as a weapon of usurpation.

Along these lines, Bob Jones University, the fundamentalist school in South Carolina, has a policy that forbids interracial dating. The University is private and takes no government money, but I.R.S. cancelled its tax exemption, on the ground that interracial dating is the so-called "public policy" of the United States.

The real issue here is not whether you and your reporter agree that interracial dating is good or is not. The real issue is that interracial dating has nothing to do with collecting taxes. Are not taxes supposed to be the only business of our friends at I.R.S.? Isn't a government that regulates dating habits well on the way to totalitarianism? If you applauded the I.R.S. ruling in the Bob Jones case, because you support, or at least condone, interracial dating, would you be just as pleased should our friends at I.R.S. use that power—power you granted—to encourage the breeding of "super" people? As you know, that has happened before—and the man who did it claimed righteously that everything he was doing was "legal."

9

WHO IS LIABLE?

As we have seen, there are two main elements to every tax in the Internal Revenue Code. First, there is the matter of *what* is taxed, from cigarette tubes to tires. We have answered that question in our analysis of income. Second, there is the matter of *who* is taxed. In other words, the Code also tells us who is required to file the pertinent form; who is required to pay the tax; who is liable. Remember that the person who enjoys the thing taxed, may not be the same person who is liable for the tax. For instance, the recipient of the gift is the one who enjoys it; but the donor of the gift is the one who is liable for the tax. The employee allegedly enjoys the fruits of the Social Security tax, but the employer is liable for half of it. So the obvious question arises: Who is liable for the income tax?

Throughout this book, you have read about a mostly mythological creature named Person Required. Person Required is the dignitary who is liable to file the pertinent form and pay the income tax, the tax on profit and gain. Despite all the honorable mentions, however, we still don't know for sure who Person Required is. Surely Congress wouldn't write a tax, debate a tax, pass a tax—and then not require anyone to pay it! No, it wouldn't. The fact is that nowhere in the gargantuan Internal Revenue Code is Person Required identified—is anyone made liable for the income tax—with one exception.

Let's set the stage for that exception with an examination of the jurisdiction of the federal government. No doubt because of the fulsome collectivism in the nation's government schools, most Americans probably believe that federal jurisdiction is all-pervasive, and that the states are meant to be mere administrative appendages of Washington. The truth is about 179 degrees away. The Constitution restricts the federal government to only a few specified powers. In the use of those powers, the federal government is supreme, but *only* there. Indeed, beyond those powers the federal government has no jurisdiction whatsoever.

On May 3, 1854, President Franklin Pierce said as follows in a veto message of the federal government's power to tax: ". . . It is not a substantive general power to provide for the welfare of the United States, but is a limitation on the grant of power to raise money by taxes, duties, and imposts. If it were otherwise, all the rest of the Constitution, consisting of carefully enumerated and cautiously guarded grants of specific powers, would have been useless, if not delusive. It would be impossible in that view to escape from the conclusion that these were inserted only to mislead for the present, and, instead of enlightening and defining the pathway of the future, to involve its action in the mazes of doubtful construction. Such a conclusion the character of the men, who framed that sacred instrument will never permit us to form. Indeed, to suppose it susceptible of any other construction would be to consign all the rights of the States and of the people of the States to the mere discretion of Congress, and thus to clothe the Federal Government with authority to control the sovereign States, by which they would have been dwarfed into provinces or departments and all sovereignty vested in an absolute consolidated central power, against which the spirit of liberty has so often and in so many countries struggled in vain."

President Pierce also quoted President Madison in the *Federalist* as follows: "The powers delegated to the proposed Constitution are few and defined. Those which are to remain in the State governments are numerous and indefinite. . . . Its [the General Government's] jurisdiction extends to certain enumerated objects only, and leaves to the several States a residuary and inviolable sovereignty over all other objects."

Finally, President Pierce said this: "In the same spirit President Jefferson invokes 'the support of the State governments in all their rights as the most competent administrations for our domestic concerns and the surest bulwarks against anti-republican tendencies,' and President Jackson said that our true strength and wisdom are not promoted by invasions of the rights and powers of the several States, but that, on the contrary, they consist 'not in binding the States more closely to the center, but in leaving each more unobstructed in its proper orbit.'"

It is worth mentioning that both Presidents Jefferson and Jackson are still heroes to today's Democrat Party.

On February 10, 1910, Idaho Senator Borah—a strong advocate of the proposed income tax—made a speech on the subject. Let's browse through it, starting at page 1696 of that day's *Congressional Record*: "[T]he state governments, in their separate and independent sovereignties, in their reserved powers, are just as much beyond the jurisdiction and control of the National Government as the National Government in its sovereignty is beyond the control and jurisdiction of the state governments."

On the next page, Senator Borah quotes from the Supreme Court ruling in *Collector v. Day*, 11 Wall. 113; 78 U.S. 122: ". . . In respect to the reserve powers the State is as sovereign and independent as the General Government." Farther down the same page (1697), Borah explains that "it is not within the jurisdiction of the National Government to exercise control over the state functions or the functions of a separate and individual sovereignty; that unlimited power to tax covering property or incomes from whatever source derived will never be construed, so long as we have an indestructible union of indestructible States, so as to embarrass or destroy each other. The fullest taxing power must be construed in the light of the objects, designs, purposes, and schemes of the Constitution as a whole."

On page 1698, Senator Borah says that the proposed Sixteenth Amendment would be construed "to cover those incomes from sources within the jurisdiction and control of the sovereignty laying the tax . . . ."

In other words, according to Senator Borah, some incomes would be from sources *not* within the jurisdiction and control of the sovereignty laying the tax—the United States—and therefore would *not* be covered. This recalls the fact that there is always a geographical, territorial component to jurisdiction. Jurisdiction always involves a physical place; always is exercised *somewhere*. To say otherwise, would be to say that you could hold back the sea without a dike. Moses did it, but he had divine support.

So, whatever the jurisdiction of the United States is, it is very limited. What is it?

In April, 1956, the U.S. Government Printing Office issued Part I of a Report of the Interdepartmental Committee for the Study of Jurisdiction Over Federal Areas Within the States, entitled, "Jurisdiction Over Federal Areas Within the States." The Chairman of the Committee was Perry Morton, Assistant Attorney General, and the Report includes a letter of transmittal from Attorney General Herbert Brownell to President Eisenhower, whose own letter praises the people who did the work.

Let's browse through this government report. At page nineteen, it describes the problems of people who live in federal enclaves, such as military reservations, within the states, complete jurisdiction over which the states have ceded to Washington: "Probably the incident of exclusive legislative jurisdiction, which has most numerous, and most serious, effects is that residents of exclusive jurisdiction areas have been held not to be residents of the State or local subdivision thereof in which such area is physically situated. As a result such persons may be denied many of the important rights and privileges which are contingent upon State residence. They are not entitled to vote, to hold public office, or to serve on juries, and their children are not entitled to receive an education in the free public school systems of the State. The right of access to State courts in matters where jurisdiction is based upon residence within the State may be denied them, and problems consequently arise in the fields of divorce, adoption, administration of estates, and juvenile offenses. There is no obligation on the State to admit residents to State-sponsored or administered hospitals or sanatoriums, nor to provide such residents with other governmental services, such as visiting nurses, public libraries, welfare services and the like. . . ."

In all these ways, the Americans who live in those federal enclaves are like citizens of a foreign nation; related to us, like Canadians, but at the same time alien.

Along these lines, page twenty six of the Report explains that in areas under exclusive, federal, legislative jurisdiction there is legal discrimination with regard to taxation, "whereby residents of such areas, persons doing business in the areas, and privately owned property contained in the areas, must receive from State and local taxing authorities treatment different from that accorded to very similarly situated persons and property on areas as to which the United States does not have exclusive legislative jurisdiction. The situation is obviously complicated by the fact that the imposition of certain taxes on private persons, activities, and properties in Federal exclusive legislative jurisdiction areas have been authorized by the Congress while other have not."

So, Congress lets the states impose certain taxes, but not others, in these exclusive federal areas. Again, we are talking about legislative jurisdiction, which means the power to make laws. If a governmental unit has no legislative jurisdiction over an area, it can't make law there.

Along these lines, sometimes a state cedes jurisdiction over an area very parsimoniously. Here is part of an Alabama cession instrument, on page 128: ". . . The state expressly reserves the right to tax all persons, firms, corporations, or associations now or hereafter residing or located upon such lands. The state expressly reserves the right to tax the exercise by any person, firm, corporation, or association of any and all rights, privileges, and franchises upon said lands; and to tax property of all persons, firms, corporations, or associations situated upon such lands. The jurisdiction ceded to the United States shall be for the purposes of the cession, and none other; and shall continue during the time the United States shall be or remain the owner thereof and shall use such lands for the purpose of the cession. . . ."

Talk about a stingy giver! Remember that the study deals entirely with federal enclaves, where Washington gains jurisdiction only with the permission of the states. If that jurisdiction in those enclaves is so cautiously circumscribed, how much jurisdiction would you guess the federal government has in state areas outside these enclaves? The answer is: about as much as Yasir Arafat has in a meeting of United Jewish Appeal.

Now, let's look at Part II of the Report, issued in June, 1957. At page six, we learn that state and federal jurisdiction are so different, the relationship between them is often governed by international law. The Report speaks of "extension to these areas of a rule of international law that when one sovereign takes over territory of another the laws of the original sovereign in effect at the time of the taking which are not inconsistent with the laws or policies of the second continue in effect, as laws of the succeeding sovereign, until changed by that sovereign."

Article I, section eight, clause seventeen, of the Constitution, allows for the creation of Washington, D.C., in which the federal government is of course supreme; and for the federal purchase of other land "for the Erection of Forts, Magazines, Arsenals, dock-Yards, and other needful Buildings." Those are the only purposes for which the federal government is permitted to buy land; nevertheless, the Founding Fathers were suspicious of the clause, in fear that the new government could use the power to disparage the rights of residents of such areas. In the North Carolina convention, James Iredell, later a Supreme Court justice, defended the clause as follows, according to page twenty four of the Report: "They [the United States government—Stang] are to have exclusive power of legislation—but how? Wherever they may have this district, they must possess it from the authority of the state within which it lies; and that state may stipulate the conditions of the cession. Will not such state take care of the liberties of its own people? . . ."

In the Virginia convention, Patrick Henry voiced a number of objections to the clause. Madison defended it as follows: ". . . I cannot comprehend that the power of legislating over a small district, which cannot exceed ten miles square, and may not be more than one mile, will involve the dangers he apprehends. . . . Is it probable that the members from Georgia, New Hampshire, & c., will concur to sacrifice the privileges of their friends? . . . The states may make what stipulation they please in it, and, if they apprehend any danger, they may refuse it altogether. How could the general government be guarded from the undue influence of particular states, or from insults, without such exclusive power?"

So, in the beginning, the purpose of clause seventeen was to defend the fledgling federal government from the states.

At page forty five, the Report tells us this: "It scarcely needs to be said that unless there has been a transfer of jurisdiction (1) pursuant to clause 17 by a Federal acquisition of land with State consent, or (2) by cession from the State to the Federal Government, or unless the Federal Government has reserved jurisdiction upon the admission of the State, *the Federal Government possesses no legislative jurisdiction over any area within a State*, such jurisdiction being for exercise entirely by the State . . . ." (emphasis added) Again, if the federal government has no legislative jurisdiction over an area, it has no power to make laws there. On the other hand, people who live in areas of exclusive, federal jurisdiction may not be citizens of the states in which those enclaves are located. Page ninety two of the Report says that the New Mexico Supreme Court ruled in 1948 that residents of the Atomic Energy Commission's area at Los Alamos were not citizens of New Mexico.

The question arises: What is the criminal jurisdiction of the federal government? At page 105, the Report says this: "Areas over which the Federal Government has acquired exclusive legislative jurisdiction are subject to the exclusive criminal jurisdiction of the United States. . . ."

Only where it has legislative jurisdiction does the federal government have power to prosecute crimes. Indeed, at page 199 of the Report, we learn of a letter written to the Chairman of the Senate Finance Committee by the Attorney General of the United States, in 1940: ". . . Criminal jurisdiction of the Federal courts is restricted to Federal reservations over which the Federal Government has exclusive jurisdiction, as well as to forts, magazines, arsenals, dockyards, or other needful buildings (U.S.C., title 18, sec. 451, par. 3d). . . ."

In other words, only if a crime is committed in one of those places, does a federal court have jurisdiction to try it. This means that almost all income tax trials are illegal.

Along these lines, let's look at Title 18, Section 7 of the Criminal Code, which deals with the "special maritime and territorial jurisdiction of the United States." That jurisdiction includes: (1) the high seas; (2) any American ship; (3) "Any lands reserved or acquired for the use of the United States, and under the exclusive or concurrent jurisdiction thereof, or any place purchased or otherwise acquired by the United States by consent of the legislature of the State in which the same shall be, for the erection of a fort, magazine, arsenal, dockyard, or other needful building"; (4) any island, rock, or key containing guano; and (5) any U.S. aircraft, owned either by the government or a private citizen, while it is in flight over the high seas "and out of the jurisdiction of any particular State."

There are also new additions (6) which announces federal jurisdiction over space vehicles in flight; and (7), which announces jurisdiction over offenses by or against a U.S. national outside the jurisdiction of any other nation.

That's it! The federal government has no other territorial jurisdiction over crimes. Question: How, then, can the federal courts conduct criminal income tax trials? Answer: They can't. Again, such trials are totally illegal, because, as we have seen, those courts have no jurisdiction to conduct them. They do so by means of the usurpation the Founding Fathers took such care to warn us against.

In *New Orleans v. United States*, 35 U.S. (10 Pet.) 662 (1836), the Supreme Court said as follows at page 737: "Special provision is made in the Constitution for the cession of jurisdiction from the States over places where the federal government shall establish forts or other military works. And it is *only* in these places, or in the territories of the United States, where it can exercise a general jurisdiction." In *New York v. Miln*, 36 U.S. (11 Pet.) 102 (1837), the

Court explained at page 139 that "a State has the same undeniable and unlimited jurisdiction over all persons and things within its territorial limits, as any foreign nation . . . ."

There is also *U.S. v. First National City Bank*, 321 F.2d 14 (1963), in which judge Moore speaks for the second circuit at page twenty three of "the settled principle of statutory construction that legislation is meant to apply only within the territorial jurisdiction of the United States unless a contrary intention appears. . . ."

In the same vein, page 107 of Part II of the Report says the federal government has power to make criminal the following acts outside its jurisdiction: espionage, sabotage, interference with the mails, destruction of federal property, frauds on the federal government, etc. Beyond these, it has no power. Remember that this two-part Report was prepared by the government.

What have we learned so far? We have learned that jurisdiction—the power to govern (to make laws and try crimes)—and territory are inseparable. The location of an entity is crucial. We have also learned that, while federal jurisdiction is supreme where it operates, it operates in very few places, such as outer space, where it belongs.

How does all this apply to the income tax? As we have seen, Congress imposed income taxes during the War Between the States. We have examined them from the point of view of income (what is taxed). Now, let's reexamine them from the point of view of jurisdiction, of liability (who is taxed).

In 1861, in the first session of the 37th Congress, the government gave us the nation's first income tax (12 Stat. 292). In Chapter 45, at page 309, the law said as follows in Section 49: *And be it further enacted*, That, from and after the first day of January next, there shall be levied, collected, and paid, upon the annual income of *every person residing in the United States*, whether such income is derived from any kind of property, or from any profession, trade, employment, or vocation carried on in the United States or elsewhere, or from any other source whatever, if such annual income exceeds the sum of eight hundred dollars, a tax of three per centum on the amount of such excess of such income above eight hundred dollars . . . . Upon the income, rents, or dividends accruing upon any property, securities, or stocks owned in the United States by *any citizen of the United States residing abroad*, there shall be levied, collected, and paid a tax of five per centum . . . ."

Section 50 of the law speaks of "internal duties or income tax." So Congress called the income tax an internal duty—to escape apportionment—and it hit the incomes of persons residing in the United States and citizens of the United States residing abroad. As we have seen, an income tax can be both direct and indirect. Here it is a duty, which is indirect. A duty usually refers to an item that is imported into the country.

In 1862, the second session of the 37th Congress passed another tax. In 12 Stat. 432, Congress said as follows in Chapter 119, Section 86, at page 472: "*And be it further enacted*, That on and after the first day of August, eighteen hundred and sixty-two, there shall be levied, collected, and paid on all salaries of officers, or payments to persons in the civil, military, naval, or other employment or service of the United States, including senators and representatives and delegates in Congress, when exceeding the rate of six hundred dollars per annum, a duty of three per centum on the excess above the said six hundred dollars . . . ."

This salary tax was of course quite direct, yet it was not apportioned. Didn't that omission make it illegal? No, such a tax was perfectly legal because the government was taxing its own. Here we see an instructive, early example of the fact that status is a crucial element of income tax. Who are you? Where are you? The answers will help determine whether you are subject to the tax. If you work for the federal government, you shouldn't be surprised when the government hits you with a tax.

Still in 1862, the law described the targets of the tax as follows in Section 90, at page 473: "annual gains, profits, or income of every person residing in the United States, whether derived from any kind of property, rents, interest, dividends, salaries," et cetera. There were also "annual gains, profits, or income, rents, and dividends accruing upon any property, securities, and stocks owned in the United States by any citizen of the United States residing abroad . . . ."

Again, the tax was levied on persons residing in the United States and citizens abroad.

In 1864, the first session of the 38th Congress passed another income tax. In 13 Stat. 223, Chapter 173, Section 116, at page 281, the things taxed are described as "annual gains, profits, or income of every person residing in the United States, or of any citizen of the United States residing abroad . . . ."

In 1894, the second session of the 53rd Congress passed the income tax the Supreme Court considered in *Pollock*. In 28 Stat. 509, Chapter 349, Section 27, at page 553, we read about "the gains, profits, and income received in the preceding calendar year by every citizen of the United States, whether residing at home or abroad, and every person residing therein . . . ."

Finally, in 1913, the first session of the 63rd Congress passed the income tax the Supreme Court considered in *Brushaber*. In 38 Stat. 114, Chapter 16, Section IIA, Subdivision 1, page 166, the law hits "every citizen of the United States, whether residing at home or abroad, and to every person residing in the United States, though not a citizen thereof . . . ."

What did the term "person" mean in that legislation? What was the meaning of the term, "citizen of the United States?" Because we have allowed the independent nations of Alabama and California, and all others in between, to degenerate into the lowly departments President Franklin Pierce feared, those meanings—still applicable—lie dormant under decades of legislative detritus. Let's resurrect them.

On April 14, 1873, the U.S. Supreme Court ruled in what are known as the *Slaughter-House Cases*, 83 U.S. (16 Wall.) 36; 21 L.Ed. 394. This of course was just a few years after the close of the Civil War, the taxes of which were no doubt still in the forefront of memory. Indeed, the Civil War income tax had expired only the year before. Justice Miller wrote the ruling, and in a discussion of the Fourteenth Amendment he wrote as follows at page 407: ". . . It had been said by eminent judges that no man was a citizen of the United States except as he was a citizen of one of the states composing the Union. Those, therefore, who had been born and resided always in the District of Columbia or in the territories, though within the United States, were not citizens. . . ."

Such people were not nationals of any other country, and they were not aliens, but, as you see, they were not citizens of this country, because such citizenship did not yet exist in more than rudimentary form. Because the states were independent nations that had created the federal government as their agent, Americans were citizens of the several states. There was no other citizenship in our nation. We saw an expression of this in the War Between the States, when General Robert E. Lee, invited to command the Union forces, chose instead to command those of the Confederacy, because of his loyalty to Virginia.

This defect, if defect it was, was cured by the Fourteenth Amendment. The blacks, whose liberty was the putative reason for the war, had been liberated. However, a situation remained almost as intolerable as the slavery now happily extinguished; for the blacks, while free, were still not citizens of their country. So it was that the first clause of the first section of the Fourteenth Amendment said this: "All persons born or naturalized in the United States and subject to the jurisdiction thereof are citizens of the United States and of the state wherein they reside."

Still at page 407, Justice Miller says this: "The first observation we have to make on this clause is that it puts at rest both the questions which we stated to have been the subject of differences of opinion. It declares that persons may be citizens of the United States without regard to their citizenship of a particular state . . . ."

Now, there were two citizenships; an artificial, juridical, government-created citizenship: citizenship of the United States; and the natural citizenship of a state. Before the Fourteenth Amendment, the concept of national citizenship, still puny, was dependent on citizenship of a state. Now, national citizenship stood on its own.

Notice, however, that the Amendment did not affect those people "who had been born and resided always in the District of Columbia or in the territories, though within the United States."

Now, they were "citizens of the United States," but not of any particular state. The Amendment only made all people in the states citizens of those states. The people in the District and the territories maintained the same status as the people in those federal enclaves covered in that government study dated 1957. As you will recall, such people couldn't vote, because they weren't state citizens.

At the next page, 408, Justice Miller explained that "the distinction between citizenship of the United States and citizenship of a state is clearly recognized and established. Not only may a man be a citizen of the United States without being a citizen of a state, but an important element is necessary to convert the former into the latter. He must reside within the state to make him a citizen of it, but it is only necessary that he should be born or naturalized in the United States to be a citizen of the Union.

"It is quite clear, then, that there is a citizenship of the United States, and a citizenship of a state, which are distinct from each other and which depend upon different characteristics or circumstances in the individual."

So, if you live in the District of Columbia, in an American territory—or even in some other nation—you are only a "citizen of the United States," not a citizen of any particular state.

Now, let's move along to *Baldwin v. Franks*, (7 S.Ct. 656; 120 U.S. 678) in which the Supreme Court ruled on March 7, 1887. Chief Justice Morrison Waite wrote the ruling, and at page 662 (690) he said this: ". . . The person on whom the wrong to be punishable must be inflicted is described as a *citizen*. In the constitution and laws of the United States the word 'citizen' is generally, if not always, used in a political sense, to designate one who has the rights and privileges of a citizen of a state or of the United States. It is so used in section 1 of article 14 of the amendments of the constitution . . . . But it is also sometimes used in popular language to indicate the same thing as resident, inhabitant, or person. That it is not so used in section 5508 in the Revised Statutes is quite clear . . . ."

In short, "citizen" and "person" are not the same things at all. What, then, is a "person"? Five years later, on April 4, 1892, the

Supreme Court ruled in *Logan v. U.S.*, 12 S.Ct. 617. At page 626, Justice Gray wrote as follows: "In Baldwin v. Franks . . . it was decided that the word 'citizen,' in section 5508 of the Revised Statutes, as in the original act of May 31, 1870, c. 114, §6, was used in its political sense, and not as synonymous with 'resident,' 'inhabitant,' or 'person,' and therefore did not include an alien. . . ."

In short, a citizen of the State of Alabama is one thing in law; while a person or alien is totally another.

Now, let's move along to January 17, 1940, to *Powe v. United States*, 109 F.2d 147, in which Judge Sibley spoke as follows for the Fifth Circuit at page 149: "In its construction it is proper to apply the rule that criminal laws are to be construed strictly, and to bear in mind that other rule that a construction is to be avoided, if possible, that would render the law unconstitutional, or raise grave doubts thereabout. In view of these rules it is held that 'citizen' means 'citizen of the United States,' and not person generally, nor citizen of a State . . . ."

Again, a "citizen" and a "person" are two different people. Still further along these lines, there is the case of *Anderson et al. v. Scholes et al.*, 83 F.Supp 681, in the U.S. District Court in the 3rd Division of Alaska, on April 11, 1949, before Alaska became a state. At page 687, Judge Dimond said this: "Can a person be considered a 'citizen' of Alaska in the same constitutional sense as that of a 'citizen' of a State? The distinction between a State and a Territory is obvious, because a State in some of its aspects and within constitutional limits is sovereign. No such claim has ever been made for any Territory . . . . So we usually speak of residents of Alaska, not of its citizens. The residents of Alaska may be, and most of them are, citizens of the United States. Perhaps that is all. Alaska does not yet enjoy the political status which would bring its residents within the constitutional meaning and definition of 'citizens' as applied to citizens of the United States who are domiciled in the States and therefore citizens of the States."

Indeed, just as one may be a "citizen of the United States" and not a citizen of a State; so one apparently may be a citizen of a

State but not of the United States. On July 21, 1966, the Court of Appeal of Maryland ruled in *Crosse v. Board of Supervisors of Elections*, 221 A.2d 431; a headnote in which tells us: "Both before and after the Fourteenth Amendment to the federal Constitution, it has not been necessary for a person to be a citizen of the United States in order to be a citizen of his state. . . ." At page 434, Judge Oppenheimer cites a Wisconsin ruling in which the court said this: "Under our complex system of government, there may be a citizen of a state, who is not a citizen of the United States in the full sense of the term. . . ."

Now, let's look again at the tax laws. The laws taxed, and still tax, "persons residing in the United States," and "every citizen of the United States, whether residing at home or abroad." In view of *all* the precedent we have examined, this means the tax hits aliens (persons) residing here or having income here; and citizens of the United States (U.S. nationals) who live either in some other country, in a U.S. territory, or "at home" in one of the federal enclaves where they suffer the disadvantages mentioned in that government report.

A direct tax could legally target the labor of such aliens and juridical "citizens"—without apportionment—because such people are not state citizens, and do not have access to the protection of apportionment. The federal government does have power to tax your labor directly, *by apportionment*, but *only* by apportionment. Without apportionment, it may directly tax only aliens who live here or have income here; and "citizens of the United States," who live either abroad or "at home" on federal ground. Remember that the Fourteenth Amendment says a "citizen of the United States" is someone who is not just born or naturalized in the United States, but someone who is also "subject to the jurisdiction thereof." This means you can be born here, can be a state citizen and a U.S. national; but not a "citizen of the United States." People born or naturalized here, but who live in Washington, D.C., in a U.S. territory, in a federal enclave or another country are "subject to the jurisdiction thereof," because they are not state citizens, and lack the protection thereof.

So, the trouble with the income tax is that our friends at I.R.S. are inflicting it on state citizens without apportionment. In *Pollock*, the Court said as follows, in 157 U.S. at 582: "Nothing can be clearer than that what the constitution intended to guard against was the exercise by the general government of the power of directly taxing persons and property within any state through a majority made up from the other states. . . ." That is exactly what is happening now.

Indeed, you will remember that in the 1913 Act, Congress levied a tax on "every person residing in the United States, though not a citizen thereof." What does the term "United States" mean? In Section H of the 1913 Act, in 38 Stat. at 177, Congress defined the term as follows: "That the word 'State' or 'United States' when used in this section shall be construed to include any Territory, Alaska, the District of Columbia, Porto Rico, and the Philippine Islands, when such construction is necessary to carry out its provisions." The 1916 Act contained a similar provision.

Does the word "include" here mean that the things mentioned are just examples of what is meant by "United States?" No, "include" means *only* what is mentioned. Remember that in 1911, in *Montello Salt Company v. Utah*, 221 U.S. 452, 31 S.Ct. 706, the Supreme Court ruled against the State of Utah and found that "including" means "to confine within," meaning that the word includes only what is specified. In other words, the first income tax was imposed only on citizens and residents of the "United States"; only within federal jurisdiction.

Along these lines, let's look at Chapter 6, Section 15, of the Gold Reserve Act, which the second session of the 73rd Congress passed on January 30, 1934. It begins: "As used in this Act the term 'United States' means the Government of the United States; the term 'the continental United States' means the States of the United States, the District of Columbia, and the Territory of Alaska . . . ."

So, "United States" does not mean the several States. It just means the government. Congress knew how to include the States if it had wanted to. Instead, it imposed the income tax in the

"United States," not in the States, because it had no jurisdiction there.

Do we have any "expert" support? Well, whom would you consider an "expert?" Would you consider a man who wrote authoritative works on the 1894 tax, the 1913 tax and subsequent income taxes an expert? Would you consider a man who wrote other textbooks on federal law and who lectured on federal jurisprudence at the Yale Law School an expert? We would. He is Roger Foster, a New York attorney, author of *Foster's Federal Practice, Foster's Federal Judiciary Acts* and other works.

In *A Treatise on the Federal Income Tax Under the Act of 1913* (Rochester, New York, Lawyers Co-operative Publishing Company, 1915, second edition), Roger Foster and his co-author, Everett V. Abbot, another attorney, say this, at page 152: "The tax applies to all citizens of the United States, wherever resident, to all residents of the United States irrespective of their citizenship, to the income of all property owned and of every business, trade or profession carried on, in the United States by persons residing elsewhere. *It is levied in Alaska, the District of Columbia, Porto Rico and the Philippine Islands*. . . . The Act expressly directs: 'That the word "State" or "United States" when used in this section shall be construed to include any Territory, Alaska, the District of Columbia, Porto Rico, and the Philippine Islands, when such construction is necessary to carry out its provisions.'. . ." (emphasis added)

What do our friends at I.R.S. say about all this? Is there any reflection of it in the Internal Revenue Code? Yes, there is. Let's return to our original question: In all of the income tax provisions of the Internal Revenue Code, who is the "person required"? Is anyone "made liable" for the income tax? Yes, someone is.

Turn with your reporter now to Section 1461 of the Internal Revenue Code: "Every person required to deduct and withhold any tax under this chapter is hereby made liable for such tax and is hereby indemnified against the claims and demands of any person for the amount of any payments made in accordance with the provisions of this chapter."

Notice that the person made liable is the person required to deduct and withhold any tax "under this chapter." What tax is required to be deducted and withheld under this chapter?

Section 1461 is in Chapter 3 of Subtitle A, which deals with income taxes. Chapter 3 concerns withholding of tax on nonresident aliens and foreign corporations. Who is the "person required to deduct and withhold" that tax? Section 1441 of that Chapter has the answer. Subsection (a) tells us this: "Except as otherwise provided in subsection (c), all persons, in whatever capacity acting (including lessees or mortgagors of real or personal property, fiduciaries, employers, and all officers and employees of the United States) having the control, receipt, custody, disposal, or payment of any of the items of income specified in subsection (b) (to the extent that any of such items constitutes gross income from sources within the United States), of any nonresident alien individual, or of any foreign partnership shall (except in the cases provided for in section 1451 and except as otherwise provided in regulations prescribed by the Secretary under section 874) deduct and withhold from such items a tax equal to 30 percent thereof . . . ."

In all the pages of the Internal Revenue Code, this is the only liability established for income tax.

What are the "items of income" specified in subsection (b)?: "The items of income referred to in subsection (a) are interest . . . dividends, rent, salaries, wages, premiums, annuities, compensations, remunerations, emoluments, or other fixed or determinable annual or periodical gains, profits, and income . . . ."

Time after time, defendants have told federal judges in court that "wages are not income," that "salaries are not income," that "compensation is not income." As we have seen, the judge bangs his gavel, says that all these things *are* income—and sends the defendant to prison. Now, in Section 1441(b), we see that the judge is correct; that wages, salaries and compensation are indeed income—but the judge doesn't tell the defendant *whose* wages, salary or compensation are income. He doesn't tell the defendant—a state citizen—that the defendant's wages, salary or compensation are *not* income. If you ask the judge why he doesn't, he would explain that it would be inappropriate for a judge to argue a defendant's case.

So, the defendant goes to prison because he didn't state his case correctly. He was wrong when he said that wages aren't income. They are. The trouble is that the wages that are income in the law, are the wages of an alien. If the defendant is an alien, then his wages are subject to the tax. If he isn't, then he has to say so (use it or lose it).

So, who is liable? Who is required to file the return and pay the tax? The "person required" is the withholding agent described in Section 1441. He is required to do those things because he now is holding cash that doesn't belong to him; cash he has withheld from the wages, or the salary or compensation, of an alien. He is acting as a fiduciary, and has voluntarily accepted the responsibility of passing that cash along to the government. What happens if he doesn't?

Put what we have just learned beside Section 7203. The withholding agent, an employer, for instance—who is now holding revenue he has deducted from the wages of an employee (who is an alien)—is the "person required" to file the return and pay the tax. If he doesn't, if he keeps the cash he has deducted, he goes to prison as 7203 prescribes.

Along these lines, in 1893 the House Ways and Means Subcommittee on Internal Revenue conducted hearings on the proposed income tax of 1894. Among the subcommittee members was Sereno Payne, co-author of the tariff. Among the witnesses was the Hon. Thomas G. Shearman, who at page eleven explained the philosophy behind the decision to make the withholding agent liable: "Reflection will show, and experience proves, that a vast amount of income is received under circumstances which enable others than the income receiver to know precisely how much he receives. Now, if the Government, instead of inquiring from the person who *receives* the income how much he receives, would inquire of the person who *pays* it to him *how much he pays*, it is obvious that the latter will have nothing to gain by a false statement . . . .

"All dividends upon the stock and all interest upon the bonds of corporations would obviously fall in this category. This is so universally recognized, that *every government which collects an income tax at all makes it a prime object to collect that tax as far as possible through the medium of corporations*, requiring them to deduct the tax from all dividends and interest paid. . . ." (emphasis this paragraph added)

For instance, in *Coastal Chemical Corporation v. United States*, 546 F.2d 110, the Fifth Circuit ruled on January 28, 1977 that Coastal was liable for the tax on gross income it had paid to a Mexican company named Acomex. Coastal was the "withholding agent" and should have withheld. It didn't, but was liable for the tax anyway, and had to pay it. So, as we have seen, one entity can enjoy the income, but another can be liable for the tax.

Now, let's go back to Section 1441. It says that the withholding agent shall deduct and withhold that 30 per cent tax on the wages, etc., of any nonresident alien only "to the extent that any of such items constitutes gross income from sources within the United States." So, first, the item from which the tax must be withheld must be gross income. We now know what that is. Second, to be subject to withholding, that item must derive from sources within the United States.

What is "the United States"? As we have been seeing throughout this treatise, words in law often mean something entirely different from what they mean in ordinary conversation. Lawyers call such words in law "terms of art." That is why the defendant in court may be talking about one thing; while the judge and the lawyers may be using the same words, but talking about something else. So it is with "the United States."

Remember that the income tax laws define the term "United States" twice. "United States" means "any Territory, the District of Columbia, Porto Rico, and the Philippine Islands." With the restoration of the independence of the Philippines after World War II, that nation of course departed from the "United States." With that exception, the law's definition of "United States" still applies. Indeed, remember also that *Montello* defined "include" in 1911, just two years before Congress wrote the meaning of "United States" into the law. Just as ignorance of the law is no excuse; so, we can reasonably speculate that Congress was aware of that Supreme

Court ruling when it wrote the definition of "United States" into the law just two years later.

This means that Section 1441 refers to items of gross income from sources within a U.S. Territory, the District of Columbia, Porto Rico, etc. Places like Salt Lake City, Huntsville, Alabama and Bellflower, California are not within the "United States," but within the States.

We have tried to cushion the shock of this blockbuster by laying considerable foundation. Remember that Article I, section eight, clause seventeen, of the Constitution, gives Congress exclusive legislative jurisdiction only over the District of Columbia and over places ceded by the States for the erection of "Forts, Magazines, Arsenals, dock-Yards, and other needful Buildings." Remember the two-part government study on federal legislative jurisdiction, which showed that the States dole out such jurisdiction in federal enclaves with as much caution as a drunk doling out bourbon at a Baptist convention. Remember the Attorney General's description of the limited criminal jurisdiction of the federal courts. Finally, remember that 18 U.S.C. §7 (the Criminal Code) says that the territorial jurisdiction of the United States includes just a few places, including "any island, rock, or key containing deposits of guano." Guano is the manure of sea birds and bats, and, while we cannot testify from personal experience, we do speculate that it is immensely unpleasant, especially since, as we have seen, our friends from I.R.S. are standing in it. If you nevertheless insist on deriving income from guano, may God bless you, but we disclaim any responsibility.

Remember also that Section 1441(a) mentions subsection (c), paragraph (1) of which says this: "No deduction or withholding under subsection (a) shall be required in the case of any item of income (other than compensation for personal services) which is effectively connected with the conduct of a trade or business within the United States and which is included in the gross income of the recipient under section 871(b)(2) for the taxable year."

Let's look at Section 871. It imposes "a tax of 30 percent of the amount received from sources within the United States by a nonresident alien individual." Section 871 is in Subchapter N of Chapter 1 of Subtitle A of the Code. So is Section 861, which begins: "The following items of gross income shall be treated as income from sources within the United States . . . ." Among those items is "Compensation for labor or personal services performed in the United States."

In short, Section 861 explains which items of gross income shall be treated as income from sources within the United States; Section 871 imposes a tax of 30 percent on amounts received from sources within the United States by a nonresident alien individual; Section 1441 says who shall withhold it; and Section 1461 makes that person liable.

Finally, there is Section 874(a): "A nonresident alien individual shall receive the benefit of the deductions and credits allowed to him in this subtitle only by filing or causing to be filed with the Secretary a true and accurate return, in the manner prescribed in subtitle F (sec. 6001 and following, relating to procedure and administration), including therein all the information which the Secretary may deem necessary for calculation of such deductions and credits. . . ."

So, if the alien wants to enjoy the available deductions and credits, he must file a return to get some money back, or cause his employer to file one. If he doesn't he won't get that refund. He won't, or at least shouldn't, go to prison. Along these lines, we shall see that in September, 1946, I.R.S. said in the *Federal Register* that when an employer files a W-2, all filing requirements have been satisfied. That announcement binds I.R.S. and it has never been revoked.

So, we have arrived at the final secret of the income tax. In the beginning, 1861, and thereafter, it was a tax on aliens, whose presence in this country is of course under the jurisdiction of the federal government; and citizens living either in some other country or in some U.S. Territory or federal enclave. Such a tax can hit such a citizen directly because he is not a citizen of a State; he is a "citizen of the United States." A state citizen has the protection of apportionment. A "citizen of the United States" does not.

Remember that the federal government has full power to tax a State citizen directly, but it must do so by means of the apportionment rule.

In *Pollock*, the Supreme Court shifted emphasis from the status of the taxpayer—either state citizen, national citizen or alien—to the source of his income; and held that a tax on the income was also a tax on the source, requiring apportionment. In other words, *Pollock* held that a tax on income was direct. *Pollock* thereby extended the protection of apportionment to aliens and citizens abroad. *Brushaber* did not at all dismantle apportionment. It merely reclassified the income tax as indirect, thereby again allowing the federal government to impose it—without apportionment—on aliens and citizens abroad.

That's what it remains today. It never did and doesn't now have anything to do with state citizens. If administered legally, it would be about as important a tax as the tax on cigarette tubes, whatever they are.

What do our friends at I.R.S. say about all this? Surely they must have some devastating answers. Let's turn first to volume 1 of the *Federal Tax Regulations* (West, St. Paul, 1987). Regulation 1.1-1, at page forty five says that "Section 1 of the Code imposes an income tax on the income of every individual who is a citizen or resident of the United States . . . ." On the next page, we learn that "[i]n general, all citizens of the United States, wherever resident, and all resident alien individuals are liable to the income taxes imposed by the Code whether the income is received from sources within or without the United States. . . ."

So, who is a citizen? Page 47 tells us: "Every person born or naturalized in the United States *and subject to its jurisdiction* is a citizen. . . ." (emphasis added)

So, our friends at I.R.S. say that you may be born in the United States, and therefore be a U.S. national, but still not be subject to its jurisdiction. When are you not subject to its jurisdiction? You are not subject to its jurisdiction when you are a state citizen. You are subject to its jurisdiction when you live in "the United States," in a federal enclave or U.S. territory, or in some other nation.

What would you guess is the function of the Criminal Investigation Branch of the Internal Revenue Service? Would you take the word of the *Internal Revenue Manual*? On January 6, 1987, our friends at I.R.S. inserted Section 1132.75 at page 1100-40.1 of that document. It says: "The Criminal Investigation Branch enforces the criminal statute applicable to income, estate, gift, employment, and excise tax laws . . . involving United States citizens residing in foreign countries and nonresident aliens subject to Federal income tax filing requirements . . . ."

At the next page, in Section 1132.93, also dated January 6, 1987, our friends at I.R.S. explain the duties of the Collection Branch: "Executes the full range of collection activities on delinquent accounts which includes security delinquent returns involving taxpayers outside the United States and those in United States territories, possessions and in Puerto Rico. . . ."

Finally, in 1987, in the Eleventh Circuit, in *United States v. Ward*, the government did not respond to attorney Lowell Becraft's brief on these matters for a full 135 days. Then it huffed and it puffed and it brought forth this: "The basis for the appellant's motion for a judgment of acquittal, lay in his own tortured theory as to the government's lack of jurisdiction over him. He arrives at this conclusion through a patently ludicrous argument involving phrases and definitions used out of context, together with deliberate ignorance of relatively simple tax regulations. *The government is unable to find any case law directed at this specific tax protest theory. The government is unable, therefore, to offer case authority* for the universally accepted proposition that a citizen of the United States, working and residing in the United States, subject to federal law, earning wages, and responsible for filing an income tax return, is liable for taxation. The argument itself is frivolous in the extreme and should be dealt with summarily by this court."

That's it. That's the government's answer! Whoever wrote the brief for our friends at I.R.S. has no authority whatsoever; yet he expects to be taken seriously by the court. He deserves the same dismissal we would expect were we to state the conclusion—without the mountain of authority we have cited here—that the income tax is imposed on aliens here and citizens abroad. In short, our friends at I.R.S. have no answer whatsoever!

What can Americans do about all this?

10

USE THEM OR LOSE THEM

Under a basic principle of American law, you must assert your rights to enjoy them. As the old saying puts it, "Use them or lose them." If you don't use them, they will atrophy and die. If you don't assert your rights, clearly, vigorously, and on time, the government assumes you don't want them. It assumes by your silence that you have surrendered them. After a while, it begins to say you never had them. When somebody else with more courage than you have tries to assert them, the government treats him like a weirdo and criminal.

In a perverse way, some of this is reasonable. Suppose that at a gathering, in front of everyone else, somebody points at you and says, "Charlie, you're a rotten crook, a subversive, and maybe even an agent of the Internal Revenue Service!" Everyone will gasp and whisper, "A crook or a subversive we can take; but an I.R.S. agent? Charlie!" "He seemed so normal!" Everyone will automatically look at you to see your reaction. If there isn't any, if you sit mute, if you don't indignantly deny that you are one of our friends at I.R.S., won't people naturally assume there's some truth to the accusation? If there isn't, if your accuser is wrong or lying, then why on earth didn't you answer? As poet John Dryden put it long ago: "Secret guilt by silence is betrayed."

That's the way it is in normal human relations, and that's the way it is in law. If you don't assert your rights—vigorously and on time—the government routinely assumes that you have waived them. If you do assert them, the government may not be happy, but you are doing nothing wrong. How does all this apply to the income tax?

Suppose you mistakenly believe that the Federal Reserve Notes in your pay envelope constitute income—just because they came in—and that, although you are a state citizen, your income is subject to the tax without apportionment; and in the grip of those spurious beliefs, engendered by years of training for servitude in the government schools, you file a return. Notice that the return asks you to sign under penalty of perjury. What does your signature on such a document mean? It means you are swearing in the face of five years in prison that the sum you have listed as income, is in fact income. How likely is it, do you think, that our friends at I.R.S.—who routinely commit the serious felonies we have looked at, and many more—will call you to explain that you don't have income but wages, a wash, an equal exchange with no gain, and that as a state citizen you are exempt? Obviously, they will take your word for it. If you swear it is income, they will officially believe it is income.

What our friends at I.R.S. essentially ask you every year is: Did you make bourbon whiskey last year? Did you live in Madagascar? If you did, the law requires you to file a form and pay a tax. If you didn't, you can forget the whole thing. If you didn't, but you swear you did, for any reason from panic to ignorance, our friends at I.R.S. won't argue.

Your signature on that return also means you are voluntarily surrendering your rights. When you sign that return, you are giving the government advance permission to drag you into court for perjury if it likes, which proves that government "favors" are dangerous. Perhaps you believe that the "favor" is worth the risk, in which case, take it and sign; but do so at least with your eyes wide open. Specifically, when you sign, you are waiving, even revoking, your rights under the Fifth Amendment. The fact that those rights are "unalienable" means that the majority, the government, can't cancel them. Only you can. Today's judges like to talk about a so-called "Fifth Amendment privilege." However, there is no such thing. Remember that a privilege in law is something you get from government; and what the government gives, it can take away. On the contrary, there is a Fifth Amendment *right*, which was there long before the government was founded. The Fifth Amendment was ratified to guarantee that right. Indeed, did not the Founding Fathers write in the Declaration of Independence that the purpose of government is "to secure these rights"? The term "Fifth Amendment privilege" is just another symptom of the present degeneracy of the courts.

What does the Fifth Amendment say? It says that no one "shall be compelled in any criminal case to be a witness against himself." Our friends at I.R.S. say this means that you can't be forced to testify if your answers would incriminate you. If you have nothing to hide, they say, if you have done nothing incriminating, as you claim—then you have no Fifth Amendment protection, and you must testify. Fifth Amendment protection applies only if you *have* done something incriminating.

As you have no doubt already realized, the flaw in all this is that, according to I.R.S., you have Fifth Amendment protection only if you're guilty. If you are innocent, says the Internal Revenue Service, you don't have it.

The best answer to this is just to *read* the Amendment. Again, it does *not* say you won't be compelled to testify against yourself only if your answers are incriminating. The term "self-incrimination" isn't used. It says you can't be forced to testify, whether your answers are incriminating or not. The Founding Fathers were worried about forced testimony, no matter what kind it was. They knew that in other parts of the world testimony extracted by torture was common practice. In many parts of the world, it still is. They knew that, under torture, under extreme pressure, even innocent men—men who are not concealing income—will confess. The typical Soviet show trial blatantly testifies to this. Surely we need no footnotes to assert that the Founding Fathers did not intend the Fifth Amendment to protect the guilty and harass the innocent.

What are you doing when you sign a return under penalty of perjury? You are testifying against yourself. Remember that the

Privacy Act Notice in the I.R.S. instruction booklet says the information on your return may be given to the Department of Justice. In 1926, the case of *Sullivan v. United States*, 15 F.2d 812, went to the Court of Appeal, which said this: "There can be no question that one who files a return under oath is a witness within the meaning of the Amendment. . . ."

So, when you file a return under penalty of perjury, you are testifying against yourself as surely as you would be if you were sitting in the witness chair in court. Indeed, if you lie on the return—which we strongly encourage you *not* to do—that is where you could wind up. The mystifying question therefore arises: how can the government force you to testify against yourself by signing a tax return under penalty of perjury, when *the Fifth Amendment clearly forbids the government to do that?*

The answer is that the government is *not* forcing you to do it. You do it voluntarily. Remember? You do it voluntarily, as Chief Justice Earl Warren said. Now do you see why our friends at I.R.S., from the Commissioners on down, keep saying we have a voluntary system? The only way our friends at I.R.S. could get around that would be to arrange the repeal of the Fifth Amendment. The next time our friends at I.R.S. call you in, ask whether the information you provide could be used against you in court. Your agent will involuntarily produce a lupine, salivary smile and say, "Yes." Then ask whether the law requires you to provide information that can be used against you. Our friends at I.R.S. will no doubt terminate the interview.

The 1976 case of *Garner v. United States* is instructive. You will find it in 424 U.S. at page 648. Mr. Garner was a professional gambler, which he entered on his return. He wanted to be friends with I.R.S. After a while, the government put him on trial for violating federal gambling laws, not tax laws. At his trial, Garner stonewalled. He argued that he wasn't a gambler. So, the government introduced his tax returns, on which he had testified that he *was* a gambler, and used them to convict him.

Garner appealed to the Supreme Court, arguing that the information on his tax return had been forced from him—had been required—and therefore that the government could not use it against him, because to do so would violate the Fifth Amendment.

The Court agreed that Garner's tax return was testimony: "The information revealed in the preparation and filing of an income tax return is, for purposes of Fifth Amendment analysis, the testimony of a 'witness'. . . ." However, the Court disagreed with Garner's contention that his testimony had been forced. The Court said he had given it voluntarily; and, therefore, that the government could use it to send him to prison: "In summary, we conclude that since Garner made disclosures instead of *claiming the privilege* (sic) *on his tax returns*, his disclosures were not compelled incriminations. He therefore was foreclosed from invoking the privilege (sic) when such information was later introduced as evidence against him in a criminal prosecution." (emphasis added)

So, Garner could have claimed his right to silence. He legally could have done so on the return. However, if you voluntarily give the government evidence against yourself, you can't call it back. To take effect, a right must be invoked, and you are the only one who can invoke it. Indeed, in the same case, Justice Powell, who wrote the ruling, refers to a series of earlier Supreme Court rulings, also dealing with gamblers, in which "the Court held that the privilege (sic) could be exercised by simply failing to file." Question: Do gamblers have more rights than the rest of us? Remember, this is the U.S. Supreme Court talking. Its message is: Use it or lose it!

This remarkable principle, in which a right or power not invoked is considered waived, works both ways. Gerald Ladd worked for Armstrong World Industries in upstate New York. In 1980, he filed a W-4 form indicating he was exempt, in the sincere belief that his wages were not subject to the tax. As we have seen, many years of federal court rulings, from the Supreme Court on down, back him up.

His employer asked our friends at I.R.S. for guidance, but they gave none. In 1981, Mr. Ladd filed exempt again. Again his employer asked I.R.S. for advice and received none. Mr. Ladd went to I.R.S. headquarters to ask about his alleged liability. He also wanted to know how he could file a return without surrendering any of his rights. Typically, I.R.S. refused to answer any of his questions. He also went to a private attorney, who was also a city judge. The attorney told him that the government could not require him to surrender a right guaranteed by the Constitution. The attorney also claimed not to know how to file a 1040 return *without* surrendering rights.

Meanwhile, I.R.S. turned Mr. Ladd's case over to Mark Sweeny of the Criminal Investigation Division. In September, 1981, Sweeny sent Ladd's file to the U.S. Attorney, with a recommendation that Mr. Ladd be prosecuted on criminal charges. For more than two years,the U.S. Attorney did nothing. Mr. Ladd kept submitting exempt W-4s. His employer kept asking for advice. Our friends at I.R.S. never responded. Indeed, Sweeny told the I.R.S. W-4 coordinator *not* to respond.

Sweeny also told Ladd's employer not to inform Mr. Ladd that a summons had been issued for his employment records. At his trial for willful failure to file, Mr. Sweeny admitted that he had never advised Mr. Ladd that he could face prosecution for his exempt W-4 filings. Sweeny also admitted that he had never advised Mr. Ladd of his right to counsel. Sweeny admitted that such notices are required by I.R.S. policy.

Mr. Ladd argued that he had been entrapped and that I.R.S. actions proved his lack of willfulness. Since I.R.S. had refused to tell him his actions were wrong, he could only have assumed them to be right. Since his exempt W-4s had apparently been accepted without complaint, he could only have assumed there was nothing wrong with them.

The jury deliberated for almost eight hours, and, on September 11, 1984, in Syracuse, returned a not guilty verdict on all four counts. Presumably this proves that Mr. Ladd's contentions were correct.

Why had I.R.S. lost? It had lost because it couldn't tell Mr. Ladd he was wrong. It couldn't because he wasn't. So, it remained silent. It stonewalled. It couldn't—and didn't—invoke its powers. Its silence was as good as acquiescence. It lost by default. In short, just as Garner lost his case because he had failed to invoke his right to silence; so, our friends at I.R.S. lost their case because they had failed to speak up. Again, the word from on high is: Use it or lose it!

You lose it when you sign an income tax return under penalty of perjury, because when you do so, you tell our friends at I.R.S. that you are either taking some government favor; or you are making bourbon, bets or cigarettes; or you are either a citizen of the United States living abroad or an alien living here. You are testifying under oath that you are subject to I.R.S. authority, subject to its jurisdiction.

One of the lessons of ancient history says we should beware of Greeks bearing gifts. Today, we have nothing to fear from Greeks. The danger today is government bearing favors, such as incorporation—which makes you a creation of state government— and other privileges, real and concocted. Although there are other ways to enjoy the benefits incorporation brings, we are not here arguing against incorporation. Perhaps your circumstances make incorporation the right choice for you. We are simply advancing the modest, and we think sensible principle, that if you do incorporate, it is wise to be aware of all the ramifications.

It is important to note that just about every dictator pretends to distribute allegedly "free" handouts to his victims. He boasts that these "privileges" prove he's a nice guy. In fact, they are instruments of enslavement. The late Roman emperors distributed bread and circuses to pacify the plebians. In his autobiography, Benito Mussolini, the founder of Fascism, boasts on page after page about the so-called "free" handouts he gave the Italian people: everything from maternity benefits, to unemployment insurance, to government recreation. These things certainly do *not* prove that Fascism was beneficial. They don't change the fact that Fascism was a system of Socialist dictatorship. Mussolini was much admired by the Roosevelt Administration, before he struck a deal with Hitler, because, among other things, "at least, he made the trains run on time." Adolf Hitler himself, boss of the National *Socialist* German Workers Party, the Nazis, also boasted about distributing "free" handouts. Indeed, even the cheap crook who extorts money from local shopkeepers, smirkingly offers to sell them "protection." Every con artist promises some benefit. If he didn't he couldn't get to first base.

Along these lines, consider the I.R.S. Doctrine of Fair Share. At some point toward the end of the illegal, criminal trial of a so-called "illegal tax protester," the attorney for the Tax Rebellion, known as the assistant U.S. attorney, will probably point at the working woman on trial and righteously tell the jury that she is trying to avoid paying her "fair share" of the government's bills. Because the defendant didn't pay her "fair share" of federal spending, you must pay *more* than your fair share, says the prosecutor. That's why you should convict her, the prosecutor says.

The prosecutor thereby tries to divide the jury and defendant, by means of an admittedly powerful argument. All of us automatically and rightly feel revulsion for someone who won't pay his fair share. He's a chiseler. He wants a free ride at our expense. So, is the attorney for the Tax Rebellion right?

Consider first the I.R.S. assertion that the people will pay more because the defendant paid less. In other words, says the prosecutor, your taxes will go up. Will they? Yes, In fact, they'll explode. As your intrepid correspondent sets this down, in the fall of 1987, your servants in Congress are maneuvering to nail you with another big tax increase, which will be the next chapter in the Reagan "tax cut" of 1986. Why? Because the federal budget in recent years has become a farce, a formality, a fraud. Taxes will explode—now that most of the deductions have been abolished—because federal spending is exploding in defiance of the budget, to finance your friends and mine, the multinational banks.

Indeed, federal spending is exploding *because* taxes are too, as much as the other way around. At first, we know, that sounds like a joke, but it isn't, and we shall present the proof later in detail. Doesn't the government spend everything that isn't nailed down, and a lot that is? Don't your taxes add fuel to the spending fire? In fact, here's the clincher: Remember that before the income tax, the nation had virtually no debt. Now—*with* the income tax—we have a crippling debt. The debt has more than doubled during the watch of "conservative" Ronald Reagan. The famous bottom line is: The more money you send your government, the more it will plunge you into debt.

So, the Tax Rebellion lawyer is right when he says your taxes will go up. They will go up anyway, not because the working man didn't pay—but because our leaders are spending our nation into bankruptcy. What the defendant does or doesn't pay is irrelevant. If everyone in this country were to pay every penny I.R.S. says he owes, your taxes would still be exploding. In fact, a few chapters hence this book will make clear—from the mouths of our friends at I.R.S. themselves—that the income tax isn't used and isn't needed to finance the government. Stay with us and we'll show you what they themselves say are its true purposes.

Meanwhile, let's look at another aspect of the I.R.S. Doctrine of Fair Share. In the courtroom, the Tax Rebellion attorney will tell the jury that the individual who hasn't filed and hasn't paid (because the individual is a state citizen and his or her receipts consisted entirely of wages or compensation) is a freeloader, because he is enjoying government services without paying for them. Again, this is a powerful argument. None of us likes a freeloader. Indeed, many Americans say they are irritated because so much of their tax money goes to freeloaders, both domestic and foreign, by means of endless federal handouts.

So, this is a legitimate question. You will find the answer in *Hale v. Henkel*, 201 U.S. 43, which the Supreme Court heard in the fall of 1905. At page 74, Mr. Justice Brown said this: ". . . The individual may stand upon his constitutional rights as a citizen. He is entitled to carry on his private business in his own way. His power to contract is unlimited. He owes no duty to the State or to his neighbors to divulge his business, or to open his door to an investigation, so far as it may tend to criminate him. *He owes no such duty to the State, since he receives nothing therefrom, beyond the protection of his life and property*. His rights are such as existed by the law of the land long antecedent to the organization of the State . . . . He owes nothing to the public so long as he does not trespass upon their rights." (emphasis added)

Again, the key to the sovereignty of the American individual is that he receives nothing from government. If he does receive something—if he takes such bait as agricultural subsidies—he loses that sovereignty; in the same way an addict loses his independence to the pusher by means of that first, "free" fix. If the individual refuses the handouts he keeps his sovereignty, because it is simple business law that an individual cannot be held to a contract unless he specifically agrees to it. No one else can legally commit you to buy a service.

Remember, however, that Justice Brown *did* mention one thing the individual *does* get from government: the protection of his life and property. Obviously, Justice Brown is speaking of police protection, one of the few legitimate functions of government. Isn't *that* certainly a government benefit—a benefit the government is *required* to provide? If our working woman needs help, and calls the police, are they not required to come?

On December 21, 1981, seven members of the District of Columbia Court of Appeal, known informally as the "second highest court in the land," ruled in *Warren v. District of Columbia*, 444 Atlantic 2d, beginning at page one. What happened?

Three Washington, D.C. women sued the District Police Department, because it had failed to provide them with police protection, after one of them had called headquarters to get it. The Superior Court dismissed their suits, so they appealed, but the Court of Appeal also ruled against them. Throughout its ruling, the court cited a fundamental, legal principle you need to be aware of.

Here's headnote one, at the beginning of the case: "Government and its agents are under no general duty to provide public services, such as police protection, to any particular individual citizen, but, rather, duty to provide public services is owed to public at large, and, absent special relationship between police and individual, no specific legal duty exists."

Are you now in a state of shock? We're sorry, but, as you see, that's what it says. The government owes public services only to the public as a whole, not to any particular individual. Government owes nothing to the individual, ***because the individual owes nothing to government***. Government is not required to provide police protection to an individual, unless there is a special relationship between them. For instance, if both sides sign a contract, in which the individual agrees to pay certain fees for the purpose, in return for which the government agrees to provide certain protection, that special relationship presumably would be established. Notice, however, that ***the mere payment of taxes does not establish it.***

At page ten of *Warren*, we learn of numerous other cases in which this fundamental, legal principle applied. For instance: ". . . The same rule has been applied in finding no special duty to protect a young man from violence in a city park . . . to protect a young lady from the threats of her estranged boyfriend . . . ." And so on.

No doubt you are wondering why the women in *Warren* called the police. Did they want the police to fix a flat tire; or get a cat out of a tree; or help them cross a busy street; or resolve some petty argument; or was there some other, equally frivolous reason the police failed to respond?

No, the reason they called the police was nothing like that. What happened was that two men, Marvin Kent and James Morse, broke into the women's home late at night, where they found Miriam Douglas and her four-year-old daughter asleep. Associate Judge Nebeker, who wrote the ruling, says this: ". . . The men entered Douglas' second floor room, where Kent forced Douglas to sodomize him and Morse raped her."

Remember, they did this in front of her four-year-old daughter!

Then the beasts kidnapped Mrs. Douglas, along with Carolyn Warren and Joan Taliaferro, and forced them at knifepoint to go to Kent's apartment. Judge Nebeker continues: ". . . For the next fourteen hours the women were held captive, raped, robbed, beaten, forced to commit sexual acts upon each other, and made to submit to the sexual demands of Kent and Morse."

What would you call it? An outrage? An atrocity? Yes, you could call it those things and more. The normal man confronted with it would no doubt be sorely tempted to drag Messrs. Kent and Morse into the street, beat them for an hour or so with a baseball bat, and then hang what was left from a tree for the edification of other ghouls. Could the reader conceive of a situation that cries out more loudly for police protection? If the incident we have just set forth does not deserve police protection, what does? As we have seen, however, the women were not entitled to it. The District of Columbia Police Department was not required to provide it. We have this on the authority of the second highest court in the land.

Judge Nebeker kissed the women off as follows on page two: ". . . [N]otwithstanding our sympathy for appellants who were the tragic victims of despicable criminal acts, we affirm the judgments of dismissal."

Indeed, even if there *is* a "special relationship" between victim and police, the latter are not required to protect the former. Staff writer Ed Bruske, of *The Washington Post*, reported as follows on October 25, 1983: "A divided 10-member D.C. Court of Appeal has ruled that the wife of a District police officer cannot hold the city liable for a 1974 shooting incident in which her husband killed her father and wounded her, her son and another policeman.

". . . The court ruled yesterday that although the woman, Garnett P. Morgan, had sought and received help from her husband's superiors in dealing with the couple's domestic problems before the incident, she was not entitled to police protection that would have prevented the shooting." "In its ruling, the court relied on previous decisions in which the obligation of police to provide protection has been limited to informants and others enlisted to help police."

In short, the police may decide arbitrarily to protect you. They may decide just as arbitrarily *not* to protect you. Government doesn't owe you police protection or any other service, just as you owe nothing to the government. Whatever service government provides you is an arbitrary coincidence. This is true no matter how much income tax and other tax you pay or don't pay. The taxes you pay and the services the government provides have nothing to do with each other. This is the shocking answer to the I.R.S. Doctrine of Fair Share. The next time you hear a Tax Rebellion attorney bring it up, you will know he is just blowing smoke.

11

INSIDE THE BEAST

How does all this apply to the daily administration of the income tax? On July 28, 1969, the Seventh Circuit Court of Appeal ruled in *U.S. v. Dickerson*, 413 F.2d, in which Judge Cummings wrote as follows at page 1116: "Only the rare taxpayer would be likely to know that he could refuse to produce his records to IRS agents. . . ."

Yes, that is what his honor said. He had to say it, because, *remember*, you can't be forced to supply evidence against yourself. Imagine the result if millions of Americans started to invoke the right his honor mentions. Just this one act could bring the totalitarian juggernaut to its knees. Judge Cummings also quotes a tax expert named Lipton with approval as follows: ". . . The average citizen, moreover, believes that the government prosecutes only the recalcitrant, uncooperative individual who is unwilling to pay what he owes. Who would believe the ironic truth that the cooperative taxpayer fares much worse than the individual who relies upon his constitutional rights?"

In other words, the sovereign American who relies upon his constitutional rights has nothing to lose. The taxpayer who testifies against himself has *everything* to lose. He has nothing to gain from cooperation. Remember, this comes from a court of appeal.

Indeed, the amazing fact is that our friends at I.R.S. admit almost everything we have been telling you, in almost the same words, in a document known as the *Handbook of Tax Audit Guide-*

lines. The *Handbook* is supposed to guide the agent as he conducts investigations. The agent is supposed to refer to it. Our friends at I.R.S. tried to keep it secret, which is easy to understand. The Foreword is signed by Mortimer Caplin, who at the time was Commissioner. The reader will recall that Caplin now says the Code is "horrendously complex," and uses Arthur Andersen & Company to prepare his return. In the Foreword to the *Handbook*, he told Revenue Agents this: "The material contained in this Handbook is confidential in character. It must not, under any circumstances, be made available to persons outside of the Service. It is issued for your use as a revenue agent and must be returned upon transfer or separation."

The *Handbook* was liberated only after a successful Freedom Of Information Act suit. What does it say?

Here, for instance, is Section 242.11: "The purpose of the Fifth Amendment provision that no person shall be compelled in any criminal case to be a witness against himself is to ensure that no one will be forced in any manner or at any time to give testimony that may expose him to prosecution for a crime. It applies equally whether incrimination be under Federal or State law, and whether the privilege is invoked in the Federal or State courts. . . .

". . . The right to refuse to answer incriminating questions applies not only to court trials, but to all kinds of criminal or civil proceedings, including administrative investigations. . . ."

As it happens, an administrative investigation is the kind our friends at I.R.S. conduct. Notice also that the protection is available in both criminal and *civil* proceedings. In short, the *Handbook* tells the agent that a target doesn't have to tell him anything. Consider also that, because of the deliberate obfuscation of the Code, *anything you say* could be "incriminating." You have no way of knowing which is which. Remember that these rights are available only if you claim them.

Now, let's go to Section 242.12: "An individual taxpayer may refuse to exhibit his books and records for examination on the ground that compelling him to do so might violate his right against self-incrimination under the Fifth Amendment and constitute an illegal search and seizure under the Fourth Amendment. . . ." Remember, that's the Internal Revenue Service talking, in a previously secret document. Here, again, we see that the solution is already on the books. However, these rights will not invoke themselves. Only the individual American can invoke them. The courts can't, and our friends at I.R.S. won't. So, as always, the buck stops with you, Pilgrim. If you don't invoke them, they will atrophy and die. Imagine again the effect if enough Americans simply invoked the rights they already have.

What happens if the target receives an I.R.S. summons or court order to appear? The same section of the *Handbook* says this: "The privilege (sic) against self-incrimination does not permit a taxpayer to refuse to obey a summons issued under Internal Revenue Code Section 7602 or a court order directing his appearance. He is required to appear and cannot use the Fifth Amendment as an excuse for failure to do so, although he may exercise it in connection with specific questions. He cannot refuse to bring his records, *but may decline to submit them for inspection on Constitutional grounds. . . .*" (emphasis added)

This means that no one—no one—is required by law to submit to an I.R.S. audit. If summoned to an audit, say our friends at I.R.S., the target must appear, and must bring his records, *but he is not required to show them.* Practically, this means you could appear with your dirty laundry under your arm, as long as it is nicely wrapped. Imagine the result if enough Americans knew this—and invoked it. Indeed, notice that I.R.S. is talking here about people who have filed returns, thereby accepting I.R.S. jurisdiction. The question of audit presumably wouldn't even arise for people who are not subject—who have not been making bourbon—and have not filed.

If you do choose to participate in an audit, you may want to record it for your grandchildren, when they ask what you did in the Great War. The rules say you have the right to do so, but they don't say how—so you may want to use a small, *hidden* tape recorder. The individual you face will probably know less about what he is doing than you do—when you have finished this book. He may be relatively new on the job, and already wondering how he got into this mess; the rate of attrition at I.R.S. is as high as a kite in a tornado. He or she will probably say things he wouldn't dare say if he knew you were recording—things that could make spectacular listening in court.

As we have seen, our friends at I.R.S. maintain extensive, secret records on each of us, many of them having nothing whatsoever to do with collecting taxes. So, you may want to ask a few questions yourself. For instance: What reports do you maintain on me? What do you have on me in the Individual Master File? What do you have on me in AIMS? What is my DIF score? Your friendly agent will of course refuse to respond, but you can later file a Freedom Of Information Act request for a copy of his report. The experience will at least constitute an instructive example of your tax dollars at work.

Section 242.132 of the *Handbook* tells the agent to say this: "In connection with my investigation of your tax liability . . . I would like to ask you some questions. However, first I advise you that under the Fifth Amendment to the Constitution of the United States I cannot compel you to answer any questions or to submit any information if such answers or information might tend to incriminate you in any way. I also advise you that anything which you say and any documents which you submit may be used against you in any criminal proceeding which may be undertaken. . . ."

Did the Special Agent tell you this when you met? If not, he broke his own rules. If he did tell it to you, you knew at the time that when you talked to him you were as much as sitting on the witness chair in court. If you talk, you can't say later that you didn't know. Indeed, the same section of the *Handbook* also tells the agent this: "If at any stage of an interview the subject indicates that he wishes to exercise his rights to withhold his *testimony* or records, or to first consult with an attorney, the special agent will terminate the interview." (emphasis added)

Notice that you are a *subject*. Of the king? Of the investigation? Notice also that what you say is *testimony*. We certainly are not advising you not to testify before our friends at I.R.S. Indeed, we are not advising you to do anything at all, either way. Advice of this kind is the province of your attorney, if you have one. For some reason peculiar to your situation—which we can't imagine—you and your attorney may decide that such testimony would be wise. We make nothing more than the modest assertion that, if you do choose to talk with our friends at I.R.S., it would be wise to understand from the start that what you say is testimony.

We also ask a modest question: If there's no good reason to talk to (testify before) our friends at I.R.S., why do so? Remember that we're not talking here about disobedience, but about rights, rights the Founding Fathers and their successors risked everything to secure. If you don't invoke them, you're saying they really weren't worth the trouble. You're spitting at the faces on Mt. Rushmore. You're saying you want to be a slave. Did not the Founding Fathers warn us about usurpation—usurpation by the people who run the government?

Section 242.15 of the *Handbook* is especially interesting: "The privilege (sic) against self-incrimination must be specifically claimed, or it will be considered to have been waived. . . ." In other words, if you don't know that, and say nothing about it, your silence on the subject tells the agent that you are surrendering your right not to testify against yourself. You surrender that right without ever knowing you did so. To preserve the right, you must vigorously invoke it.

The *Handbook* tells the agent about the *Nicola* case, in which a man named Nicola permitted a revenue agent to examine his books and records. Mr. Nicola was indicted for income tax evasion and invoked his Fifth Amendment right for the first time at the trial. According to the *Handbook*, the court said as follows in 72 F.2d at page 780: ". . . The constitutional guarantee is for the benefit of the witness and unless invoked is deemed to be waived. . . . [I]t was necessary for him to claim immunity before the government agent and refuse to produce his books. After the government had gotten possession of the information with his consent, it was too late for him then to claim constitutional immunity."

Again, how much clearer could it be? The court here actually tells the target that to invoke his rights, he must refuse to show his books.

Finally, Section 263, paragraph two of the *Handbook* tells the Special Agent this: "When a taxpayer or a witness refuses to submit requested information, all surrounding circumstances should be fully considered before a summons is issued. The likely importance of the desired information should be carefully weighed against the time and expense of obtaining it, the probability of having to institute court action, and the adverse effect on voluntary compliance by others if the enforcement efforts are not successful." Paragraph three speaks of "the problems of future cooperation of others."

So, public relations is an important factor. The *Handbook* tells the agent to be very wary of attacking someone who knows the things you are reading here. Such a person could win, which would expose so-called "voluntary compliance" as a sham. Each time our friends at I.R.S. put the hit on a target who refuses an audit—refuses with impunity—the risk of exposure is multiplied. Another way of saying this is that our friends at I.R.S. will get away with as much as you let them. A defendant in a tax trial is tried as much for public relations as he is for taxes.

Now, let's consider the question of assessment. Assessment follows liability, which establishes who is required to pay a particular tax. When that is established, assessment nails the "person required" with a specific amount. Question: What happens when the person required to file a return fails to file it? Answer: Section 6020(b)(1) of the Internal Revenue Code tells us, "If any person fails to make any return required by any internal revenue law or regulation made thereunder at the time prescribed therefore, or makes, willfully or otherwise, a false or fraudulent return, the Secretary shall make such return from his own knowledge and from such information as he can obtain through testimony or otherwise."

The Secretary is of course the Secretary of the Treasury, who is the Commissioner of Internal Revenue's boss, and our friends at I.R.S. maintain vehemently that this section does not require him to make a substitute return when the "person required" fails to make one. You have just read the section. What do *you* think it means? If it doesn't mean what we say it does, what does it mean? We assume that since Congress bothered writing it, it must mean something, or are we wrong?

Why is all this so important? It is so important because, again, the Secretary's return is a substitute for a return that is *required*; which means that if the Secretary doesn't make one, no return was in fact required.

In 1935, the U.S. Supreme Court ruled in *Bull*, 295 U.S. 247. At page 259, Justice Roberts said this: ". . . Some machinery must be provided for applying the rule to the facts in each taxpayer's case, in order to ascertain the amount due. The chosen instrumentality for the purpose is an administrative agency whose action is called an assessment. . . . *Once the tax is assessed*, the taxpayer will owe the sovereign the amount when the date fixed by law for payment arrives. . . ." (emphasis added)

If the taxpayer owes the amount only when the tax is assessed, then obviously *before the tax is assessed, he owes nothing*—and remember that *it is the Secretary's duty to assess the tax.*

Along these lines, Section 6201(a) tells us this: "The Secretary is authorized and required to make the inquiries, determinations, and assessments of all taxes . . . imposed by this title . . . which have not been duly paid by stamp at the time and in the manner provided by law. . . ."

How does the Secretary make the required assessment? Section 6203 says this: "The assessment shall be made by recording the liability of the taxpayer in the office of the Secretary in accordance with rules or regulations prescribed by the Secretary. Upon request of the taxpayer, the Secretary shall furnish the taxpayer a copy of the record of the assessment." Have you requested a copy of the record of the assessment? Has the Secretary furnished one?

Finally, there is Section 6303(a): "Where it is not otherwise provided by this title, the Secretary or his delegate shall, as soon as practicable, and within 60 days, after the making of an assessment of a tax pursuant to Section 6203, give notice to each person liable for the unpaid tax, stating the amount and demanding payment thereof. . . ."

Has the Secretary given you such notice? If not, has he made an assessment? If not, are you the "person required"?

Now, let's look at the one I.R.S. form that Americans probably encounter even more often than the ubiquitous 1040: the W-4, which you are told to complete when you work for someone else. Since you have read this far, you no doubt already understand it. What does it say? It says that if you are exempt from withholding, you should write the word EXEMPT, all in capital letters. The form says that because it has to, because you may in fact be exempt. You may be a state citizen without income. What our friends at I.R.S. ask you every year, if you are a wage-earner, by way of the W-4, is: Are you a resident alien or a citizen living abroad? If so, are you earning income derived from some source? If you are, you may pay the tax on that income by means of withholding from your wages. If you are not, you may enter EXEMPT and forget the whole thing. That is how the authors of withholding explained it, as you shall see.

The W-4 instructions mention dependents and allowances. Notice that while dependents are allowances, allowances are not necessarily dependents. Allowances may also be business losses and other deductions; so, you may have no dependents at all, but still have many allowances. The W-4 must be structured like this, because, remember, income is gain, not receipts. If it were just receipts, there would be no need to calculate losses and expenses. There is, because income is gain.

By means of the W-4, you pay regular installments of tax on your income. The tax is measured by, and calculated on, your wages in part (by bracket, for instance); but, as we have seen, the tax is a tax on income, not wages; on gain, not receipts. As we shall see from the mouths of the authors themselves, your wages constitute a convenient, constantly replenishing fund from which the tax can be extracted (withheld). The W-4 instructions speak of "non-wage" income, and of "income other than wages, such as interest and dividends, capital gains, rents," but they never actually say that wages are income for purposes of this tax. You are left to make that assumption yourself, after many years of brainwashing in the government schools. Notice, however, that you sign the W-4 "under penalties of perjury," which gives our friends at I.R.S. the chance to haul you into court. How can the government force you to sign such a thing? Doesn't that violate the Fifth Amendment?

The government is not forcing you to sign it, Pilgrim. It's voluntary. Remember? For instance, if you are a resident alien, presumably you are here voluntarily. No one is forcing you to stay.

The first paragraph of the W-4 instructions, headed, "Privacy Act and Paperwork Reduction Act Notice," says this: "If you do not give your employer a certificate, you will be treated as a single person with no withholding allowances as required by law. We ask for this information to carry out the Internal Revenue laws of the United States. We may give the information to the Dept. of Justice for civil or criminal litigation and to the States and the District of Columbia for use in administering their tax laws."

So, if you are a resident alien and therefore subject to withholding, you could file a W-4 that lists your dependents and any non-wage allowances you may accumulate in business after work and on weekends. As we have seen, you must do this in order to enjoy a partial refund. If your non-wage activities generate so many allowances, which, remember, are not the same as dependents—allowances you can prove—that they amount to more than the tax you would have to pay without them, our friends at I.R.S. want you to say so and not pay a thing. We'll explain later how such genuine allowances can be accumulated. If you list more than a dozen or so on your W-4, your employer is told by I.R.S. to assume that you are numbering non-existent children and to reject it. In other words, he is instructed to presume that, because you work for wages, you are too dumb to do what he is doing: business. Are you that dumb? Our presumption, because you are reading this book, is that the answer is "No." Will you sit still for this I.R.S. insult?

If you are EXEMPT—because you enjoy the protection of state citizenship—I.R.S. tells you to say so. For those of you who do file W-4s, our friends at I.R.S. typically compound the confusion, by means of line 6a, for instance; which asks you to swear for the purpose of exemption that, "Last year I did not owe any federal income tax and had a right to a full refund of all income tax withheld." The purpose of that line is, typically, to trick the target into the erroneous belief that, because he may have filed a 1040 and paid income tax last year, he is ineligible to write EXEMPT on his W-4 this year. This of course is an absurdity. What he did last year may be totally unrelated to what he is doing now, because his situation may have changed. Last year, our resident alien or federal citizen may have made no income; so, he was not required to file. This year, our resident alien or federal citizen may be making income, so he is required to file. He may have made income last year, and be making none now. Or, he may have become a state citizen. If you sold a piece of real estate last year, does the county demand that you pay this year's property taxes; because, although you may not own it now, you did own it last year?

Line 6a is of course directed at the honest worker for wages who either is a state citizen or had no income, no gain, last year, but who, because of ignorance engendered in the government schools by our friends at I.R.S., made a contribution to the federal government we all know and love, by permitting his employer to withhold from his pay. Now, he knows that he "volunteered"—he's reading this book, as you are—and he's angry. Our friends at I.R.S., as always, are trying to confuse him, but the fact is that he could check the box on line 6a in consummate, good faith, because, in fact, he didn't owe any income tax last year, and was in fact entitled to a full of refund of all income tax withheld.

In recent years, more and more workers have been learning about this, and filing EXEMPT, so, in 1980, our friends at I.R.S. adopted a new program to intimidate employers ("withholding agents"). They told employers to disregard an employee's sworn W-4, and withhold on the basis of one allowance, whenever the employee claims EXEMPT and receives more than $200 a week.

However, an I.R.S. *Manual Supplement*, dated July 31, 1978, told I.R.S. agents as follows about EXEMPT W-4s: "The employer has no legal obligation to intervene with the employee."

Yet, our friends at I.R.S. as usual are acting illegally, because they are pressuring employers to do exactly that! This also means that when you employers do succumb to intimidation and intervene with the employee, you do so voluntarily; which could leave you twisting slowly in the wind in the event of a suit for damages. Some employees have sued in recent years, but our friends at I.R.S. have offered the defendants no protection.

According to Associated Press, on October 31, 1980, Herbert Mosher, I.R.S. District Director for Massachusetts, said of the new I.R.S. policy on W-4s, that, "I.R.S. could not enforce a penalty on employers who refused to cooperate with this policy." Doesn't this prove there's no law that requires an employer to reject a W-4? If there were, there would be a penalty, but there isn't. Why, then, would an employer cooperate?

District Director Mosher also said this: "But, let's face it, no employer wants to incur the wrath of the I.R.S." In other words, he actually admits that I.R.S. policy is one of illegal intimidation. The reader is invited to imagine the result, were just about any other government agency to make such an outrageous admission.

Indeed, in 1972 U.S. District Judge Huyett said as follows of the W-4, in *United States v. Malinowski*, 347 Fed. Supp., at page 352: ". . . The employer is not authorized to alter the form or to dishonor the employee's claim. The certificate goes into effect automatically . . . ."

In other words, not only is the employer not required to dishonor the employee's W-4; the employer is *not permitted* to do it. Why should that be so? It should be so because when the employer dishonors the employee's W-4, the employer in effect is calling him a liar, with no court finding to back him up. Remember that the W-4 is a sworn statement. The employer who rejects it is saying in effect that a sworn statement is a lie; that the employee who swore to it is committing perjury. Indeed, in its illegal policy of employer intimidation, I.R.S. is also encouraging the employer to play policeman—to play judge—which the government everywhere else discourages us from doing. However, if the employer gets into trouble doing so, our friends at I.R.S. will abandon him.

Since word of all this has been leaking out, the government wrote into the 1982 Tax Equity and Fiscal Responsibility Act a section that imposes a $500 fine on anyone who files a tax form that our friends at I.R.S. label "frivolous." That's what our friends at the Tax Rebellion would call your paperwork, were you to insist on their obedience to the law we have cited. Soon after T.E.F.R.A. took effect, your obedient servant was in Birmingham, Alabama, to conduct a seminar on the subject, and told a television crew that a worker has considerable recourse to the $500 fine. Good journalists that they are, the television people went to an "impartial source" for an "objective rebuttal": H & R Block. The man from H & R Block told them that such a worker has no recourse; that the fine is automatic; that there is nothing the worker can do about it—and, furthermore, that your obedient servant doesn't know what he is talking about. Later, on the air, the station anchorperson mournfully added the footnote that if yours truly had his way, we wouldn't have any roads; the only trouble with which is that the income tax doesn't pay for the roads.

What does T.E.F.R.A. say? It says that if someone challenges a $500 "frivolous" fine, a hearing must be conducted, in which the burden of proof is on the Internal Revenue Service. New Code Section 6703(a) says as follows of the fine: "In any proceeding involving the issue of whether or not any person is liable for a penalty, the burden of proof with respect to such issue shall be on the Secretary." Section 6703(c) says that a worker hit with that $500 "frivolous" assessment has the option of paying $75 and filing for a refund. If it is denied, he has six months to go to court. During all that time, I.R.S. action stops.

So, again, there is plenty of recourse. It's in the law. Would it be far afield to conclude that Congress, which wrote those sections, wants us to use them and would not be surprised if we did? However, neither the Congress nor the courts—and certainly not our friends at the Tax Rebellion—will encourage you to do so. You are sovereign and the buck starts with you. Again we ask you to imagine the result were enough aroused, informed Americans to invoke these sections of the law. How long could the law last, with the courts crammed with such matters?

Finally, notice that you don't have to file a W-4 at all. You don't have to testify against yourself. If you don't, our friends at I.R.S. will confiscate some of your wages. Should you sue to get them back? Consult your bar association monopolist. How much are your privacy and independence worth?

The W-2 is of course closely related to the W-4. The W-2 is the withholding statement the employer furnishes annually to the employee. On September 11, 1946, our friends at I.R.S. said as follows of the W-2 at page 177A-39 of that day's *Federal Register*: ". . . The original is used as an optional income tax return by the employee in lieu of Form 1040." Again, the resident alien may file a 1040 to take advantage of deductions, but he doesn't have to. If he wants to let the federal government keep all the money withheld, he may do so.

At page 177A-41, of the same day's *Federal Register*, our friends at I.R.S. said this of the 1040: ". . . A return must be made on this form, unless Form W-2 is filed . . . ." These regulations have never been revoked or superseded, and still stand.

A word should be said about Social Security. Subtitle C of Title 26 (the Internal Revenue Code), is headed: "Employment Taxes." Chapter 21 of that Subtitle deals with the Federal Insurance Contributions Act. Note 3 in that Chapter cites *Avis Rent A Car System, Inc. v. U.S.*, D.C.N.Y. 1973, 364 F.Supp. 605, on the nature of the tax: "This chapter imposes both an income tax on individuals with respect to their employment and an excise tax on employers with respect to having individuals in their employ."

Indeed, Section 3101(a) tells us this: "In addition to other taxes, there is hereby imposed on the income of every individual a tax equal to the following percentages of the wages . . . ." Section 3101 (b) says as follows: "In addition to the tax imposed by the preceding subsection, there is hereby imposed on the income of every individual a tax equal to the following percentages of the wages . . . ."

Notice that the tax is on the income. The tax is not on the wages. Income is profit (gain). If there is profit (gain), there is income, and anyone subject to the jurisdiction of the United States must pay the tax thereon. If there is no gain (profit), there is no income, and no tax. If there is income, the tax is calculated on the amount of the wages, and is taken from the wages; but, again, the tax is on the income, not the wages. The tax is merely measured by the wages. The tax is not on the wages, but is "equal to the following percentages of the wages."

To understand this relationship better, imagine that you are Farmer Brown, who raises apples. Good morning, Farmer Brown! To take your produce to market, you have a choice between the long way around by road and bridge, or the much shorter route across the river on my ferry. Since time is money, you choose the latter conveyance, and we strike a deal in which, for each trip on my ferry, you pay me a percentage of the apples you have picked that week. If your reporter happens to be the government and calls your payment a tax, such tax would be governed by your use of the ferry, not your accumulation of apples. The tax would be measured by apples and paid in apples, but would not be a tax on apples. It would kick in only when you use the ferry. If you don't use it, there would be no tax.

So, the same principles apply here that we saw apply to the income tax. Indeed, remember that the law says "Social Security" is also an income tax; income tax under another name. Your true income tax is your income tax plus your Social Security tax. Notice also that the tax on the employer is an excise, while the tax on the individual is an income tax—which construction must mean that the latter is direct. If it is direct, it must be apportioned, because *Brushaber* held that the rule of apportionment still applies to all direct taxes.

The question arises: Shouldn't we reasonably *want* to pay the Social Security taxes, since we receive specific benefits therefrom; benefits to which we are entitled, paid from the reserves?

Look again at Sections 3101(a) and (b). The caption on the first says, "Old-age, survivors, and disability insurance." The caption on the second says, "Hospital insurance." The trouble is that the captions are not part of the law. The captions are inserted by the annotators to make the reading easy. The law passed by Congress —the law we must obey—is only the language that begins after the caption. That language, as you see, says nary a word about any kind of insurance. Again, the funds the government collects thereunder are simply additional income tax the government spends.

Wait a minute! What about the reserves—the reserves composed of all those "insurance premiums"—the reserves in those Social Security silos, so bountiful, so high, that no mortal man could ever see the top of them? What about the specific benefits to which we are entitled?

The answer is: There is no reserve. There never was. There is no drawer in Washington, D.C. with your name and number on it, into which a clerk regularly deposits your Social Security "contributions." That's why Social Security is always broke and still is, despite the latest Reagan "solution." Like all the other income tax you have paid, your Social Security tax was merely collected and spent. People who get checks from Social Security now, are paid with taxes presently collected. Needless to say, if a private insurance company conducted business in such fashion, your alert insurance commissioner would close it down so quickly, and throw its directors into a prison so secure, that the travail of *The Man In The Iron Mask* would seem in comparison like a Caribbean vacation.

Here's how the outrage happened. In the 1930s, Social Security's advocates were faced with the problem of selling it to the Supreme Court and to the people. Americans of that era were different in some important respects from the millions of grovelers we have today. Although President Herbert Hoover had constructed all the bureaus and imposed all the bureaucracy Governor Franklin Roosevelt—preparing to run for President as an "arch-conservative"—said he had; the idea of permanent, government handouts to every conceivable faction for any inane purpose had not yet taken firm root. Business still was required to stand or fall on its own. Americans were still expected to handle their own dandruff. "Socialism for the rich" did not yet exist, with such notable exceptions as the Federal Reserve. At the other end of the economic spectrum, Americans hurt by the deliberately engineered

Federal Reserve Depression of 1929, combined with Roosevelt's subsequent betrayal of his Free Market promises, still considered their liberty more important than government grants. They did not willingly go on "relief," as welfare was then known. If, finally, they had to take it, they took it because they had to; they kept it a secret and got off it as soon as they could. It was still an embarrassment. By and large, Americans of the day, regardless of color or persuasion, would have been shocked by the prospect of millions of Americans and several generations happily breeding at government expense. Around World War I and thereafter, black illegitimacy, for instance, was lower than white illegitimacy today.

The advocates of the new Social Security income tax could not sell it to such a people with a promise to put them on "relief." Instead, they devised a brilliant gimmick, in which the new handouts would be called "insurance." The use of that one word of course conjured up a spurious connection to a real insurance company, complete with presumed reserves, growing assets and investments, stability and probity. Again, however, there is no reserve. The so-called "trust funds" contain pieces of paper bearing promises, signed by politicians. There is no drawer bearing your name, containing your money. What the American people were sold—and are still being sold—was a word.

On the other hand, the advocates of the Social Security income tax knew that the Supreme Court, which would rule on its constitutionality, would not condone an "insurance" scheme conducted by the federal government. Today, of course, Washington competes with private business in many ways, but in 1935 such a thing was still considered alien, even by influential people in government. The Constitution gives the government no power at all to run an insurance company.

So the Social Security press agents and attorneys told the people one thing, and the Supreme Court another. Indeed, they told the Court exactly the opposite. They told the people it was "insurance," and they told the Supreme Court it was "welfare," the opposite of insurance. They said "welfare" was permissible under the "general welfare clause" in the preamble to the Constitution.

We realize all this may be hard to believe. Would you believe the government? Compare what follows to what the government tells *you*.

There were two Social Security cases. One was *Steward Machine v. Davis*. On March 20, 1937, Judge Sibley said as follows of Social Security taxes, for the Fifth Circuit: ". . . They enter the Treasury as free funds set apart to no special use and subject to be applied to any congressional appropriation. . . . The appropriations are not of the proceeds of this tax or of any particular fund, but are general appropriations from the Treasury. No appropriation corresponds in amount with or is offset by this tax so as to justify a court in regarding the two as vitally joined in spite of the separability section of the act."

Later, in 301 U.S. 548, at page 585, Justice Cardozo said this for the Supreme Court: "The proceeds of the excise when collected are paid into the Treasury at Washington, and thereafter are subject to appropriation like public moneys generally." (The excise he referred to was the one paid by the employer.)

The other Social Security case was *Helvering v. Davis*, 301 U.S. 619. At page 635, Justice Cardozo said this: ". . . The proceeds of both taxes are to be paid into the Treasury like internal revenue taxes generally, and are not ear-marked in any way. . . ."

Indeed, here now is what the Social Security lawyers told the Court. You will find it in *Landmark Briefs and Arguments of the Supreme Court of the United States: Constitutional Law,* (edited by Professors Philip B. Kurland and Gerhard Casper, Arlington, Virginia, University Publications, 1975), on page 262 of which you will find the following, from page forty two of the government's brief in Steward: ". . . Being mingled in the Treasury with other internal-revenue collections, these proceeds, . . . are not ear-marked or related in any way to some special purpose, but are subject to any appropriation for the general support of the Government." On the next page, the government says this: "These receipts pass unrestricted into the Treasury of the United States and are available for the general support of the Government. . . ."

Charles E. Wyzanski, Jr. was Special Assistant to the Attorney General. On April 8, 1937, he told the Supreme Court this, at page 420: ". . . This tax collects money from individuals and puts it into the Federal Treasury, to be used for any purpose whatsoever. . . ." At page 423, Assistant Attorney General Robert H. Jackson told the Court as follows: ". . . The appropriation is not measured by the proceeds of the tax. The tax is not earmarked for this purpose. There is no equivalence between the amounts set aside by this section and the proceeds of the tax."

At page 439, Jackson said as follows of unemployment compensation: ". . . This law operates upon the taxpayers who are citizens of the United States and subject to its taxation. . . ."

Notice again that there are citizens of the United States who are *not* subject to its taxation. By now, the reader understands this.

In *Helvering v. Davis*, page seventeen of the government brief says as follows at page 495: "These taxes are true taxes, their purpose being simply to raise revenue. No compliance with any scheme of Federal regulation is involved. The proceeds are paid unrestricted into the Treasury as internal revenue collections, available for the general support of the Government. . . ."

In short, the government here specifically denied that Social Security had anything to do with insurance.

So, Social Security isn't insurance. It's just another tax. You have no "account." There is no reserve. Again, the government said all this. We're just repeating it. Doesn't this prove the government lied? Isn't it exactly the opposite of what the government tells *you*? Would your government lie to you? Does King Kong have bad breath?

Along these lines, at page 419 of *Landmark Briefs and Arguments*, Wyzanski argued as follows to the Supreme Court: "The direct tax is, of course, a tax upon the individual. But the 1862 amendment to the 1861 direct tax provided that the direct tax upon the individual might be assumed by the State in which he lived, and might be paid by the State, not to the Treasury directly but by payments toward raising troops and supplying troops with their equipment—in other words, as a credit against individual direct taxes, there was allowed the amount which the State expended for the purpose of enrolling and supplying troops. That is very similar to this situation where, as a credit against an individual person's tax, there is allowed the amount which he contributes to the State for unemployment compensation, which takes care of the general welfare of the United States."

In short, unemployment compensation involves a direct tax, which is levied without apportionment. The Supreme Court has ruled that no direct tax—including the income tax—may be levied without apportionment. Therefore the unemployment compensation tax—a direct tax on individuals—is illegal, according to the government itself. Wyzanski tries to substitute the "general welfare" clause for the rule of apportionment. It can't be done. If it could, the Constitution would say so. It doesn't.

Nevertheless, the people bought the Social Security complex, and today we have it; but remember that the law says Social Security is just another group of income taxes, which one is required to pay only if he has income.

Finally, remember that, although Social Security, with typical prevarication, calls itself an "entitlement," it doesn't entitle you to anything. The taxes you pay do not necessarily govern the benefits you receive. What you receive when Social Security sends you a check, is merely what Congress at the time decides to hand out. As we have seen, Congress has full, legal authority to decide to send you nothing.

Surely Congress would never do that. Wouldn't the political risks be too great? Yes, they would be—*now.* However, would Congress do it in some future, manufactured emergency; in another deliberately engineered Federal Reserve crunch? Would they do it to save *themselves* from their own profligacy? Remember that we're talking about people who have given corruption a bad name. Even now, are we not beginning to hear for the first time cautious comments from the cognoscenti to the effect that Social Security for the elderly may be too onerous after all?

On May 27, 1976, W. Allen Wallis, Chairman of the 1975 Advisory Council on Social Security, testified before the Joint Economic Committee of Congress. At page eighty seven of those hearings (94th Cong., 2nd sess., 1977), Professor Wallis said this: "Many people think that the social security taxes taken out of their wages and sent to Washington each month provide for their old-age pensions and other social security benefits. This simply is not the case. . . . When you pay social security taxes you are in no way making provision for your own retirement. You are paying the pensions of those who already are retired.

"Once you understand this, you see that whether you will get the benefits you are counting on when you retire depends on whether the Congress will levy enough taxes, borrow enough, or print enough money, and whether it will authorize the level of benefits you are counting on.

"The situation is in no way analogous to putting money each month into a private insurance company . . . ."

Why do many people have these erroneous ideas? They have these erroneous ideas because our government leaders have been lying to them for more than fifty years.

12

CORRUPTION IN THE COURTS

By now, you are no doubt asking an unsettling question: If everything we have told you is as the Congress and the Supreme Court have said it is, why don't the lower courts stop the outrageous usurpation? Why don't the judges tell our friends at I.R.S. to administer the law on the books and no more? The answer is that the judges by and large have slavishly and ignorantly acquiesced in the usurpation of their crucial independence; the lack of which the Founding Fathers complained about in the Declaration, and went to war for five years to get. The result is that many federal judges have timidly degenerated into mere I.R.S. clerks.

We have already seen a remarkable symptom of this in the juristic cabal's stilted, injudicious defense of I.R.S. illegality. Now, let's go behind the scenes. Godfrey D. Lehman is a San Francisco ad man and journalist, who, on the weekend of May 8 and 9, 1987, attended a Tax Procedure Institute in that city. The sponsor of the Institute was the California Continuing Education of the Bar, affiliated with the California Bar Association and the University of California Extension. The subject of this particular conference was: "How to Handle Civil and Criminal Controversies with the I.R.S., F.T.B., & in Court." The Franchise Tax Board is the state tax agency in California.

In the magazine piece he did on the subject, entitled, "Government By Fear," Godfrey Lehman reports that in the closing minutes of the conference, Roger M. Olsen, Assistant Attorney General, Tax Division, Department of Justice, Washington, D.C., told about seventy five tax attorneys and other experts this: "We encourage voluntary compliance by scaring the heck out of you!"

When our people were big and the government was small, the government was afraid of the people, as it should be. Today, our people are small, the government is big, and the people are afraid of it. Apparently, the tax experts were not at all surprised by this confession of intimidation that would land the officials of any other government agency in prison or the street.

Later, Godfrey Lehman confronted Olsen: "If it's voluntary, doesn't that mean we don't have to file at all?"

"It's voluntary to a point. The law says you have to file."

"Would you cite the law?"

"Section 7203 of the Internal Revenue Code."

Godfrey Lehman surprised him by producing the Code, and read: " 'Any person required under this title to pay any estimated tax . . . .' It doesn't say who is a person required."

Godfrey Lehman writes as follows: "Olsen took the book and spent a few minutes searching. Apparently this professional perpetrator of terror, towering several slender inches over six feet above me, was unfamiliar with the legal basis for his frequent prosecutions. Finally he made his discovery: '6011.'

"I read to him again: 'That says, "When required by regulations prescribed by the Secretary any person made liable . . . ." But it doesn't say who is a person made liable.'

"Olsen decided then that, 'It's not in the Code. It's in the regulations.'

" 'What is the cite?'

" 'It's the law. The courts have decided it. I can't talk to you now. I have to catch a plane.'

" 'Bon voyage.' "

Notice Roger Olsen's admission that it isn't in the Code. However, the Code is the law. If it isn't in the Code, then it just isn't in the law. Olsen is admitting that his actions are *ultra vires* and illegal.

Now, who would you guess was a witness to Olsen's confession that terror is official Justice Department policy? Would you believe that United States District Judge William A. Ingram, of San Jose, California, not only was present, but was a co-panelist at the conference? He was. Yet, as far as we know, tax trials are still proceeding as usual in "his honor's" court, prosecuted by Roger Olsen's underlings. Title 18 of the U.S. Code defines a crime called "misprision of felony," under which anyone with information about a felony is required to report it to law enforcement. If he doesn't, he is guilty of a felony himself. As best we can tell, Judge Ingram has not reported Roger Olsen's felonious confession, so "his honor" is presumably also a felon awaiting trial and conviction. It is important to note that Ingram is just one of scores of judges who are up to their ears in such crimes.

What else could Ingram have heard? He could have heard Jay Weill, chief of the tax division in the San Francisco office of the Department of Justice. Godfrey Lehman tells us this: "In the case of a fessing up former 'protester' who could not be contrite enough to tell the court, 'I've been bad,' the I.R.S. worked on scaring him for a whole week until he broke. 'I didn't understand why it took so long,' Weill said."

The reader no doubt will also be glad to hear (did Judge Ingram?) the following examples of the psychology of the tax attorneys the people hire to defend them at great expense, such as Bruce I. Hochman, of Beverly Hills: ". . . One prosecutor reported that during a luncheon break in a protracted trial the defendant's attorney observed gleefully that he would be able to put two kids through college with his trial fees, the possibility of his client's conviction notwithstanding. Hochman responded: 'I plead nolo contendere to that. I have four kids in college.' (Laughter) Indeed, when I revealed the doubtful character of the 'income tax' to several lawyers privately I was told, 'I hope that doesn't get out. If it does I won't be able to charge $200.'

"'Do you have children?' I asked.

"'Yes.'

"'And you don't care if you enslave them?'

"'They won't be enslaved. I'll teach them what I do.'"

No doubt this explains why Jesus said, "Woe unto ye lawyers"; why Rabelais excoriated them; why Shakespeare had a character say they should all be killed.

Now, let's look at a letter dated February 12, 1981, from Harold M. Edwards, U.S. Attorney for the Western District of North Carolina, to Woodrow Malone, Acting District Director of the I.R.S. in Greensboro: "Included in this grand jury will be agents of the Federal Bureau of Investigation." ". . . Upon the request of the United States Attorney, the Internal Revenue Service will furnish the United States Attorney and the Tax Division, U.S. Department of Justice, with its expert advice for a determination by them as to what course of action should be recommended to the grand jury."

The grand jury is supposed to be a separate branch of government—run by the people—the main purpose of which is to investigate crimes committed by officials of government. It has been totally perverted by such officials. It is gone. Today, it is just another weapon the prosecutor uses against the people. In your reporter's own incredible case, the prosecutor, Mark Healy Bonner, illegally used grand jury subpoenas. To her credit, Judge Consuelo B. Marshall threw three of the five charges out for that reason; but not before the jury had heard the "evidence" now found illegal. The reader can only imagine, as in a nightmare, what would be done with him were he to impersonate the grand jury. Yet, as far as we know as we set this down, Mark Bonner is still not in prison, where he belongs. We shall have more to say about Bonner's illegal activities later.

On another occasion, your intrepid correspondent sent a certified letter to the Los Angeles grand jury, expressing our eagerness to testify about information in our possession that top government officials have been committing serious crimes. Would you believe we didn't get even a peep of a response? We didn't. Why don't you try it. The grand jury clerk, who wouldn't even tell us her name when we called, would not even guarantee that the letter would be delivered to the foreman to whom it was addressed. Isn't the interception of mail—even by the U.S. Attorney—a federal offense? You will remember that the government is committing exactly that, with the collaboration of the U.S. Postal Service. Meanwhile, the people have zero access to their grand jury.

Later, we visited Manuel Real in his chambers. Manuel Real is Chief Judge of the Central District of California, and we certainly expected him to harangue us, hurling thunderbolts from his Los Angeles aerie, high atop the federal building there. We told Judge Real that the U.S. Attorney has completely perverted the grand jury. He replied that the grand jury is "independent," and that he could do nothing. He was not at all shocked to hear of the perversion; was not even surprised and requested no details. We repeated that the grand jury's independence has been usurped, and reminded him that he is the Chief Judge of the district. He replied that he merely "supervises" the grand jury, but does not "interfere." We asked him whom, then, we should see to correct the situation. He actually suggested that we take it up with the U.S. Attorney, the man who is committing the perversion. When we pointed out this discrepancy, his honor suggested we write to the Department of Justice in Washington. We said that the grand jury clerk won't even tell us her name over the telephone. His honor said that wasn't important, and that teenagers do the same thing. We responded with some vigor that he and your reporter are not teenagers; that we are adults who are supposed to be running the country. "His honor" sheepishly admitted that was so.

In short, we came to be lectured and stayed to chide. We came expecting Zeus. We found instead Alcibiades, without charm or brilliance. His honor appeared to be either befuddled or frightened or both.

Did you also know that when your number is drawn for service as a juror in a tax case, the prosecutor knows almost as much about you as you do yourself—including whether or not you have had any tax trouble? Look with us now at an I.R.S. document entitled *Disclosure of Official Information Handbook*. Paragraph (22)70, dated January 15, 1982, on page 1272-298.5, is headed: "Disclosure Concerning Prospective Jurors in Federal Judicial Tax

Proceedings." Paragraph (22)71 tells us this: "(1) IRC 6103(h)(5) permits an attorney of the Department of Justice (including a United States Attorney) or any person (or the legal representative of such person) who is a party to a judicial tax proceeding to which the United States is also a party, to ascertain whether a prospective juror in such proceeding has or has not been the subject of any audit or other tax investigation by the Internal Revenue Service. Under this provision, the response is limited to an affirmative or negative answer to the inquiry."

On the next page, paragraph (22)73 says in (2)(b) that a request for such information should include "the title and docket number of the case to which the prospective jurors have been or may be assigned." There is also paragraph (22)75, which begins as follows: "Upon receipt of the request, the disclosure officer will have the alphabetical registers searched for the social security number of each prospective juror (generally the requester will not have the jurors' social security numbers). Once the number has been located, the disclosure officer will coordinate searches of appropriate records to ascertain whether each juror has been the subject of an audit or other tax investigation."

The purpose of all this of course is to prevent such a person from serving as a juror in a tax case; which raises the question of what ever happened to a jury of one's "peers." The reason the Founders gave us such a jury, is that only someone who has walked a mile in your moccasins can fully appreciate your case. The word *peer* means *equal*. Only someone who has some idea of what you are talking about, and what you have experienced, can reasonably rule. On the contrary, by means of these investigations our friends at I.R.S. are trying precisely to prevent your peers from serving; thereby denying you *and your peers* that basic right. The next time the judge examines you in voir dire in federal court, be aware that the simpering prosecutor already knows your key answers.

What do our friends at I.R.S. say about this? They don't say anything we know of. They try to ignore it. If forced to say something, they would probably say this: "Then, do you want a convicted murderer on the jury in a murder trial? Do you want an embezzler to judge an embezzler?" No, we don't and we won't get one, because, under law, such felons lose their civil rights, including the right to serve as jurors. Do you really believe that this question did not occur to the Founding Fathers? Remember that we are not talking about denying felons that right. We are talking about denying it to law-abiding people who pay taxes, and who have experienced the system in which the defendant is enmeshed. We are talking about true peers. To equate them to convicted felons is absurd. Felons have been convicted of serious crimes. The peers we speak of have not been convicted of anything. The reason the right they are denied is so important, is that juries make the law and therefore rule the country, whether they know it or not, as we shall see.

All right, we have proved that the judges know for sure what is happening; we have proved the perversion of the grand jury and petit jury selection. Now, let's move into the courtroom and look at the effects.

Your obedient servant sued our friends at I.R.S., asking the court to order them to tell us how much they thought we owed, if they thought we owed anything. On January 14, 1985, in Los Angeles, Judge Pamela Ann Rymer granted the government's motion to dismiss. Her honor's tentative ruling began as follows: "Plaintiff seeks a writ of mandamus that would order the defendant to arrange a hearing to determine whether he is subject to the *exercise* tax in accordance with Title 26 . . . ." (emphasis added)

I told her honor I hadn't known there was a tax on exercise; but that, as a confirmed exerciser, I would be happy to pay it. She replied in some huff that the word "exercise" used for "excise" was of course a typographical error, which we are sure it was—an error generated by ignorance—but we invite you to see what happens when *you* make such an error. At the least, you may be treated to the disgusting, judicial condescension we have already examined, because you are not a member of the bar association monopoly.

In another case in Los Angeles, in 1984, Ron Matheson was the defendant. Mr. Matheson ran an organization in Orange,

California, called the Freedom League, which teaches the law. The trouble is, our friends at I.R.S. don't want the people to know the law. They say that ignorance of the law is no excuse, but they are frightened when you study the law. So, they tried to shut Ron Matheson up, by hauling him into court on four charges of willful failure to file.

The judge in the Matheson case was David Kenyon. In a conference in chambers, where the jury was of course not present, Mr. Matheson complained to him that the prosecution was using his 1975 and 1976 returns against him. Kenyon explained that he agreed with Matheson's contention that those returns were voluntary. Since they were voluntary—not compelled—said hizzoner, they could be used against him. On the other hand, said the judge in effect, Mr. Matheson *was* guilty of *not* filing in later years, because he was required to.

In other words, the words mean whatever the government wants them to mean at the time. When using your tax returns against you, the government says you filed them voluntarily. If you had filed them under compulsion, the government of course couldn't use them against you, because of the Fifth Amendment. When it comes to years you *don't* file—probably because by now you have found out about Taxscam—the government tells the jury that you were compelled to. The judge hears all this—and lets the Tax Rebellion lawyer get away with it!

Another Matheson complaint was that the I.R.S. Privacy Act Notice in the 1040 instruction booklet was unclear. As we have seen, it was, and then some. In a conference in chambers, the Tax Rebellion lawyer conceded that the Notice had been unclear and needed change. This of course vindicated Mr. Matheson; but, later, on the bench, Judge David Kenyon told the jury that the I.R.S. Notice Mr. Matheson had read did satisfy the law.

Indeed, now here's the clincher. The Matheson defense wanted to show the jury several placards, on which photographs of sections from the Internal Revenue Code were printed in large type. There was no interpretation on the placards; no exhortation. Again, all they bore were photographs of the exact language of the law, about which no question was raised; but the judge wouldn't let the jury see it, pretending to be afraid it would confuse them. The Tax Rebellion lawyer argued that showing the law to the jury would constitute "publishing" it—which would be "illegal"—and Kenyon bought his argument. Isn't something seriously wrong when the government won't let the jury see the law? Meanwhile, the Tax Rebellion lawyer told the jury this: "You may presume that all persons know the law."

The jury found Mr. Matheson guilty of all charges. Because of Judge Kenyon's malicious obstruction, the jurors were never allowed to hear what the case was really about; never allowed to hear all the evidence.

Now, let's look at *United States v. Kilpatrick*, 570 F.Supp. 505, in which federal Judge Fred Winner issued a ruling in Denver on August 25, 1983. With the connivance of lawyers from the Tax Division of the Department of Justice in Washington, two of our friends from I.R.S. were sworn in as "agents" of the grand jury that was hearing testimony in the matter they were investigating. A grand jury is of course supposed to be impartial. It is not part of the prosecution. Yet, these two agents of the prosecution infiltrated it. In *Kilpatrick*, his honor did explain that "ignorance of the law is not a defense available to a prosecutor."

So staggering was the misconduct of its agents, that our friends at I.R.S. tried to hide it by preventing the printing of the case in the permanent court reports. For a time, they actually succeeded. For instance, in the ruling the government tried to suppress, Judge Winner said this: "Richard Birchall is a lawyer formerly with the Tax Division who practices in New Jersey and who did some work for defendant and his company. He was subpoenaed to testify before the grand jury, and he showed up in Denver pursuant to the subpoena. He says that he met Mr. Snyder and the agents in a bar and they downed a few drinks paid for by Mr. Snyder. During this session Mr. Snyder supposedly disregarded the secrecy rules and, having done so, he told Mr. Birchall he was a potential target. He added that there was testimony about a personal relationship of Mr. Birchall's, a comment which was bothersome to the witness because of marital problems of Mr. Birchall. These communications are of a nature (if they were made) designed to bring about hurried cooperation from a witness, and especially from a witness who is a former Tax Division lawyer practicing tax law in the private sector."

Mr. Snyder is of course one of the Tax Rebellion attorneys, and his honor apparently is talking about old-fashioned blackmail. His honor writes that Mr. Birchall "testified that he thought that he was being threatened by Mr. Snyder."

Indeed, attorney Birchall testified that Snyder "tried to persuade him to breach his ethical duty of confidentiality and he attributed to Mr. Snyder a remark that even if the defendant wasn't guilty, the government would 'break him' with the cost of the defense."

Because of such outrages, the federal government has metastasized into the biggest lawbreaker in this country today. The sissies in the Mafia don't even come close.

Another witness in the *Kilpatrick* case was Roland Hjorth, Professor of tax law at the University of Washington Law School, who testified before the grand jury on Kilpatrick's behalf. Judge Winner says this: ". . . His views of tax law differed markedly from those of Mr. Snyder, who bragged on frequent occasions that he had never taken a course in taxation and knew almost nothing about it. Nevertheless, Professor Hjorth was browbeaten and ridiculed by Mr. Snyder, and some of the conversation so out of place for an ethical prosecutor took place during a recess in the hearing of some grand jurors. . . ."

Professor Hjorth also testified that in view of Snyder's unethical conduct, he would never appear as an expert witness again.

Judge Winner remarks as follows: ". . . Intimidating witnesses by telling them that their testimony disgraces them and implying that the Tax Division of the Department of Justice will take after the witness and will complain to the University of Washington Law School because an expert testified to his expert opinions does no credit to our government. . . . I hope that we haven't gotten to the point that disagreement with the legal concepts of the IRS provides grounds for attacks by that bureaucracy because sometimes the IRS is wrong."

As we have seen, however, his honor's hopes have fallen on stony ground, because that is exactly what our friends at I.R.S. are doing. What would the government do to you—a private citizen—were you to commit blackmail, for instance?

The I.R.S. agents who had infiltrated the grand jury also wrote letters on the stationery of the U.S. Attorney in Colorado, in which they revealed matters under grand jury scrutiny. One of the agents served a subpoena duces tecum to produce records on a witness, who told the agent he had no such records in his possession. The agent replied, "You're a liar." The witness, James Treece, was himself a former U.S. Attorney for Colorado, and Judge Winner remarks: "[A]lthough I doubt that Mr. Treece was intimidated, other witnesses would have been."

What would the government do to you—a private citizen—were you to impersonate a U.S. Attorney?

Another I.R.S. prosecutor, named Scharf, also did some police work of his own, the trouble with which is that when a prosecutor turns policeman, he loses his prosecutorial immunity. Judge Winner writes as follows: "While in Puerto Rico, Mr. Scharf conducted a surveillance of some little girls and tailed them to their home. This let him question their mother as to the whereabouts of his prey who happened to be her husband, and who is a Bank of Nova Scotia employee. Of course, Mr. Scharf must have known that the wife couldn't have been compelled to testify to her husband's whereabouts . . . . As an investigative technique tailing the little girls and quizzing the wife may have been brilliant police work, but I am quizzical as to the propriety of a lawyer questioning someone he knows he couldn't question in court because of an absolute privilege which . . . can be waived only with full knowledge of the incompetence to testify. It seems to me that whatever may be the obligations of an IRS agent, a prosecutor owes a duty not to question a wife about her husband's whereabouts . . . ."

The federal rules say that a grand jury transcript is to remain under the control of the U.S. Attorney and *only* the U.S. Attorney.

In this case, instead, the transcript remained with our friends at I.R.S., in a room they had obtained from the General Services Administration. Had the U.S. Attorney wanted to see the transcript, he would have had to get a key from the Special Agents.

So it's no mystery that the Justice Department worked so feverishly to prevent permanent publication of this case.

Judge Winner also wrote as follows of the prosecutors: "There is testimony that Mr. Snyder threw his jacket on the floor and mouthed obscenities at me as I left the bench. I didn't see anything like that, and the conduct is denied. I don't know whether he did or didn't do any such thing.

". . . I started to leave the bench, and Mr. Scharf yelled at me (he says that he spoke in a loud voice, but the dictionary I have suggests that the difference between a loud voice and a yell is quibble). Mr. Scharf's discourtesy amused me more than it offended me, but, according to that which has been said in the post trial hearings members of the public were distressed that a government lawyer would shout at the judge from the spectators section of the courtroom. I thought that my court reporter's comment as we left the courtroom was discerning. She said that if her five year old son did something like that he would be sent to bed without his supper."

If you want to know what could happen to you—a private citizen—for yelling at a federal judge in court, try it, if you can afford to spend considerable time away from home. Did Mr. Scharf get his supper? We'll tell you in a minute.

Meanwhile, Judge Winner said this: "It is argued that in the presence of the jury one of the agents stared at and laughed at the defendant. The prosecution says that this didn't happen, and that if it did, I would have seen it. I didn't see it, but that doesn't mean that it didn't happen, because no judge sees everything which goes on in a courtroom. This is especially so because I was concentrating my attention on Mr. Scharf's glowering as he sat in the second row of the spectator's section, and I doubt that defense counsel could see him. . . ."

By now, you may well figure you've heard it all, and that no more prosecutorial outrages remained to be committed. On the contrary, his honor says this of Mr. Scharf: ". . . He then made the most ridiculous demand I have ever heard in the almost 50 years since I graduated from law school. Mr. Scharf directed that I instruct the jury to 'cease its deliberation' until he could have his hearing. . . . To accede to this absurd demand would have created irretrievable error under Rule 43 . . . ."

Remember that no other government agency would be allowed to get away with all this, or even a part of it. We are pleased to commend Judge Winner and his colleague, Judge Kane, for throwing the Kilpatrick conviction out, although the man they vindicated had to spend $6 million for the purpose, as persecutor Snyder had snidely predicted he would.

Now, what was done to Snyder and Scharf? As far as we know: nothing. Mr. Scharf got his supper. They didn't even draw a reprimand. We would not be surprised to hear that our friends at I.R.S. threw a party in their honor.

Indeed, the reason all this should again be on the front page—and the reason we have included it in this chapter on the subject of judicial corruption—is that on June 28, 1987, a panel of the Tenth Circuit Court of Appeal voted 2-1 to reject all these grounds for dismissal cited by District Judge Kane, and to reinstate all the charges. Chief Judge Holloway agrees there were repeated abuses of grand jury rules, but says they didn't taint the jurors' independent judgment. The message to the Tax Rebellion attorneys is clear: You can get away with everything Snyder and Scharf did for their I.R.S. clients, and then some.

In the *Runte* case, in western Louisiana, in December, 1983, the trial judge ruled that his jurisdiction to hear it is found in Section 7203 of the Internal Revenue Code. However, that Section contains not a word either way about the jurisdiction of the federal courts. Is the judge as ignorant as he seems? If so, how does a man that ignorant get to be a federal judge? Or, did the judge just take a dive for I.R.S.?

Indeed, in John F. Runte's appeal from a conviction of willful failure to file, attorney H. Gayle Marshall wrote that "the trial Court Judge placed the retained counsel for the defendant . . .

under a 'gag order' and ordered that the United States Marshal physically take counsel for the defendant and sit him down. Upon defense counsel's attempt to make a motion to the Court, the Court further cut him off and ordered the United States Marshal to escort counsel for the defendant from the Courtroom if he rose from his chair one more time, whether to make a motion or to present any item of evidence of whatever representation on behalf of the defendant. . . ."

Yes, it is unbelievable to the point of disorientation, we know, but that is what the man says. Question: If the defense attorney wasn't allowed to say anything, why was he present? The answer is that he was present to conceal the fact that this was a *kangaroo* court. He wasn't allowed to talk for fear that the fraud would turn into a fair trial. Does not this outrage in western Louisiana resemble the "show trials" in Communist-occupied Russia and Nazi Germany?

Why is all this happening? Why have so many judges cravenly become I.R.S. clerks, in defiance of law? The smelly farce could be explained, at least in part, by what has become known as the Croasmun Memorandum. It sounds like the title of a Robert Ludlum novel, and maybe one day it will be. In fact, it was a memo dated February 26, 1973, sent by Western Regional I.R.S. Commissioner Homer O. Croasmun, to participants in a conference on the "Tax Rebellion" movement. In it, we are told as follows: ". . . Mr. Hansen commented on the problem of federal judges appearing to be anti-I.R.S. based on a belief that I.R.S. is 'highhanded.' Mr. Howard reported on a change of attitude in federal judges in San Francisco after he met with a number of them and discussed the gravity of the Tax Rebellion Movement and the importance of giving prison sentences as deterrents."

Remember that our friends at I.R.S. are running the Tax Rebellion, in that they willfully refuse to obey the tax laws. To conceal their lawlessness, they call Americans who discover it "tax rebels," or "illegal tax protesters." Notice that the date of the Croasmun Memorandum corresponds roughly in chronology to the bizarre perversion from sense to nonsense in many of the income tax rulings we have examined. How many federal judges have our friends at I.R.S. seen? How many of them have Roger Olsen's storm troopers scared the heck out of? What do they tell the judges in those meetings? As we have seen, they intimidate lawyers and witnesses and members of Congress. Why not judges?

Surely you will remember Harry Claiborne, chief federal judge in Las Vegas. A while back, he was on the network news every evening. Federal agents feloniously broke into his home and stole records, in an operation that recalls the break-in by the Watergate "plumbers" at the office of Daniel Ellsberg's psychiatrist. Judge Claiborne was convicted and sent to prison for an income tax mistake committed by his accountant. The most damaging testimony against him came from a fugitive racketeer whom the government had bribed to return from Brazil; a man the government ordinarily would not believe if he told them the time. A national reporter (not your obedient servant) came to Las Vegas to cover the story. When he found out what it was, he skulked out of town. An I.R.S. official was asked to participate in the frameup. It so sickened him, he refused and was transferred. Propelled by the usual, smelly hypocrisy, the Senate impeached Judge Claiborne and threw him off the bench, while he sat in the federal prison camp at Maxwell Air Force Base, in Alabama.

Why did all this happen? It happened because Las Vegas is full of pit bosses and other people who live on tips, and because Judge Claiborne refused to serve as the typical I.R.S. patsy. What's your guess as to the message this case was calculated to send to other federal judges? Indeed, remember that a federal judge is the closest thing to a king we have in this country. In some ways, he has more power than the President. If you disobey his orders, you go to the clink. If he has a fight with his wife and feels like excoriating the attorneys in his courtroom, he does it, with impunity. If he decides that a female attorney in a pants-suit is improperly clothed, he tells her to leave and return in a dress—and she does it. Yes, that has happened. Imagine the President at a press conference telling U.P.I.'s Helen Thomas to do that. The President has to be a politician. A federal judge doesn't.

Yet, even with all that power, a federal judge can be terrorized and thrown into jail. The lesson the average citizen—and the average federal judge—is supposed to learn from this is clear.

Indeed, along these lines consider the case of Walter L. Nixon, Jr., Chief Judge of the U.S. District Court in Biloxi, Mississippi. Nixon presided at the criminal trial of citizen Kimbrough G. Middlebrook, on tax charges, in Meridian, Mississippi, in 1982. G. R. Stradley is the father of Mr. Middlebrook's attorney, and he filed the following sworn affidavit, which is the same as testimony, on March 15, 1982: "During the course of the trial, the presiding judge, Judge Nixon, made a statement in the presence of the jury to the effect that while the defendant, Mr. Middlebrook, may have been right, if he was allowed to get away with what he was doing, everyone else would want to do the same and the whole system would collapse."

Breathtaking, isn't it? Hizzoner was here confessing that the trial he conducted was a sham, a charade, a farce, a fraud. He was saying in other words that the law is irrelevant. Question: If the system is not based on law, *shouldn't* it collapse? If it isn't based on law, what is it based on?

Now, here's the kicker: In 1985, a grand jury indicted Judge Nixon on charges of accepting royalty interests in three oil and gas wells in 1981, from Wiley Fairchild, a Hattiesburg, Mississippi businessman, in return for potential favors. Such a favor came due in 1982, when Mr. Fairchild's son, Drew, was accused of smuggling drugs at the local airport, and Judge Nixon was accused of interceding with the prosecutor in his behalf. In 1986, Nixon was convicted on two charges of lying to a grand jury about it, and sentenced to five years in prison. In the spring of 1987, the Fifth circuit Court of Appeal upheld the conviction.

But he isn't in prison. He hasn't been impeached—although he drew a five year sentence to Judge Claiborne's two. Indeed, Nixon still enjoys his judicial salary ($81,100), and the wood-panelled chambers reserved for the District's Chief Judge. In an ironic twist, he no longer has to work for it, because when he was indicted he put himself on leave. There have been no banner headlines about him across the country, as there were about Judge Claiborne.

Why not? Was Nixon one of those judges to whom our friends at I.R.S. paid a visit? We don't know. We do know that he willingly played the part of I.R.S. pimp, which no doubt helps explain the royal treatment he is receiving.

Starting in grade school, you were told, and still are told, that one of the triumphs of our system is the abolition of debtors' prison. Did you know that, like most of what our government tells us, that boast isn't true? We do indeed have debtors' prisons. They are called Federal Correctional Institutions and prison camps. Time after time, federal judges send tax victims back to them, with instructions to "think it over," by which is meant: "Pay up and I'll set you free." The only thing you can call such incarceration is debtors' prison. If you are a private creditor it isn't available. If you are the Internal Revenue Service, it is.

Why do the judges not only tolerate, but enthusiastically collaborate in, such outrages? Why do they abjectly allow themselves to be intimidated? They do so because they have completely and cravenly surrendered the independence the Founding Fathers fought so hard to get. Among the complaints against the King that Thomas Jefferson wrote into the Declaration of Independence was this: "He has made judges dependent on His will alone, for the tenure of their offices, and the amount and payment of their salaries."

A judge worried about his government job and his government salary, will be subservient to government. That is why the Framers wrote into Article III, Section One of the Constitution a requirement that anyone who exercises the judicial powers of the United States must be appointed for life; and a prohibition against diminishing a federal judge's salary while he is in office. Hamilton explained why this must be so in Federalist Paper 78, where he wrote that "liberty can have nothing to fear from the judiciary alone, but would have everything to fear from its union with either of the other departments."

In *O'Donoghue v. United States*, 289 U.S. 516, Justice Sutherland said as follows for the Supreme Court at page 531, on May 29, 1933: "In framing the Constitution, therefore, the power to diminish the compensation of the federal judges was explicitly denied, in order, inter alia, that their judgment or action might never be swayed in the slightest degree by the temptation to cultivate the favor or avoid the displeasure of that department which, as master of the purse, would otherwise hold the power to reduce their means of support. . . ." Today, no doubt because of the pressure described in the Croasmun Memorandum, inter alia, that's exactly what has happened.

In the same ruling, Justice Sutherland quotes Chief Justice John Marshall, who said at the debates of the Virginia State Convention of 1829-30: ". . . I have always thought, from my earliest youth till now, that the greatest scourge an angry Heaven ever inflicted upon an ungrateful and a sinning people, was an ignorant, a corrupt, or a dependent Judiciary."

Are these issues still alive? On June 28, 1982, in the *Marathon Pipe Line* case, 458 U.S. 50, 73 L.Ed.2d 598, 102 Sup.Ct. 2858, the Supreme Court created turmoil when it ruled that the bankruptcy courts were illegal, because the judges thereof, while exercising the judicial power of the United States, were appointed for fourteen years, rather than for life.

In 1977, 140 U.S. district and circuit court judges sued the government in the Court of Claims, arguing that inflation had unconstitutionally diminished their judicial salaries. In *Atkins v. United States*, 556 F.2d 1028, the Court rejected their demand for a raise, but said as follows on May 18, 1977, at page 1054: ". . . We note first that while the level of inflation in the United States since 1969 has been high, its effects serious, and its existence perhaps without precedent, it still has not reached the proportions of the problem in certain European and South American nations, nor does it in any way resemble the hyperinflation of Weimar, Germany, in the early 1920's, where fortunes in nominal dollars were reduced to pittances practically overnight. Certainly, were Congress not to budge on the nominal dollar salaries it allowed judges in the face of hyperinflation, while the earnings of most others rose in rough parity with the cost of living, the threat to the ability of the judges to stay in their posts would be so great that a demand for their relief under article III would be difficult to refute. But hyperinflation, fortunately, has not yet been our nation's problem, and plaintiffs' official salaries, though seriously diminished in real value, are not presently in danger of closely approaching point zero on the scale of 1969 dollar value."

So, the Court turned them down, not because it thought they were wrong, not because it rejected the principle, but because the problem is not yet bad enough. When it gets bad enough, the Court will intervene with relief. At page 1055, the Court explained: ". . . Obviously, this situation could change, and the demonstration of massive resignation for financial reasons would very differently color plaintiffs' contention, stating a more compelling case that the strictures of the Compensation Clause had been violated. . . ."

In 1979, in *Will v. United States*, 478 F.Supp. 621, thirteen U.S. district judges, representing a class of more than six hundred such judges, sued the government to recover compensation allegedly due them. District Judge Roszkowski ruled as follows at page 623: "In this motion, we must decide whether the Compensation Clause of Article III §1 of the United States Constitution has been violated by Congress' refusal to pay plaintiffs a cost-of-living adjustment for the salary periods commencing October 1, 1976 and October 1, 1977. Because we find that Congress' refusal to pay plaintiffs a cost-of-living adjustment directly diminished the compensation to which plaintiffs were entitled, we conclude that the Compensation Clause has been violated and, accordingly, we grant plaintiffs' motion for summary judgment."

So, the judges are perfectly aware of the issue; nevertheless, they let I.R.S. diminish their compensation and turn them into grovelling clerks. Indeed, how do you guess they would receive a working woman who maintains in court that she has reduced the amount of tax she sent to the government, to correspond to the amount to which inflation has reduced her real pay? She would no doubt be dismissed with protestations of feigned ignorance, and a ruling that her argument is "frivolous." Which genius was it who said that hypocrisy is the deference that vice pays to virtue?

13

YOUR AWESOME POWER

From all of this, it no doubt appears that nothing can be done. On the contrary, one informed, aroused American could bring this juggernaut of totalitarian usurpation to its knees—and could do so without risk—simply by serving as a juror in a federal tax case and voting for acquittal. No one will know why you did it, and you can do it in perfect conscience, because, as we have seen, most of the trials by far are illegal. As a juror, you have the legal power to rule on that fact.

Today, it is universally true that, when a jury is selected, the judge tells the jurors they have power only to decide matters of fact. Did the defendant break the law or not? Did he or didn't he do what the government alleges? Those matters alone, says the judge, are what the jury may consider.

The jury may *not* consider the validity of the law, says the judge. The jury may *not* make its decision on the basis of whether it thinks the law is just or unjust. The jurors are forbidden to do that, says the judge. His honor says *he* will tell the jurors the law, and they are stuck with it. The jurors' only job is to decide whether the defendant broke it. If you have ever been a juror, you have no doubt heard some version of this. Is it true?

No, it's false—it's a lie—and its purpose in the present emergency is to reinstall dictatorial government. The same judges who have cravenly surrendered their independence to our friends at I.R.S., have used the lie to transform themselves into grinning, little caesars. The entire history of our country since before the beginning proves this.

For instance, you will probably remember the landmark case of newspaper publisher John Peter Zenger. It took place in New York in 1735, when George Washington was just three, forty-one years before Jefferson would write the Declaration of Independence, when the future united states were still colonies of England. As you will recall, Zenger was hauled into court on a charge of seditious libel. Under the law as it then existed, the facts showed him to be clearly guilty. However, lawyer Andrew Hamilton urged the jurors, in the face of the judge's charge, "to see with their own eyes, to hear with their own ears, and to make use of their consciences and understanding in judging of the lives, liberties, or estates of their fellow subjects."

In other words, Hamilton told the jury to apply what is known as common law—common sense. The jury did so and voted for acquittal, thereby repudiating the law and expanding freedom of the press. The jury disregarded the judge's instructions and ruled on both the facts and the law. Since the law was unjust, the jurors struck it down; overruled the judge. Today, other journalists still celebrate the Zenger ruling.

On July 19, 1789, Thomas Jefferson wrote as follows to M. L'Abbe Arnaud: "But we all know that permanent judges acquire an *Esprit de corps*; that being known, they are liable to be tempted by bribery; that they are misled by favor, by relationship, by a spirit of party, by a devotion to the executive or legislative power; that it is better to leave a cause to the decision of cross and pile, than to that of a judge biased to one side; and that the opinion of twelve honest jurymen gives still a better hope of right, than cross and pile does. It is in the power, therefore, of the juries, if they think permanent judges are under any bias whatever, in any cause, to take on themselves to judge the law as well as the fact. They never exercise this power *but when they suspect partiality in the judges; and by the exercise of this power, they have been the firmest bulwark of English liberty.*" (emphasis added)

By 1794, our country was a few years old. In *Georgia v. Brailsford*, U.S. Supreme Court Chief Justice John Jay, a co-author of the

Federalist Papers, told the jury as follows in 3 Dallas, at page four: "It may not be amiss, here, Gentlemen, to remind you of the good old rule, that on questions of fact, it is the province of the jury, on questions of law, it is the province of the court to decide. But it must be observed that by the same law, which recognizes this reasonable distribution of jurisdiction, *you have nevertheless a right* to take upon yourselves to judge of both, and *to determine the law as well as the fact in controversy.* On this, and on every other occasion, however, we have no doubt, you will pay that respect, which is due to the opinion of the court: For, as on the one hand, it is presumed, that juries are the best judges of facts; it is, on the other hand, presumable, that the court are the best judges of law. But still *both objects are lawfully, within your power of decision.*" (emphasis added)

So, the jurors should respect the court. The judge is there to give advice. We believe both these things make sense. However, says the Chief Justice, the jurors have power politely to *reject* that advice. The jurors are judges too, as the Chief Justice says, and, in fact, they have more power than the judge who sits on the bench.

Now, let's move along to the year 1852, when John P. Jewett and Company, of Boston, published a book entitled *An Essay on the Trial By Jury,* by a scholar named Lysander Spooner. Spooner went back to Magna Carta in 1215, when, as you will remember, the English barons forced King John to accept trial by jury, a jury of peers, or equals.

Spooner wrote as follows in 1852: "The question here arises, whether the barons and people intended that those peers (the jury) should be mere puppets in the hands of the king, exercising no opinion of their own as to the intrinsic merits of the accusations they should try, or the *justice* of the law they should be called on to enforce? No. They were engaged in no such senseless work as that. The trial by jury, be it observed, was the only real barrier interposed by them against absolute despotism. Could this trial, then, have been such an entire farce as it necessarily must have been, if the jury had had no power to judge of the justice of the laws the people were required to obey? Did it not rather imply that the jury were to judge independently and fearlessly as to everything involved in the charge, and especially as to its intrinsic justice, and thereon give their decision (unbiased by any legislation of the king), whether the accused might be punished?"

The Magna Carta he refers to was of course one of the documents that figured prominently in the birth of our own Declaration of Independence and Constitution. That is why people in the legal business still refer to it as if it were written yesterday. This is the answer to Tax Rebellion attorneys who will tell you that some of the cases we cite in this book are sixty or seventy years old and therefore inapplicable.

Remember that the origin in Magna Carta of this peer's (juror's) right to judge the law was the desire of the barons to break the tyrannical power of King John. After all, if the law says, for instance, that you have no right to own private property, no right to freedom of speech or religion, no right to keep and bear arms, and so on; then your right to a jury trial would not be worth much, if the jurors were restricted just to deciding whether you illegally owned or spoke or prayed or bore arms or not. What, then, is the judge there to do? He is there to act as a referee. He is there to supervise the proceedings and explain the law.

In *Gilbert's History of the Common Pleas*, we are told that "by the common law of the land the jury are judges as well of the matter of law, as of the fact, with this difference only, that the judge on the bench is to give them no assistance in determining the matter of fact, but if they have any doubt among themselves relating to matter of law, they may then request him to explain it to them, which when he hath done, and they are thus become well informed, they, and they only, become competent judges of the matter of law."

The trouble is that many, if not most, of today's judges are not satisfied with this. Being rotten sinners like the rest of us, they enjoy their (delegated) powers too much. They have usurped the power of the jury. They like sitting up there in black, pretending to be little gods while the people tremble. Notice that everything in the courtroom, from the architecture to the elevation of the bench, is carefully calculated to intimidate.

Critics of the fundamental doctrine of jury nullification protest that it empowers jurors who may be totally ignorant of the law to judge it; while the judge, who is (presumably) learned in the law, is compelled to sit by. Lysander Spooner's answer echoes Jefferson: "The powers of juries are not granted to them on the supposition that they know the law better than the justices; but on the ground that the justices are untrustworthy, that they are exposed to bribes, are themselves fond of power and authority, and are also the dependent and subservient creatures of the legislature; and that to allow them to dictate the law, would not only expose the rights of parties to be sold for money, but would be equivalent to surrendering all the property, liberty, and rights of the people, unreservedly into the hands of arbitrary power (the legislature), to be disposed of at its pleasure. The powers of juries, therefore, not only place a curb upon the powers of legislators and judges, but imply also an imputation upon their integrity and trustworthiness; and these are the reasons why legislators and judges have formerly entertained the intensest hatred of juries, and so fast as they could do it without alarming the people for their liberties, have, by indirection, denied, undermined, and practically destroyed their power. And it is only since all the real power of juries has been destroyed, and they have become mere tools in the hands of legislators and judges, that they have become favorites of them."

Remember that this was published in 1852. Its breathtaking timeliness is demonstrated almost daily. Isn't it a good description of Walter Nixon, for instance, the I.R.S. pimp, and of the judicial scoundrels whose perversions we have examined? Would you trust such judges with your life savings?

Lysander Spooner also says this: "There is no reason why a judge should have the power of punishing for contempt, any more than for any other offense. And it is one of the most dangerous powers a judge can have, because it gives him absolute authority in a court of justice, and enables him to tyrannize as he pleases over parties, counsel, witnesses, and jurors. If a judge have power to punish for contempt, and to determine for himself what is a contempt, the whole administration of justice (or injustice, if he choose to make it so) is in his hands. This arbitrary power, which has been usurped and exercised by judges to punish for contempt, has undoubtedly had much to do in subduing counsel into those servile, obsequious, and cowardly habits, which so universally prevail among them, and which have not only cost so many clients their rights, but have also cost the people so many of their liberties."

Today, the disaster is 135 years worse, and Lysander Spooner would probably remember 1852 fondly, in comparison, as a year of perfect freedom. Today, many craven lawyers who are paid lavishly for defense, nevertheless don't tell their clients about their unalienable rights. As we have seen, the tax lawyers laugh about keeping the truth secret, so they can keep charging their victims $200 per hour. Across the country, federal judges throw I.R.S. tax targets into debtors' prison for contempt—without trial, even without accusation—with the nauseating explanation that the victim has the key to his cell. By means of contempt, a tax victim can be sent to jail for life.

So, contempt is not a weapon proper to an American judge. It is the weapon of an absolute monarch, a dictator. It is a symptom of the fact that our system has been perverted; that sovereignty, which God delegated to you, has been usurped by government.

Let's trace the doctrine of jury nullification from Lysander Spooner's time down to our own. Before the Civil War, in 1856, the U.S. Supreme Court ruled in the famous Dred Scott decision (*19 Howard 393*) that a runaway slave, like a runaway horse, had to be returned to his "owner." That was the so-called "law of the land," but northern juries didn't buy it. They refused to convict—they overruled the Supreme Court—and the law collapsed.

Needless to say, this disturbed government officials in the courts and elsewhere. If it continued, the people might get the outrageous idea that they were running the government! So, in 1895, in *Sparf v. United States*, 156 U.S. 51, the Supreme Court ruled that although juries do have the right to ignore a judge's instructions on the law, the court should not make the jurors aware of it. On the theory that the character George Orwell would later make famous knows best—Big Brother—the king's minions were advised to keep the people in the dark.

After World War I, Prohibition came to the United States. The law said sipping whiskey was illegal. In just a few years, however, the people decided they didn't agree. They voted against the law, by serving on juries and refusing to convict. The law collapsed. Later, Congress passed Repeal, but Repeal was not what killed Prohibition. Juries killed it when they nullified the law. By means of Repeal, Congress just put an official signature on what the juries had already done. Congress typically took credit for it, which reminds us of the man running down the street, shouting, "Where's that crowd going? I'm their leader." Had the juries not acted, we probably would have Prohibition today, supported by Congressmen bribed by bootleggers.

In 1969, the Fourth Circuit Court of Appeal ruled in *United States v. Moylan*, 417 F.2d 1002. Justice Sobeloff wrote as follows at page 1005: "In the early history of the American Colonies and for a time after the Revolution juries were nearly always recognized as having the power to judge both law and fact. . . ."

On the next page, Judge Sobeloff says this: "We recognize, as appellants urge, the undisputed power of the jury to acquit, even if its verdict is contrary to the law as given by the judge and contrary to the evidence. This is a power that must exist as long as we adhere to the general verdict in criminal cases, for the courts cannot search the minds of the jurors to find the basis upon which they judge. If the jury feels that the law under which the defendant is accused is unjust, or that exigent circumstances justified the actions of the accused, or for any reason which appeals to their logic or passion, the jury has the power to acquit, and the courts must abide by that decision."

His honor even admits that jury nullification can work for good: "Concededly, this power of the jury is not always contrary to the interests of justice. For example freedom of the press was immeasurably strengthened by the jury's acquittal of John Peter Zenger of seditious libel, a violation of which, under the law as it then existed and the facts, he was clearly guilty. . . ."

There is also the dramatic 1972 case of *United States v. Dougherty*, 473 F.2d 1113. Judge Leventhal wrote the ruling for the District of

Columbia Court of Appeal, the nation's "second highest court." At page 1132, he says as follows: "[A] prosecutor disposed by unworthy motives could likely establish some basis in fact for bringing charges against anyone he wants to book, but the jury system operates in fact . . . so that the jury will not convict when they empathize with the defendant, as when the offense is one they see themselves as likely to commit, or consider generally acceptable or condonable under the mores of the community."

Notice his honor's recognition that there are prosecutors with unworthy motives; which presumably could include locking up so-called "illegal tax protesters" and preachers who won't submit, in order to win promotion.

Judge Leventhal says this: "The existence of an unreviewable and unreversible power in the jury, to acquit in disregard of the instructions on the law given by the trial judge, has for many years co-existed with legal practice and precedent upholding instructions to the jury that they are required to follow the instructions of the court on all matters of law. There were different soundings in colonial days and the early days of our Republic. We are aware of the number and variety of expressions at that time from respected sources—John Adams; Alexander Hamilton; prominent judges—that jurors had a duty to find a verdict according to their own conscience though in opposition to the direction of the court; that their power signified a right; that they were judges both of law and of fact in a criminal case, and not bound by the opinion of the court."

It is important to note that Judge Leventhal doesn't like this. He admits it, but he doesn't like it. The lawyers would call his remarks "admissions against interest." He says this, on page 1133: ". . . The old rule survives today only as a singular relic." Yet, in the very next sentence, he says as follows: "The breadth of the continuing prerogative of the jury, however, perseveres, as appears from the rulings permitting inconsistent verdicts. These reflect, in the words of Justice Holmes, an acknowledgment that 'the jury has the power to bring in a verdict in the teeth of both law and facts' . . . ." On the same page, in a footnote, his honor reports that the Constitutions of both Maryland and Indiana require that juries be told the judge's instructions on the law are only advisory.

In the face of all this, Justice Leventhal advises the trial judge as follows, at page 1136: ". . . The fact that there is widespread existence of the jury's prerogative, and approval of its existence as a 'necessary counter to case-hardened judges and arbitrary prosecutors,' *does not establish as an imperative that the jury must be informed by the judge of that power. . . .*" (emphasis added)

In other words, Judge Leventhal advises the trial judge to *pretend* that the jury *doesn't* have that power. Because of the typically sorry state of government education, the juror will not have heard about it in school; if the judge doesn't tell him, he'll never know (unless *you* force him to read this book).

At page 1136, Judge Leventhal states a reason for the secrecy that we find especially revealing and insulting. What do you think?: "Moreover, to compel a juror involuntarily assigned to jury duty to assume the burdens of mini-legislator or judge, as is implicit in the doctrine of nullification, is to put untoward strains on the jury system. It is one thing for a juror to know that the law condemns, but he has a factual power of lenity. To tell him expressly of a nullification prerogative, however, is to inform him, in effect, that it is he who fashions the rule that condemns. *That is an overwhelming responsibility, an extreme burden for the jurors' psyche. . . .*" (emphasis added)

The fact is, however, that in our great system of representative government, the individual American *is* precisely he who fashions the rule that condemns; even if he *never* serves on a jury—but especially if he does. If that is no longer true, then we no longer have our liberty. We have a dictatorship. Remember that, in our great system, the Members of Congress, who make the laws, do so in your name—exercising your power. They are representatives—*your* representatives. The court referees known as judges are servants, public servants, *your* servants. They, too, exercise your (delegated) power. From the beginning, the presumption has been that what government officials do is what you want; and would do yourself, if you had the time—but for the fact that it would be fatally cumbersome for the entire American electorate of scores of millions to meet in Washington for the purpose. That is why we hire errand boys and girls and referees—Congressmen and judges—to do it for us. If this is no longer true, our Republic is gone, and our freedom with it. Notice that when pressed to the wall, those errand boys and referees still pay lip service to all this. The buck still stops with you.

As we have seen, however, Judge Leventhal believes your ultimate responsibility to govern is "overwhelming." He thinks it's too much for you. It's an "extreme burden for the jurors' psyche." Isn't this a blatant example of paternalism? Isn't his honor saying in effect that the people are too puny to govern themselves? Doesn't that spit in the faces of the Founding Fathers? Isn't it the stuff of which dictatorship is made?

The judge is saying here that he thinks you're a wimp. Well, Pilgrim, *are* you a wimp? You weren't when you stood at the rude bridge that arch'd the flood, and when you crossed the Delaware. You weren't when John Paul Jones spoke his piece, and Charles Cotesworth Pinckney spoke his. You weren't when Santa Ana blew his trumpet. You weren't when Stonewall Jackson stood like a stone wall. You weren't at San Juan Hill. You weren't at Chateau Thierry, Bastogne and Pork Chop Hill. Indeed, despite the network news and other perversions, you still were not a wimp in Vietnam. Are you now?

Along these lines, in the same ruling, Chief Judge Bazelon says as follows at page 1143: ". . . Surely nothing is gained by the pretense that the jurors lack the power to nullify, since that pretense deprives them of the opportunity to hear the very instruction that might compel them to confront their responsibility." Notice that the Chief Judge himself calls it a "pretense." He also says this: ". . . The reluctance of juries to hold defendants responsible for unmistakable violations of the prohibition laws told us much about the morality of those laws and about the 'criminality' of the conduct they proscribed. And the same can be said of the acquittals returned under the fugitive slave law . . . ."

In other words, says Judge Bazelon, the Republic still stands. The system still works—but only if you use it. Use it or lose it.

Speaking of pretense, the reader will recall the Matheson case. Again in chambers, Matheson and his attorney asked Judge David Kenyon for a jury instruction on nullification. Both Kenyon and the prosecutor replied with straight faces that they had never heard of it. Told about *Moylan* and *Dougherty*, his honor remarked that those cases were "old." The reader will recall that the oldest of them was at the time about *fifteen* years old! As if liberty could ever go out of fashion! Kenyon has assiduously cultivated a reputation in the community as a "humanitarian," but, as you see, he spits on the people's rights, while he no doubt looks with judicial favor on Magna Carta, now 772 years old.

The reader will of course have to decide for himself, but we don't believe a federal judge can be as dumb as David Kenyon would have us think he is. Has he enjoyed a visit from our friends at I.R.S.? Has he read the Croasmun Memorandum? Indeed, Kenyon agreed with Matheson that Kentucky's alleged ratification of the Sixteenth Amendment was invalid, if not fraudulent—a ruling tantamount to an admission that Matheson was right—and then ignored his own finding and ruled that Matheson was wrong.

The powers-that-would-like-to-be encourage us to report for jury duty. We, too, encourage you to do so. When you serve on a jury, you make law *whatever* you decide. You are voting not only to convict or acquit, but also to uphold or repeal the law, whether or not you know it. The law is always on trial, along with the defendant. This may not be readily apparent when the charge is murder, for instance; only because the law against murder is universally accepted as sound, so the question doesn't come up. If you believe a law is unjust, you have the ultimate power to repeal it, by serving on the jury. Indeed, doesn't a conscientious citizen have a *duty* to repeal unjust law—like the fugitive slave law?

Consider also that what we are asking you to do is relatively modest. The fugitive slave laws, however reprehensible, *were* laws. Prohibition *was* a law. Indeed, it was a constitutional amendment. Violations may not have been immoral, as Judge Bazelon suggests, but, technically, they were violations.

What we are asking you to do here, on the contrary, is not to nullify illegal, immoral "law," but to nullify illegal practices. By doing so, you would be *supporting* and *restoring* the law. Remember that we preach obedience to the law on the books. We don't like it, and in a chapter to come we'll show you how to get rid of it, but since it is still on the books, we believe it should be obeyed. As we have seen, however, our friends at I.R.S. are "illegal tax protesters," who lead the Tax Rebellion; in that they are the ones who refuse to obey the law on the books, do everything to conceal it, and commit serious crimes to circumvent it. Remember that not only should working people on trial for tax charges be acquitted; the trials should not be taking place.

If you have been audited, or have had some other trouble with our friends at I.R.S., the prosecutor will probably kick you off the prospective jury in voir dire, as we have seen. Should that happen, you could try to enlighten your fellow Americans in the environs of the courtroom to their true powers, on your way out, if possible. You could volunteer to return as a defendant. Now, however, we are not talking to you. Now, we are talking to the millions of Americans who know something is desperately, fatally wrong; but who didn't know what it was until they arrived at this point in this book; who want to end the oppression by restoring the law—and who either have not yet had any trouble with I.R.S. (a disappearing minority), or somehow are able to survive voir dire and become jurors. What are we asking you to do?

We're asking you to be quiet about what you now know. We're asking you to take your seat on the jury with perfect docility. (A simpering grin would help. Just imitate the prosecutor.) We're asking you to hear the evidence. And we're asking you to vote for acquittal. Many fine Americans these days ask themselves and each other in discouragement what just one person can do. Pilgrim, just one person with knowledge enough and fortitude enough can at least hang a jury and prevent a conviction. A string of such defeats for the Tax Rebellion would cause Congress to jump on the Restoration Bandwagon and typically pretend to be driving.

Because of the reprehensible tactics of our friends at I.R.S., millions of Americans today are afraid to exercise their rights; but they can apply the doctrine of jury nullification without risk—because the government has no way of learning why a juror voted as he or she did, as Judge Sobeloff said in *Moylan*. When the judge says you have no power to rule on the law—in other words, when he lies—simply smile, play dumb (as David Kenyon does), vote for acquittal without explaining why and go home, knowing that you have struck a blow for yourself and Patrick Henry. Imagine the result if I.R.S. couldn't get convictions. Imagine the result if juries around the country voted to acquit.

For instance, in upstate New York, the government accused Jack Pierce of willful failure to file. A citizens' group took newspaper ads to educate the people to their unalienable rights and powers as jurors. The government tried to evade the effects of that blitzkrieg by changing the venue of the trial. But the people and the newspaper ads also changed venue. As Joe Louis said of one of his opponents: "He can run, but he can't hide." There was nowhere else to run, so the trial took place. Our friends at I.R.S. turned it into a circus.

They testified that Jack Pierce was conducting meetings in which he distributed material that was harmful to the tax system. Under cross-examination, the meetings turned out to be about constitutional taxation, and the "subversive" material turned out to be the Declaration of Independence and the Constitution.

Mr. Pierce had proved his good faith by filing a Claim for Refund form. Chief Judge Lloyd F. MacMahon, of the Southern District of New York, a hired gun apparently sent upstate for the purpose, allowed the claim to be entered in evidence, but refused to allow the supplement, a fourteen-page explanation that Pierce had filed with the claim. His honor, who seems to be a disciple of Judge Leventhal's, said it might confuse the jury.

On May 27, 1983, after several hours of deliberation, the jury unanimously acquitted Mr. Pierce of all charges, to which his honor MacMahon said as follows: "In my forty years on the bench, this is the greatest disservice I've ever seen a jury do against this country."

The jurors cheered. Remember that this happened in upstate New York, land of taxes. Of course, the Prostitute National Press typically gave the story no coverage. Again, most of what they print and broadcast on the subject, with rare exceptions, consists of press releases prepared by our friends at I.R.S. Isn't it peculiar that the moguls of the media will go to the ends of the earth—will literally go through garbage, lots of it—to expose the malfeasance of almost every government agency; but will take at face value whatever I.R.S. says, however nonsensical?

Nevertheless, the victory for law in the *Pierce* case was won. You can multiply it by the tens and hundreds. Wouldn't you like to be part of such fun? You *can* be.

14

WHY DOES WASHINGTON TAX?

The restoration of the law would mean a considerable decrease in the revenue now illegally confiscated from the people. True, American workers would again enjoy the use of their entire paychecks; but the crucial question arises: How would the government finance itself? Some experts tell us that when the rate of tax is reduced, the amount of tax collected increases; as you see, however, we are not assuming that will happen when the tax law is restored. This book is addressed to genuinely patriotic Americans, so we're sure we all agree—Democrat and Republican, liberal and conservative—at least, we should, that it would be monumentally stupid, even subversive, to make a change, however right and pleasant, were it to cause our wonderful government—ordained by God—to collapse or even stumble. We have the greatest system of government ever devised on this earth. As patriotic Americans, we certainly want to preserve it. To do anything less, would be to spit in the faces of the Founding Fathers we claim to revere—which would turn us into clones of our friends at I.R.S.

So, this is a truly crucial question. With the income tax once again administered legally, how would our friends at I.R.S. confiscate the receipts they seize now? The answer is: They couldn't. Why *should* the government get what it gets now? The handouts so many Americans enjoy are paid with a fearful price. The cost of the federal government is now in the neighborhood of a quarter of the Gross National Product. (If you add up all the taxes you pay—federal, state and local, hidden in the purchase price of things you buy or listed separately—you would find that your true tax rate is between fifty and sixty per cent; more if you account for inflation.) Washington spends your tax money on such jokes as the $9,992 National Science Foundation study of bullfights in Spain, which, according to N.S.F., "will entail ethnographic descriptions and comparisons of the local vs. national bullfighting formats," etc. Wisconsin Senator William Proxmire gave it his Golden Fleece award for September, 1987, and said at the time that he was equally suspicious of a $28,578 research project on the role of non-marriage in rural Irish family systems.

Nationally syndicated columnist and author Donald Lambro has made a career both distinguished and humorous of exposing such jokes, such as $8 million to study weeds, and $9.3 million to David Rockefeller's Chase Manhattan Bank to help build an office tower. Do you really believe the government would collapse were the beneficiaries of such largesse forced to finance their own jokes? Washington also provides billions in cheap loans to help Fortune 500 corporations sell their products abroad, just one example of "Socialism for the rich." As the late Illinois Senator Everett Dirksen is alleged to have said, "A billion here, a billion there, pretty soon you're talking about real money." With one hand, Washington gives billions, literally, to the International Monetary Fund and the multinational banks. With the other, our friends at I.R.S. take a bigger percentage of your wages than the lord of the manor took from the medieval European serf; even bigger than the take of the ante-bellum slaveowner here. Washington even gives your tax dollars to our mortal Communist enemies, by financing construction of the Kama River truck factory in the Soviet Union, for instance, where the Soviets make the heavy, military trucks they are using to commit genocide in Afghanistan. Then Washington says we must dramatically increase our military budget to counter the "Soviet threat." Because of all this—and much more like it we don't have room to mention—the famous American standard of living is now noticeably falling. Doesn't it take both husband and wife working to maintain the standard the husband alone was able to provide just a few years ago? The cure for such outrages isn't more money but different policy.

Indeed, this entire discussion, while valid and important, is somewhat irrelevant, because the fact is that the federal government *doesn't need* the income tax to operate.

Remember that we got the income tax in 1913, and that it did not become an important factor until 1942. Before the income tax we had practically no debt—as you will recall, Washington generally had more money than it knew what to do with—and we won all our wars. Can you name one year in our history during which the government was paralyzed because we had no income tax? One month? A week? How about one day? During this period, America became the greatest nation known to history. Of course, there was relatively little "Socialism for the rich," and other such thefts. Since the income tax, we have lost two wars, and the national debt, inspired by the tax, is bringing the government to its knees.

So, again, the income tax isn't needed to run the government. Obviously, there is another reason for it, a hidden reason, a reason the people who control the government do everything to conceal. What is that reason? What is the true purpose of the income tax?

A glimpse of the answer emerged briefly during the war we fought as an ally of Hitler's former ally, Stalin, also known as World War II. On August 21 and 22, 1942, in the second session of the 77th Congress, a Senate Finance subcommittee conducted a confidential hearing on the proposed provisions of the 1942 Revenue Act. The testimony was classified and was released only about thirty five years later. On the cover of the copy your reporter is now looking at, it says: "Declassified, See Exchange & Gift Div., Declassification File No. 100." Why on earth would hearings on the 1942 Revenue Act be withheld from public scrutiny for so long? At the hearings, a gentleman named Meyer Jacobstein, of the Brookings Institution, told the Senators as follows at pages 99-100:

"It is obvious that it is necessary to mop up the excess purchasing power of the community, not only because of its effect on the price situation but because the Treasury needs the money and needs it quickly. Obviously if the Treasury can collect from the consumers as the purchases are made the Treasury has the use of those funds long before it would obtain them by the income-tax method.

"Now, there are many ways, of course, of mopping up this surplus purchasing power. The income tax, unfortunately, does not reach large groups of people. . . .

". . .

"If you want to mop up purchasing power the thing to do is to go after purchasing power. . . ."

So, according to Meyer Jacobstein, of the influential Brookings Institution, the main purpose of the tax he proposed was not so much to finance the government as it was to "mop up the excess purchasing power," in order to prevent prices from getting out of control. Notice that he apparently proposed a species of sales tax, because the income tax *did not touch many people*. Along these lines, Senator Danaher asked about a coupon system tied to purchases by the public. Jacobstein replied (p. 101): "[L]ooking at the coupon system by and of itself, it seems to me that it is a workable method of reaching the largest number of people quickly, for siphoning off purchasing power into the Treasury . . . ."

At the same hearing, Charles O. Hardy, also of the Brookings Institution, told the Senators this (pages 101-02): "Now, as has been stated a moment ago, this is a forced loan, using the mechanics of the sales tax both for distributing the burden and for the mechanics of collection. . . .

"I would like to say just a word on the result of doing it this way as compared with making it a tax and calling it a day. The basic necessity of running this system, either out of taxes or forced loans, one or the other, is simply, in effect, that we have to bring about a readjustment of consumption in the country to the amount of consumers' goods and services that we can spare the resources to produce under war conditions. First, we have got to devote our productive energies to the war. If we do not devote a large part of the purchasing power correspondingly to the war, then we have got the choice of either making the adjustment by an inflationary rise of prices, which is also a form of sales tax only it is paid to the dealer and producer instead of being paid to the Government, or you can use the mechanism of the sales tax, as far as I can see, by mopping up the increased purchasing power that is created by the rising amount they receive in their pay checks. . . ."

It sounds reasonable, does it not? After all, we *were* in a war. We *had* been attacked, after provocation by Washington to the point of Japanese desperation. Notice that, here at least, Hardy says nothing about raising revenue to finance the government. Like Mr. Jacobstein, he is concerned about "mopping up" purchasing power to prevent inflation that could threaten the value of the currency.

Also at the hearings, witnesses testified in favor of accomplishing this purpose by linking the income tax to something new, called "withholding." One of them, Randolph Paul, of the Treasury Department, explained at page 119 that, without it, many taxpayers would default, putting "Bureau prestige" in jeopardy: ". . . You can file liens on his salary, and so on, which will certainly be an unpopular procedure. We are just afraid, without collection at the source, with our present rate and our present spread of the incidence of taxation, that the system will break down. I do not think I put it too strongly when I say not only Bureau prestige is involved but the future of the income tax may be involved. . . ."

Another Treasury Department official who strongly supported withholding at the hearing, was Milton Friedman, of the Division of Tax Research. This is the same Milton Friedman who today is a "monetarist," and says that paper "money" is better than gold, if it is properly managed. And if we had some ham, we could have some ham and eggs, if we had some eggs.

Again, during a war you do what you must. That is why dictators love war. In war, they do as they like and then claim there was no choice. Along these lines, at page 106 of the hearings, Mr. Hardy said this: ". . . It would give an opportunity for complete registration of the population, which could be used for a great many purposes. . . ." The trouble here is that, in *United States v. Butler*, 297 U.S. 1, the Supreme Court ruled on January 6, 1936 that a tax, to be legitimate, must be a "pure" tax; its purpose must be strictly to raise revenue for the government. At page sixty one, Justice Roberts said this: ". . . A tax . . . signifies an exaction for the support of the government. The word has never been thought to connote the expropriation of money from one group for the benefit of another. . . ." As we have seen, however, the perversion that started in World War II consisted precisely of the fact that the income tax was now being used for other purposes.

Along these lines, we have already alluded to the fact that taxes cause deficits. Now come Richard Vedder and Lowell Gallaway, both Ohio University economists, whose recent study shows that the more money Congress is given, the more it overspends. As the average personal tax rate increased over the past twenty years, so did the federal deficit as a share of the gross national product. The professors found that for every dollar in new taxes, Congress enacted $1.58 of additional spending. Just as the taste of blood drives sharks into a frenzy; so, the more taxes that pour in, the more the frenzy to spend and the greater the deficits.

If taxes cured deficits, we would see tax increases and reduced deficits; or, at least, a national debt that is not increasing. Instead, we see tax increases, and a debt that is exploding. In 1980, at the dawn of the Reagan Revolution, spending was $590 billion. In 1987, as your reporter sets this down, spending is expected to be $1.015 trillion, an increase of 72%. The deficits during those years have been staggering, and the national media have told us the reason was the Reagan "tax cuts." Was there a tax cut? In 1980, the government took $517 billion in taxes. In 1987, it will take about $842 billion in taxes. Where your reporter went to school, 842 is considerably bigger than 517, and, we believe, still is. So, during that period taxes increased 63%, while spending increased even more—9% more. There has been no tax cut. There have been changes, yes; but, taxes are exploding.

Indeed, remember the experiments of 1982 and 1984? Taxes were raised. Did our leaders use that revenue to reduce the deficit? No, they used it to increase spending.

So, the trouble with federal finances is not at all insufficient tax. The trouble is *too much tax*. Again, taxes cause spending. Giving more taxes to the pious frauds in Washington, allegedly to "solve" the deficit problem, is like making the Hillside Strangler dean of women at the university, with instructions to solve the problem of rape.

This means that the conscientious reader serving on a tax jury, can vote in perfect conscience to acquit the worker on trial; not only because the trial is illegal, but because the taxes the prosecutor talks about so reverently, not only don't finance the government—they increase the debt.

Indeed, now that there is no precious metal whatsoever behind our currency, the question arises with consummate force: Why oppress the people with the totalitarian methods we have mentioned? Why continue the liens, the garnishments, the jeopardy assessments, the intimidation and prison terms, that have reduced so many of the American people to quivering wimps? Since our "money" now does consist entirely of paper, why doesn't the government simply print whatever it "needs?" If this question never has occurred to the reader, it hasn't only because it is so blatantly obvious, like the glasses you can't find on the end of your nose.

When our money was gold and silver, we had to pay our taxes in those things. This meant that we physically had to deliver certain amounts of those precious metals to the government. Precious metals are relatively rare. That is why they are precious. Relative rarity is one of the essential qualifications a commodity must have to serve successfully as money. If it isn't relatively rare, people won't place value in it. They would laugh derisively, with good reason, if we tried to use grains of sand on the beach as money. Such a monetary unit wold be meaningless, precisely because it is so plentiful. Self-confessed monetary wizards that they are, our government leaders cannot make precious metals, which is why they hate them when you have them.

However, they *can* print bigger and bigger numbers on as much paper currency as they like, because paper and ink are relatively limitless in supply. So, why don't they? For years, they have told us, in government school, for instance, that the national debt is not a problem, because "we owe it to ourselves"—so, why don't they just print billion dollar bills and pay it off? When they "need" more "money" to operate—to give the Soviets, for instance—why don't they just print it?

They do. In effect, they not only print without stint—and without monetary backing—by means of even phonier credit schemes they also increase government purchasing power immeasurably. For instance, page E-28 of a document entitled *Special Analyses: Budget of the United States Government, Fiscal Year 1988*, prepared by the Executive Office of the President, and published by the U.S. Government Printing Office, says this: "The Federal Deposit Insurance Corporation (FDIC) began to issue notes in June 1986 as part of some agreements with prospective purchasers to buy failing banks. The FDIC ordinarily tries to arrange for the private purchase and assumption of failing banks rather than liquidate them and pay off the depositors, in part because purchase and assumption agreements are usually less expensive to the Government. Under purchase and assumption agreements, the FDIC normally pays cash to the buyer in order to bring the value of the assets of the failing bank up to the value of the liabilities assumed by the buyer. The FDIC has, however, in some cases issued notes in place of cash to the buyer of a failing bank. These are one-year, interest-bearing notes, redeemable for cash upon demand."

Why the rigmarole? Why doesn't F.D.I.C. just issue cash, Federal Reserve Notes? Because it doesn't have them! There are about $200 billion in Federal Reserve Notes, while F.D.I.C. "guarantees" $1.4 trillion in deposits. This is the legacy of fractional reserve banking, in which the government has allowed the banks to kite checks. The last time you borrowed "money" from your bank, did it give you cash? Probably not. It probably just added the sum to your account. In the beginning, fractional reserve banking performed the "miracle" of making "money" in an inkwell. Then it did so with a typewriter. Now, it does so with a computer.

The government's analysis of the budget continues as follows: "The issuance of these notes is thus a method of paying the Government's bills, just as is the disbursement of cash. Accordingly, under standard budget concepts, the issuance of these notes should be treated as outlays and borrowing. The FDIC transactions were not, however, reported in this manner to Treasury and consequently were not recorded in Treasury's published reports as outlays or borrowing. . . ."

Why weren't they? Why the coverup? Is someone at the Federal Deposit Insurance Corporation breaking the law? What didn't he know, and when didn't he know it? When will a special committee of Congress hold hearings?

On page E-32 is Table E-10, which reports that in 1986 F.D.I.C. issued $472 million of these notes. Indeed, the Table estimates that in 1987 even more of the notes will be issued, in the amount of $3,954,000,000. Why? The government's budget analysis doesn't say so, but the obvious answer is: because the "experts" expect even more banks to fail during that year. Of course, all that "money" would be added to the national debt you now owe.

In fact, Table E-10 also reports that these F.D.I.C. notes are not subject to the statutory limit, which means that the experts can print any amount of them they want. Is that what they will do when the domino effect begins cascading through the banks; when they begin to collapse not by ones, but by dozens? Do monkeys like bananas? Is Moscow Red?

It is reasonable to speculate that should a general banking collapse occur, you, the depositor, would be paid off, all right; not in the cash you were promised, but in these F.D.I.C. notes—and, as sure as Marx didn't make green apples, they would no longer bear interest (no law says they must). The process would of course amount to repudiation, but the media would routinely print F.D.I.C. press releases, to the effect that the government "always keeps its word."

Again, this is just one example of how the government inflates, which inflation is causing the price explosion that is collapsing the currency. "Honest," crooked governments inflate honestly by printing currency. Ours does so indirectly—by means of such schemes as these F.D.I.C. notes—to conceal its crimes. In Germany, in the early 1920s, the government printed the mark around the clock. The genius who ran the Reichsbank and boasted that he had hired three shifts for the purpose, drew several standing ovations from the Reichstag for his wizardry. He had saved Germany! It lasted less than a couple of years. In 1923, the currency collapsed and wound up on many bathroom walls. Toward the end, menu prices in restaurants changed while diners ate their meals. So did the prices while housewives waited on line at the markets. Dividend checks were not worth as much as the stamps needed to mail them.

Why, on the contrary, has our currency lasted so long? It has lasted so long because the multinational bankers have found a way to control inflation, and thereby to defer the inevitable crash—ensuring that it will be considerably worse than it would have been without their interference—a way that was either unavailable to or not considered by that 1923 German genius.

As we have seen, inflation is not rising prices. Rising prices are the effect of inflation. Inflation is the process in which large amounts of money, or substitutes therefore, are dumped into an economy all at once, thereby substantially increasing purchasing power. The Socialist billionaires spread the lie that inflation is rising prices, to protect themselves from the people's wrath. They trick us into blaming the businessman, who raises prices to protect himself from their inflation. Indeed, during the Johnson Administration they blamed housewives; they said in effect that we were suffering from inflation because American housewives were too stupid to buy inexpensive groceries.

During the Ford Administration, Alan Greenspan, now Federal Reserve Chairman, a member of David Rockefeller's world-government group called the Council on Foreign Relations, was Chairman of the Council of Economic Advisers, and extruded a scheme called Whip Inflation Now, which taught that inflation was our own fault, because we bad boys and girls were not finishing everything on our dinner plates. If this were not insulting enough, we were also told to wear W.I.N. buttons. If enough people wore such buttons, you see, inflation would be whipped. Years ago, your obedient servant spent many hours in the presence of Alan Greenspan, and I can testify for sure that he knows exactly what he is doing.

It now becomes clear that, having seen how "well" their manipulation of purchasing power worked during World War II, the Socialist billionaires decided to make it permanent. We don't have to guess about this. We have it in black and white from the horse's mouth himself.

In this case, the horse was Beardsley Ruml. In 1921, he was assistant to the president of the Carnegie Corporation. In 1922, he was director of the Laura Spelman Rockefeller Memorial. In 1931, he was dean of social science at the Rockefeller-financed University of Chicago. It was Beardsley Ruml who conceived the fatal allotment feature of the New Deal's disastrous farm program. Starting in 1937, he was for ten years a director of the New York Federal Reserve Bank, far and away the most powerful bank in the system. During the last six of those years, he was bank chairman. In 1944, he was influential at the Bretton Woods, New Hampshire, monetary conference that paved the way for the transfer of American wealth overseas.

In short, Beardsley Ruml was completely a factotum of the Rockefeller cabal, which for decades has been active in foundations, in education, in banking, in the United Nations, in Washington; and the goal of whose activity has always been to protect Rockefeller wealth, to confiscate yours, to socialize our economy and to submerge it in a world government they would run.

What did Beardsley Ruml have to say about taxes? He was the author of the "temporary" World War II withholding that is still with us, known in the beginning as the "Ruml pay-as-you-go plan." During the last year of the war, he read a paper before the American Bar Association. Later, a magazine called *American Affairs*, published by the immensely prestigious National Industrial Conference Board, published it under the title, "Taxes for Revenue Are Obsolete." In the introduction to the paper in the issue of January, 1946, the editor explained as follows at page thirty five: ". . . His thesis is that given (1) control of a central banking system and (2) an inconvertible currency, a sovereign national government is finally free of money worries and *need no longer levy taxes for the purpose of providing itself with revenue.* All taxation, therefore, should be regarded from the point of view of social and economic consequences. . . ." (emphasis added)

As we have seen, gold ties government to reality; therefore, government hates it. When gold backs paper, government must store a certain amount of the former, before it prints any more of the latter. In this context, a government "finally free of money worries" is a government that has banished gold—severed that connection to reality—and therefore can print as much as it likes.

Beardsley Ruml himself puts it this way: "The necessity for a government to tax in order to maintain both its independence and its solvency is true for state and local governments, but it is not true for a national government. Two changes of the greatest consequence have occurred in the last twenty-five years which have substantially altered the position of the national state with respect to the financing of its current requirements.

"The first of these changes is the gaining of vast new experience in the management of central banks.

"The second change is the elimination, for domestic purposes, of the convertibility of the currency into gold."

Ruml was talking about the creation of the Federal Reserve, the nation's central bank, and about the theft of the people's gold by Franklin Roosevelt. Old-timers will perhaps recall that, when Roosevelt called in the gold, soon after he took office, he told the people he would keep it only "temporarily." The unspoken, and insulting presumption, was that the government was wiser and more honest than the people. Needless to say, the government still has the gold. (Or does it? Edward Durell, the indefatigable Virginia industrialist and champion of real money, has the proverbial documentary proof that much of the stolen people's gold is missing, perhaps stolen.) Until 1971, the government paid foreigners gold on demand for Federal Reserve Notes, while denying it to you under threat of imprisonment.

The thunderbolt question obviously arises: If taxes no longer are needed to run the government—because of the sublime genius of people like Ruml—then what on earth are they for? Under the heading, "What Taxes Are Really For," the horse's mouth lists four purposes: "1. As an instrument of fiscal policy to help stabilize the purchasing power of the dollar; 2. To express public policy in the distribution of wealth and of income, as in the case of the progressive income and estate taxes; 3. To express public policy in subsidizing or in penalizing various industries and economic groups; 4. To isolate and assess directly the costs of certain national benefits, such as highways and social security."

According to Ruml, the first of these purposes is by far the most important, his explanation of which deserves quotation at length: "By all odds, the most important single purpose to be served by the imposition of federal taxes is the maintenance of a dollar which has stable purchasing power over the years. Sometimes this purpose is stated as 'the avoidance of inflation' . . . .

"The war has taught the government, and the government has taught the people, that federal taxation has much to do with inflation and deflation, with the prices which have to be paid for the things that are bought and sold. If federal taxes are insufficient or of the wrong kind, the purchasing power in the hands of the public is likely to be greater than the output of goods and services with which this purchasing demand can be satisfied. If the demand becomes too great, the result will be a rise in prices and there will be no proportionate increase in the quantity of things for sale. This will mean that the dollar is worth less than it was before—that is inflation. . . .

"The dollars the government spends become purchasing power in the hands of the people who have received them. The dollars the government takes by taxes cannot be spent by the people, and, therefore, these dollars can no longer be used to acquire the things which are available for sale. . . ."

So, we arrive at last at the final secret of the income tax; and a dirty, little secret it is. Its true purpose, unavailable to or unimagined by the German genius who printed the mark into collapse in 1923, is to protect the equally unbacked Federal Reserve currency from such profligacy. Its true purpose is to pay the people with one hand, and to confiscate with the other; thereby inhibiting the inflationary effect of ravenous government spending. The income tax allows our rulers to juggle their fiscal balls in the air a little longer, by offering a safety valve through which the inflationary pressure generated by that spending can more safely be released. The income tax does that by *transferring purchasing power from the people to the government*. Again, the income tax has nothing whatever to do with financing the government.

The next heading in Ruml's paper is, "To Distribute the Wealth," under which Ruml says this: "The second principal purpose of federal taxes is to attain more equality of wealth and of income than would result from economic forces working alone. The taxes which are effective for this purpose are the progressive individual income tax, the progressive estate tax, and the gift tax. . . . It is important, here, to note that the estate and gift taxes have little or no significance, as tax measures, for stabilizing the value of the dollar. Their purpose is the social purpose of preventing what otherwise would be high concentration of wealth and income at a few points, as a result of investment and reinvestment of income not expended in meeting day-to-day consumption requirements. These taxes should be defended and attacked in terms of their effects on the character of American life, not as revenue measures."

So, estate and gift taxes also have nothing to do with raising revenue. We presume that Beardsley Ruml told this to the American Bar Association with tongue firmly embedded in cheek. The system he supported and ran, in which the Federal Reserve monopoly over our currency enjoys the protection of the income tax, has made the Rockefeller Socialists, whom he served as factotum, wealthy beyond imagination, and certainly several light years beyond the requirements of "day-to-day consumption," while inflation devours *your* savings.

In *The Rockefeller File* (Seal Beach, California, '76 Press, 1976), Gary Allen gave us a glimpse of a life-style that beggars the inmates of the Taj Mahal. For instance, the Rockefeller estate at Pocantico Hills alone, in New York State, has seventy miles of private roads, and is said to be "the kind of place God would have built if he had had the money." After a long and luscious description of such digs, Gary Allen says this (page fourteen): "Needless to say, it takes an army of underlings to operate these elegant pads. There are 500 full-time domestics, gardeners, guards and chauffeurs at Pocantico Hills alone, 45 at the family's Seal Harbor, Maine, retreat, and 15 in Nelson's Fifth Avenue apartment. All told, it has been estimated the Rockefeller women have at their beck and call about 2,500 servants.

"Because the Rockefellers are forever on the wing—in their private jet fleets—each residence is permanently staffed, and nightly the sheets are turned down. One never knows when the boss might pop in."

The income tax makes it possible. Now, where have you heard before about redistribution of the wealth? Wasn't it in the *Communist Manifesto*? Sure it was. Give that lady a brass figlegee. Indeed, isn't a graduated income tax the second of Marx's ten steps to Communism, preceded only by government seizure of the land? Yes, it is. Give her another. What Beardsley Ruml was recommending here—euphemisms such as "the character of American life" notwithstanding—was the use of the income tax for the very purpose Marx had in mind. What that works out to mean, again, is confiscation of workers' property, which then is delivered to the people behind the Fed; confiscation of *your* property—from wages to automobiles—not David Rockefeller's. Is that what you want?

Along these lines, remember Ruml's third reason for taxes, in which friends of the Socialist billionaires are rewarded with subsidies, while enemies are hurt with penalties—exactly the system we have now; exactly what Marx recommended. Is this what you want? Are you a Communist?

A word should be said about the Federal Reserve Note and its parent, the Federal Reserve system, for which the income tax runs interference. As you know, the Constitution reserves the power over money to the Congress, which power Congress is forbidden to delegate. How would you respond, were Congress illegally to give its power to a private corporation, like Ford or

Xerox, or Occidental Petroleum or IBM, or a new corporation organized for the purpose? Suppose Congress confiscated your gold and gave it to that private corporation. Suppose that private corporation issued currency the government forced you to use, and on which it forced you to pay interest. Suppose that private corporation extended credit ("cheap money") and then called the loans; did so time after time, creating endless boom and bust; thereby farming the farmer and bringing the people to their knees —protesting all the while in a blizzard of propaganda that it was fighting these things.

How would you respond? Do we exaggerate when we speculate that you would call it the biggest scandal of all time? Are we far afield when we guess that you would demand a special prosecutor, complete with hearings, to expose the conspiracy; seizure of the corporation's assets and abolition of the corporation; long prison terms for the perpetrators, in government and out; and restoration to Congress of the money power, in obedience to the Constitution?

Pilgrim, if that is close to what you would demand, may we ask respectfully why you have not demanded it—because the private corporation we have been talking about is the Federal Reserve System.

Our Socialist billionaires gave us the Fed because they had been losing control of the nation's banks. The Fed was their successful attempt to reassert that control. In *The Triumph of Conservatism: A Reinterpretation of American History, 1900-1916* (New York, The Free Press, a division of Macmillan, 1963), Professor Gabriel Kolko writes as follows starting on page 140: ". . . The crucial fact of the financial structure at the beginning of this century was the relative decrease in New York's financial significance and the rise of many alternate sources of substantial financial power.

"Throughout the 1870's and much of the 1880's, by far the largest number of banks were national banks, with their financial standards determined in Washington. By 1896, however, nonnational state banks, savings banks, and private banks accounted for 61 per cent of the total number of banks, and private banks, and by 1913, 71 per cent of the banks. . . ."

The Socialist billionaires tried unsuccessfully to stop the hemorrhage: "In 1903 the New York Clearing House tried to impose national reserve requirements on its rapidly growing state trust companies. Seventeen of them walked out and did not return until 1912. . . . J. P. Morgan and Co. were fully aware of the diffusion of banking power that was taking place through the state banks, and it disturbed them." New York banker Henry Clews said in 1888 that "the natural development of national production of commerce is to build up independent financial centres of the interior, the effect of which can only be to check in some measure the growing ascendancy of New York." Henry P. Davison, Morgan's partner, said in 1913 that New York's share of the nation's banking resources had fallen from 23 per cent in 1902 to 18 per cent in 1912.

The key to the "success" of the Federal Reserve System, with which our Socialist billionaires have reasserted what is now total control over the nation's banking system, was a technique they have refined into an art: They foment a problem—create panic, which inhibits thought—and then pretend to "solve" it. In other words, they rob you, enslave you—and make you like it. Indeed, they usually arrange for someone else to take the blame. As we have seen, they blame businessmen for inflation. Hitler, another Socialist, was also adept at the scam. Professor Kolko writes as follows: ". . . Morgan's activities in 1895-1896 in selling U.S. gold bonds in Europe were based on his alliance with the House of Rothschild; these activities added to Morgan's reputation as a rescuer of governments. That reputation was often the key to his power, and it lasted long after the power was greatly diluted. Morgan and a few large bankers saved the New York Clearing House in 1893, and, seemingly, the United States' financial standing only a few years later. . . ."

So it was that in 1907, Morgan set the stage for the Federal Reserve, by instigating a run on the perfectly sound Knickerbocker Bank. There was a panic. Influential commentators "spontaneously" began to comment that "something must be done." In 1909, the Fed's organizers met secretly to spawn it in a resort on

Jekyll Island, Georgia, where they used only their first names to conceal their identities from the staff. Later, they would joke about their charter memberships in "the First Name Club."

Not only was it conceived in secrecy; in 1913 it was born in fraud. Just as its backers had told the people that the income tax would "soak the rich"; so, they now told the people that the proposed Fed would soak the banks. To mollify opponents who saw through the scheme, they promised changes—but didn't make them. They had promised to delay the crucial vote until those opponents returned to Congress from Christmas recess; and then rushed the scheme through Congress on December 23, 1913, with most of the Members out of town. Congressman Charles Lindbergh, father of the famous aviator, told his colleagues that they had witnessed the greatest illicit power grab in history.

Today, the Federal Reserve Note in your handbag or wallet is a total fraud. First, it isn't a note. A note is a promise to pay; but your Federal Reserve "Note" promises to pay you, the bearer, nothing. As we have seen, it does pay interest to the multinational banks behind the Fed, in exchange for the "favor" you take when you use their currency. Second, there is no reserve. The word "Reserve" looks comforting, doesn't it; and is there to remind you that the Fed is supposed to bring stability to the business cycle. In fact, hasn't there been much more "boom and bust" *since* the Fed was inflicted than there ever was before? Didn't the Fed give us the Great Depression of 1929, by inflating to explosion via stock margins and then refusing to use the "reserve" as it had promised it would? The answers to both questions are *yes*; and the fact is that there is no "Reserve" and never was. The word on your currency is nothing more than that: a reassuring public relations device, like the reassuring word "insurance" used in connection with Social Security.

Finally, it isn't Federal. The word "Federal" is there to convince you it is part of the government. Is that so? Then why has the government never audited it? Can you believe that the most powerful institution in our nation—which controls the currency—has never enjoyed an *outside* audit? It hasn't. Federal Reserve activities are kept secret even from Congress. Again, the Federal Reserve System is a private corporation; as private a corporation as General Motors or IBM.

Along these lines, there is the crucial case of *Lewis v. United States*, 680 F.2d 1239, in which the Ninth Circuit ruled on June 24, 1982. Mr. Lewis was hit by a truck owned by the Federal Reserve Bank of San Francisco, so he sued. The trouble was that he sued the U.S. government under the Federal Tort Claims Act, in the belief that the Bank is a government agency. The Court ruled against Mr. Lewis, explaining that he had mistakenly named the wrong defendant, that the government had nothing to do with it —and that Mr. Lewis should have sued the Bank, which is a private corporation.

Indeed, the Court was kind enough to list in detail all the reasons that make the Fed a private corporation. Starting at page 1241, Judge Poole said as follows: ". . . Examining the organization and function of the Federal Reserve Banks, and applying the relevant factors, we conclude that the Reserve Banks are not federal instrumentalities for purposes of the FTCA, but are independent, privately owned and locally controlled corporations.

"Each Federal Reserve Bank is a separate corporation owned by commercial banks in its region. The stockholding commercial banks elect two thirds of each Bank's nine member board of directors. The remaining three directors are appointed by the Federal Reserve Board. The Federal Reserve Board regulates the Reserve Banks, but direct supervision and control of each Bank is exercised by its board of directors. . . .

"Each Bank is statutorily empowered to conduct these activities without day to day direction from the federal government. Thus, for example, the interest rates on advances to member banks, individuals, partnerships, and corporations are set by each Reserve Bank and their decisions regarding the purchase and sale of securities are likewise independently made.

"It is evident from the legislative history of the Federal Reserve Act that Congress did not intend to give the federal government direction over the daily operation of the Reserve Banks . . . ."

The daily operation of those Banks is revealing: ". . . Unlike typical federal agencies, each bank is empowered to hire and fire employees at will. Bank employees do not participate in the Civil Service Retirement System. They are covered by worker's compensation insurance, purchased by the Bank, rather than the Federal Employees Compensation Act. Employees traveling on Bank business are not subject to federal travel regulations and do not receive government employee discounts on lodging and services."

At page 1242, his honor says this: "Additionally, Reserve Banks, as privately owned entities, receive no appropriated funds from Congress. . . .

"Finally, the Banks are empowered to sue and be sued in their own name. . . . They carry their own liability insurance and typically process and handle their own claims. In the past, the Banks have defended against tort claims directly, through private counsel, not government attorneys . . . ."

In short, the Internal Revenue Service is the collection agency for a private corporation. Is I.R.S. itself a private corporation? We don't have the answer, but we certainly do have a good question.

So, when you vote as a juror to acquit that innocent worker in court, you not only do so in the secure knowledge that you are not hurting the government—because it doesn't need his money—you also strike a blow to stop the illegal usurpation of the money power, and to restore that power to Congress, where it legally belongs.

15

WITHOUT THE INCOME TAX

Suppose we went all the way. Suppose we didn't just persuade our friends at I.R.S. to administer the law legally, but repealed it (assuming as always that the Sixteenth Amendment was actually ratified and that we actually have a law). If there were no income tax, how would the federal government finance itself?

We have a proposal we admit is quite revolutionary: Why not finance it legally, the way the Founding Fathers said it should be financed in the Constitution? Remember the Constitution? It's the law of the land. Anything the government does that violates the Constitution is null and void the moment it is done. Before the income tax, the federal government was almost always financed as the Constitution says it should be. So, our "revolutionary" proposal is really quite modest. It consists merely of restoring the system under law we were supposed to have all along.

The Founding Fathers based our system on The Bible. In Genesis 47:24, Joseph, Pharaoh's prime minister, tells the Egyptian people this: "And it shall come to pass in the increase, that ye shall give the fifth part unto Pharaoh, and four parts shall be your own, for seed of the field, and for your food and for them of your households, and for food for your little ones."

The Egyptians took the deal because they were starving. They sold themselves into slavery to eat, in exchange for which they had to pay Pharaoh a tax of only 20%. As slaves, they were allowed to keep 80% of their receipts. Notice also that the thing taxed was the "increase," the profit/gain. Were the authors of the Sixteenth Amendment familiar with that verse?

Remember that the Lord Himself requires only a tithe—only *ten* per cent. Indeed, in Exodus 30:15 the Lord spake unto Moses as follows: "The rich shall not give more, and the poor shall not give less than half a shekel, when they give an offering unto the Lord, to make an atonement for your souls." A shekel at the time was worth 88 cents. As you see, the Lord is considerably more generous than the Internal Revenue Service. Notice also that the Lord is not a Marxist. In the divine scheme of government, everyone—rich and poor—pays the same percentage.

The Bible says man is basically rotten and sinful; so, the Founding Fathers gave us the system of checks and balances. They didn't trust man. They didn't trust themselves. The checks and balances divided the power, to prevent the despicable creature they didn't trust from seizing it all. Because they believed man is rotten and sinful, the Founding Fathers were wary of con men. Jefferson is supposed to have said: "Let us hear no more of trust in man, but bind him down from mischief with the chains of the Constitution." Franklin is supposed to have told a woman outside Constitution Hall that the Fathers had given her a republic, "if you can keep it."

Today, sure enough, the system has been subverted. The old, satanic perversion according to which man runs things—creates himself—has been installed. We are told that man is basically a wonderful fellow who can be trusted, and that where any regeneration is necessary the government can achieve it. The belief that man is the "master of his fate" goes hand in glove with dictatorship, because such a belief finds expression in bigger and bigger government, the ultimate expression of which—total government—*is* dictatorship. So, today, children in government schools are taught that the government is god; that the government can solve all problems if only enough money is appropriated. The government schools have banished the Lord (they think) because there isn't room for two Gods in one church. The name of this satanic religion today is Humanism, which, according to its own *Manifestoes*, is a "faith," and its "church" is the government school.

How will the biblically based system of taxation work when it is restored? The first step would be to abolish the budget, which of course is a relatively new, Twentieth Century device (1921). What Congress calls a budget today is *not* a budget; it's a fraud, a farce. Congress calls it a budget to conceal that fraud; just as the Fed calls itself Federal to *conceal* the fact that it is a private corporation. A true budget is something you stick to, but many years of expensive experience teach that Washington totally ignores its so-called budget. The government spends as much as it can, without regard to what the budget says. The budget has become a license for bankruptcy. The mere existence of the budget creates an impetus to spend. Remember that before we had a "budget," before the income tax—when Congress appropriated only what was absolutely necessary—we not only had no debt; the big problem in the fiscal department was figuring out what to do with all the revenue pouring in.

The second step would be the abolition of the Fed and its unbacked, monopoly currency. Real money—precious metals—would be restored. The government would again collect most of its revenue from indirect taxes: duties, excises and imposts, just as the Founding Fathers said it should. However, the Founding Fathers were *realistic*. Since they knew that man was wallowing in sin, they were perfectly aware that emergencies would erupt—wars, for instance—at which times indirect taxes would be insufficient. So, they wisely made provision for the federal government *temporarily* to collect additional revenue at such times from direct taxes. Remember that direct taxes have always been war taxes.

In the system they devised—and which has financed our nation for most of its existence—who pays those direct taxes to Washington? As you will recall, the states pay them. How? The Constitution has the answer. Article One, Section Two tells us this: "Representatives and direct taxes shall be apportioned among the several states which may be concluded within this Union, according to their respective numbers." Each state, whatever its size, gets two Senators, but the number of Members it is entitled to in the House of Representatives is determined by the size of its population. That is the principal reason the census is taken every ten years: not to find out how many times your wife has been pregnant; not to find out how many bathrooms you have —but to find out where the people are; where they have moved in the previous ten years, in order to allot seats in the House.

In *An Economic Interpretation of the Constitution of the United States* (New York, Macmillan, 1972), Professor Charles A. Beard commented as follows, starting on page 170: ". . . The provision requiring the apportionment of direct taxes on a basis of population obviously implied that such taxes were to be viewed as a last resort when indirect taxes failed to provide the required revenue.

"With his usual acumen, Hamilton conciliates the freeholders and property owners in general by pointing out that they will not be called upon to support the national government by payments proportioned to their wealth. Experience has demonstrated that it is impracticable to raise any considerable sums by direct taxation. Even where the government is strong, as in Great Britain, resort must be had chiefly to indirect taxation. . . ."

What is the difference between taxation under the old Articles of Confederation and taxation under the new Constitution? Professor Beard says this: ". . . Real and personal property are thus assured a generous immunity from such burdens as Congress had attempted to impose under the Articles; taxes under the new system will, therefore, be less troublesome than under the old."

It is interesting to note that the government church (school) teaches today that the Constitution made the tax burden more onerous than it was under the Articles. As you see, Professor Beard, for one, says it was the other way around. Remember also that apportionment still governs all direct taxes—including the income tax. How does it work?

For instance, the State of New York for years had the biggest population. The 1940 census gave it forty-five Members of the House. Then it became the "land of taxes" and began to lose people. The 1980 census gave it only thirty-four seats in the House. Meanwhile, some of those people who had escaped from New York were going west, to California. Many of them arrived to find that "conservative" Republican Governor Ronald Reagan had buried California in taxes. Which reminds your obedient servant of the basic difference between the parties: The Democrats take us to bankruptcy haphazardly, but they do so with vigor. They're fun. With the Democrats in office, we go broke but we like it. For instance, for 1988 the Democrats fielded a squad of presidential candidates including billy goat Gary Hart, known as "Snow White and the Seven Dwarfs." Hart won the lasting gratitude of the nation by reentering the campaign just in time to rescue it from a dullness as deadly as a feminist convention. On the other hand, the Republicans would never dream of contributing such a public service. Mike Deaver is their idea of a man with a sense of humor. The Republicans take us to bankruptcy *efficiently*. They have a plan. They have a different style, but we get there just the same.

In 1940, the census gave California twenty-three Members of the House. By 1980, California had the nation's largest population by far. The 1980 census gave California forty-five seats in the House. The House of course has 435 seats, so California has 10.34% of them. Its forty-five seats are 10.34% of 435. Indiana has ten seats. They add up to 2.29% of 435. New York's thirty-four seats amount to 7.82% of 435. So it goes, down through the list of states. Each state's percentage of seats is allotted so as to correspond to its percentage of the nation's population.

Apportionment requires each state to pay the same percentage of a particular, direct levy to Washington, as the percentage of seats that state has in the House. Again, California has 10.34% of the seats. It would have to pay 10.34% of any direct tax, and so on. Indiana would have to pay 2.29%. New York would have to pay 7.82%, because it has 7.82% of the seats.

As you will recall, Chief Justice Fuller explained it as follows in *Pollock*, 158 U.S., starting at page 632: "Being direct, and therefore to be laid by apportionment, is there any real difficulty in doing so? Cannot congress, if the necessity exist of raising thirty, forty, or any other number of million dollars for the support of the government, in addition to the revenue from duties, imposts, and excises, apportion the quota of each state upon the basis of the census, and thus advise it of the payment which must be made, and proceed to assess that amount on all the real and personal property and the income of all persons in the state, and collect the same, if the state does not in the meantime assume and pay its quota and collect the amount according to its own system, and in its own way? . . . ."

Assume there is an emergency—a *true* emergency, not another no-win war concocted as an excuse to seize still more power—and that there is a shortfall between the amount the government genuinely needs to overcome it, and the amount Congress is able to raise by means of duties, excises and imposts; which are the indirect taxes the Constitution authorizes Congress to use. Having exhausted those indirect means, Congress is now allowed to use *direct* taxes.

Assume for ease in calculation that the amount of the shortfall is $100 billion. California would be required to pay $10,340,000,000 of that amount, which of course is 10.34%. New York's bill would be $7,820,000,000. Indiana's would be $2.29 billion, and so on. Washington sends the bill—the demand for payment—to the various state capitals. The states raise the money from their citizens, in whichever way they approve, and send it to Washington.

Notice that although the tax is direct, Washington is not taxing the people directly. In the apportionment process, the states act as buffers between the people and the federal government. Remember, this isn't some new system your reporter has devised. It's the system the Founding Fathers gave us. It's still the law.

Several important questions arise. First, isn't the system of the Founding Fathers old-fashioned? Suppose there's an emergency during the year. Suppose the British come again to get the guns. What happens? The answer is that Congress raises the necessary money by means of the same constitutional process, by means of a special levy, which it forwards to the states. Consider also that we would have a much better defense for much less money, because a Congress that has the sense to restore the law, to use apportionment, would also have the sense to force our allies around the world to pay their own way. Indeed, such a Congress would stop the suicidal, subversive insanity in which multinational corporations, allegedly American, make billions by sending our latest technology—even technology with military applications—to Communist-occupied Russia. For the facts on the subject, even including the serial numbers, see the monumental work of Dr. Antony Sutton, such as *The Best Enemy Money Can Buy* (Liberty House Press, Billings, Montana, 1986).

Second, what happens if a state fails to pay its bill? In such a case, the federal government intervenes directly. Federal tax collectors with assessments would show up at your doors. Here we see another manifestation of the genius of the Founding Fathers, in that this arrangement gives state officials an irresistible motive to pay, because angry citizens—who know where they live—would blame *them* for any federal intervention.

Third, isn't the apportionment machinery cumbersome? Again, yes it is, and that fact is not an accident. It was *designed to be cumbersome*. The Founding Fathers made it cumbersome to underline the fact that the federal government is permitted to resort to direct taxes only *temporarily*. So, they made it possible, but painful and difficult. They did so to express their distrust of man, and therefore of temporal government. Today, our leaders say, "Trust us." The Founding Fathers reply: "In God we trust. All others pay cash."

There are some remarkable advantages to this system of genius. For instance, it would reduce the Internal Revenue Service to the relatively small size necessary to administer the alcohol and tobacco taxes, the taxes on tires and gambling, et cetera. Many of our friends now at I.R.S. would no doubt drift into similar work under new management; as consultants to the Mafia, for instance, or as free-lance pimps. No more children would be taken hostage. The working woman would suffer no more withholding or W-4s; no more sizeable chunk confiscated from her check. No more waitresses with their pockets turned out. No more workingmen thrown into prison. No more automobiles towed from your driveways. The entire, totalitarian structure would be dismantled.

Also in the Founding Fathers' system, you would see federal spending fall, to a level so low it would amaze you today. You would find out how *little* the federal government really does need. Why and how would this miracle occur?

Today, your Congressman is no longer your representative to Washington. Instead, he is Washington's representative to you. With some outstanding exceptions, he's a federal errand boy (or girl). His job is to pacify and confuse you in Washington's behalf. So it is that your typical Congressman says he's against destructive spending, but votes for it. When you complain, the "action" he takes consists of sending your letter for response to the agency you complain about. By spending as much as he can get away with, he wins the plaudits of the national press and his Washington bosses. He continues to use the House dining room, the House barber shop, the House gymnasium, the House junket, the House bimbos, et cetera. His motive is to spend. The reason is that Washington has usurped the power to tax you directly without apportionment. The reason is that the powers of the states—which created the federal government—have thereby been emasculated.

However, the restoration of the system the Founding Fathers gave us, would see the states restored as true governmental entities, rather than the mere lines on the map they are today. The *federal* government would be restored to what the Founding Fathers intended: It would again be the *federal* agent of the states. Most of the money Washington now takes, would be left in the states where it belongs.

Congressmen who vote to increase federal spending, would thereby be voting to increase their state's tax liability, which their state treasury would have to pay. Remember that the bigger states would have to pay more than the others. When Congressmen who do vote for gargantuan federal spending—via direct, special levies—go home, they would find not just bamboozled citizens who don't know their voting records, but angry state officials who do. Those state officials would have to raise the money the Congressmen vote to spend. Remember that we're talking now about real money—gold and silver—not monopoly Federal Reserve currency. The state officials would have to go to the people to raise it. The people in turn would become angry at those officials, whose homes and offices are not far away in Washington, but around the corner. That anger would threaten reappointment or reelection to lucrative state jobs. Remember that if those state fiscal officials decide instead to do nothing at all, federal officials would collect the tax; for which the state officials would also be blamed.

How happy do you imagine those state tax officials would be with Congressmen who return from Washington boasting in private—as they do now—about how much so-called federal money they have voted to spend? Such Congressmen would be voting in effect to put those state tax officials on the spot. They would be dramatically proving to the people who pay the taxes, that so-called "free handouts" are not free, are quite expensive; that "There Ain't No Such Thing As A Free Lunch" (TANSTAAFL).

Do you begin to appreciate anew the incredible genius of the Founding Fathers? Your Congressman would quickly begin to see a choice between a balanced budget and lynching. His new motive would be to cut spending; to reduce taxes. The system of checks and balances the Fathers gave us would be largely restored. No longer would you see milk drained from your babies' bottles to study the sex life of the newt; or, to send high-technology to the Soviets. No longer would you see a so-called farm program in which the more farmers the government drives off the land; the bigger the Department of Agriculture gets; the more money it spends and the more people it hires. No longer would you see federal officials fight to give billions to the International Monetary Fund—to save the multinational banks—while millions of Americans are driven out of work.

The restoration of constitutional taxation would also bring an end to deficit spending, because the abolition of Beardsley Ruml's "pay as you go" withholding would restore truly pay-as-you-go government. The government's bills would be paid every year. There would at last be an end to the government's suicidal debt, and to the suicidal interest on that debt, which is now the third largest item in the federal budget, and amounts to about as much as it cost to run the entire federal government—including welfare and the military—for a full year, as recently as about 1970. No longer would we be mortgaging our great grandchildren's future. No longer would we have to pay interest to the secret government of the United States for the right to use our own money.

Since the restoration of constitutional taxation would also restore constitutional spending, a substantial reason for inflation would be removed, because the government would no longer have a spurious "need" to sell interest-bearing securities to the Federal Reserve, which then authorizes the printing of counterfeit, paper currency to pay the government's bills. Inflation is of course the name of that process.

Remember that we by no means are talking about some "pie in the sky" proposal. We're talking about something very practical, something that worked as designed during most of the existence of our country, until it was subverted; something that was new when the Founding Fathers devised it, and still is. Again, the incredible fact is that the system they gave us hasn't been repealed. It's still on the books, as much the law as it was when the Constitution took effect. It has been usurped. All you need do to resurrect it is invoke the law.

It can be done. It is being done as you read this, by heroes and heroines so far unsung by the Prostitute National Press, a few of whom we have mentioned here—Americans who are demanding their unalienable rights in court. However, to be an effective fighter in this battle to restore the law, you must protect yourself. If you lose your home and property, you would be making no greater sacrifice than the men who signed the Declaration of Independence—probably less—but your effectiveness could be diminished. There are perfectly legal things one can do to prevent this, and we turn to them now.

16

HOW TO PROTECT YOUR PROPERTY

The first thing you must do is learn the advantages of separate ownership. This doesn't mean your property goes anywhere; in fact, it doesn't move an inch. It does mean that your home, for instance, is beyond the reach of the extortionists. Today, for public consumption, our friends at I.R.S. try to create the impression that going "offshore" is "illegal." On the contrary, the multinational banks and other billionaire investors have been doing it legally for years. Congress wants them to do it, and has passed laws for the purpose. How often do you hear that the executives of a Fortune 500 company have been jailed for offshore dealing? Our friends at I.R.S. began to complain of "abuse" only when individuals learned how to use the techniques of the "establishment." So, again we ask: Is it legal?

On August 28, 1985, in the first session of the 99th Congress, the Permanent Subcommittee on Investigations of the Committee on Governmental Affairs, of the U.S. Senate, ordered the printing of Report 99-130, entitled, *Crime and Secrecy: The Use of Offshore Banks and Companies*. Buried all the way back in an appendix, starting on page 143, is a section headed, "Legitimate Uses of Offshore Centers," which is worth quoting at length: "It is essential to understand who uses offshore financial centers and the reasons why, since legislation designed to counter the abuses of offshore banks and companies must be tailored to avoid disruption of the legitimate markets.

"The primary beneficiaries of offshore financial centers, particularly through legitimate tax advantages, are multinational corporations. . . ." "Legitimate markets," and "multinational corporations," are polite ways of saying "establishment monopoly."

The report says there are three main ways offshore corporations are used to reduce taxes: profit creation, profit diversion and profit extraction. For instance, companies established in low tax havens can create profit by manufacturing or substantially transforming goods for sale or use elsewhere. If such sales are not made for a related party, the company usually will not be considered a foreign based sales company, and the profit derived therefrom will escape taxation under Subpart F. This was what the De Lorean car company did. Is that at least one of the reasons the government destroyed the company and tried twice—unsuccessfully—to put De Lorean in prison? Was the real problem the fact that De Lorean apparently is not a member of the tight, little group? Did he borrow from the "right" banks or perhaps use too much private money?

In profit diversion, taxable profits are diverted from a high tax country to a low tax country: ". . . Major companies use controlled foreign corporations to implement profit-diversion. Assets that are transferred to these controlled corporations can under certain circumstances, be repatriated as loans to U.S. entities. An advantage of this practice is the maintenance of anonymity. Companies also divert income to such entities as holding companies and sales companies. By retaining substantial stock ownership, holding companies may, again under certain circumstances, be used as investment vehicles or as conduits for the collection of income in the terms of dividends, interest, royalties or licensing fees. The controlled company can then distribute funds to the parent, reinvest, or lend to affiliates."

For instance, in October, 1982, McDermott International merged with its Panamanian subsidiary, which acquired all the shares of the parent company, to "reduce taxes on foreign earnings and improve operating flexibility." There is also *Hospital Corporation of America v. Commissioner*, 81 Tax Court 520 (1983), in which we learn that H.C.A. won a contract to manage a hospital in

Saudi Arabia, and transferred the contract to its new Cayman Islands subsidiary. Our friends at I.R.S. argued that the profits derived therefrom could be blamed on H.C.A., but the Tax Court found the arrangement legitimate.

Taxes can also be reduced when a subsidiary in a low tax country charges management fees, royalties, interest and so on, against profits created by its parent in a high tax country.

The Senate report also says this: "Another traditional way for a multinational corporation to use an offshore company is as a 'financial vehicle.' For example, major banks use offshore financial centers to minimize taxes on loans. Officials at Chase Manhattan Bank explained that Chase has offices in 75 countries and makes loans in over 125 countries. . . . As a matter of policy, Chase tries to book loans to their customers in countries where taxes are the lowest in an effort to reduce foreign taxes."

You can do all these things, adapted to your own circumstances. Remember, the thing that is illegal is tax evasion, which means lying on a tax form. Tax avoidance—in which one takes advantage of low-tax breaks Congress has made available—is perfectly legal. In fact, taxes are not the only reason to go offshore: "In addition to accepted legal techniques of minimizing taxes, offshore centers offer users privacy, freedom from currency controls and banking regulations, and higher interest rates on deposits with lower rates on borrowing. . . ."

If all these advantages are legal for Chase Manhattan and David Rockefeller, they are legal, period. Section 957 of the Internal Revenue Code defines a "controlled" foreign corporation as a foreign corporation in which a U.S. shareholder owns more than 50% of the voting power. If a certain U.S. shareholder—you, perhaps—owns *less* than 50% of the voting power, that foreign corporation is not "controlled," and legally escapes tax treatment as such. It can legally own property and hire someone to manage it. Our friends at I.R.S. can not seize property from someone who is not liable in the lien.

Yes, we know your mother didn't raise you to be a janitor, but, again, the name of the game these days isn't ownership, it's control. Today, not enough hard-working Americans realize that. What counts today isn't who owns something, but who gets to use it; who gets to enjoy it. In many cases today, ownership is a disadvantage. Ownership merely establishes you as a target for the predatory beasts who control our government.

Here is proof that you can operate offshore as well as Chase Manhattan: On November 5, 1979, Special Agent Donald Jensen, of the Tax Rebellion, wrote a memo to the Chief, Criminal Investigation Division, in Seattle, in which he discussed "the promotion of a tax shelter scheme that is designed to utilize foreign trusts to eliminate income and estate taxes on income generated by an individual taxpayer's business or profession."

At page eleven of the memo, Jensen wrote this: "Successful prosecution of this case will result in newsworthy, precedent setting case law necessary in this abusive tax shelter area. . . . Knowledge that upper income taxpayers are not paying taxes because of this type of situation only pushes other taxpayers to become a part of the tax resistance movement. . . .

"Knowledgeable attorneys and accountants are incensed at the inability of the IRS to expediently counteract such schemes. Our apparent inaction has caused many of the attorneys and accountants embarrassment, and in some cases, to lose clients. . . . If this program is allowed to continue without strong action by the IRS, the results on voluntary compliance could be disasterous (sic)."

Notice that there was a public relations aspect to the case. There always is. Each selected case is an important part of the Reign of Terror. Jensen wanted to imprison the people who are teaching Americans how to go offshore; how to use tax advantages made available by Congress. Did Nelson Rockefeller, who paid zero taxes, go to prison? No, he became Vice President.

Why was Jensen demanding action? He was demanding it because bar association monopolists—lawyers—were suffering embarrassment, when clients learned without their help what the law really says. He was demanding action because those lawyers—lawyers like the ones Godfrey Lehman confronted in San Francisco—were losing clients and money. So, the overinflated claptrap our friends at I.R.S. extrude about your "fair share" is nothing more than that. There is no elevated, moral crusade here. Our friends at I.R.S. are merely acting as enforcers for a gang of shysters who enjoy a lucrative monopoly supported by guns. This is a tawdry story Hollywood has made many times about the Mafia.

The *Dahlstrom* case (83-1297) went to court and the defendants were convicted, although the government's own witness, Karl Kroque, testified that the trusts were indeed valid, legal entities. In September, 1983, the Ninth Circuit overturned the convictions, and on May 14, 1984, the Supreme Court denied the government certiorari. In other words, Dahlstrom was right. If arranged properly, it is perfectly legal to go "offshore."

On March 9, 1984, Assistant U.S. Attorney Thomas Flynn filed a petition in district court in Sacramento, in which he told Judge Raul Ramirez that a tax target was doing as follows: "2. That the Internal Revenue Service has determined that the defendant has liquidated substantially all of her real estate holdings and other assets including selling her residence and the Century 21 Real Estate franchise that she once owned.

"3. That the Internal Revenue Service has information that defendant has placed some of these assets in off-shore trusts beyond the reach of the United States."

Obviously, the lady did not move the real estate, which must mean that the real estate, although still here, is protected. Notice that the prosecutor himself is complaining that he can't touch her property.

On November 16, 1984, a remarkable story appeared on the front page of *The Los Angeles Daily Journal*, which is the daily newspaper of the legal profession in that city. Written by Charlotte Low, it is worth quoting at length: "In a 2-1 decision Thursday, the Ninth U.S. Circuit Court of Appeal approved a controversial arrangement that allowed a couple to avoid more than $2.5 million in taxes by transferring stock to an offshore trust."

It seems that in 1971, Sidney and Vera Stern established a trust in the Cayman Islands, and gave it about 130,000 shares of Teledyne. The stock was virtually the only asset of the trust. The trustee was an affiliate of a company in the Bahamas, which promised to pay them lifetime annuities. The Sterns retained the power to change the trustee and to give financial advice to the trust. They could also borrow from it freely. The Tax Court ruled against the Sterns, but the Ninth Circuit overruled.

Charlotte Low writes as follows: "The Ninth Circuit's action in overturning that ruling is significant because it suggests there are ways taxpayers can legally use foreign trusts to defer or reduce taxes on significant portions of their income.

"As long as the taxpayers meet certain 'formalities' barring them from directly controlling the trust's assets and the annuity payments are not tied to the income the trust generates, transfers can be 'valid sales in exchange for annuities,' Judge Joseph T. Sneed, a former tax professor at Stanford University, wrote for the Ninth Circuit majority." Judge Sneed held as follows: "*Trusts may not be recharacterized merely because the transactions were part of a prearranged plan designed to minimize tax liability or because the transferred property constituted the bulk of the trust assets.*" (emphasis added)

The question arises: If our friends at I.R.S. are so hostile to all this, why don't they instruct their sissies in the Congress to change the law; to declare offshore illegal? Remember that the same law that governs you governs Chase Manhattan. If offshore were made illegal, it would be illegal for Rockefeller, too. Remember also that the people who run Chase and other multinational banks are the same, wonderful people who run the Federal Reserve, the protection of whose monopoly paper currency is the main purpose of our friends at I.R.S. There is no chance that they will bite the hands that feed them. There is also the fact that, were offshore advantages made illegal, foreign investment in our country would be crippled. If foreigners were to stop buying a considerable share of the U.S. government paper they buy now, either you or the Fed would have to buy it, or it would remain unbought; in which case the subversive effects of the Federal Reserve inflation would become even more apparent than they already are, bringing the day of doom for its currency closer even quicker. The Fed resembles more and more the husband who has cheated so much, he can't even remember what lies he told his wife.

You will probably be surprised, and no doubt delighted, to learn how easy it is to go offshore. Should you wish to do so, your obedient servant can put you together with the nation's leading consultants on the subject, who operate in strict conformity to federal law and are ready to take you by the hand. For information on the legal use of foreign entities to reduce taxes and limit liability, call (714) 980-3165, or write your reporter at P.O. Box 1220, Alta Loma, California, 91701.

For many years, the collectivists have been encouraging incorporation. They even have been demanding that churches incorporate, and many churches, deluded by the deception that there is no other way, have done so. The problem is that incorporation turns the entity incorporated into a ward of the state. However, there is a way to enjoy the advantages of incorporation, without suffering the disadvantages. You can form a business trust. Indeed, before the ascendancy of the collectivists in our country, the trust was routine. You will recall, no doubt, that Teddy Roosevelt gained fame not only as a "rough rider" but as a "trust buster." The trust is the private, non-governmental version of the corporation. It has suffered official disfavor—and you may not have heard of it—because the collectivists don't like it. They prefer monopoly. *They* have trusts, but say they are illegal for *you*. However, trusts are perfectly viable and can work for you. Again, for more information call that number or write that address. Many churches, newly awakened to the danger, have been regaining their independence by disincorporation. If your church would like to do so, the American Coalition of Unregistered Churches will help. Dr. Greg Dixon, the Christian warrior who is pastor of the mammoth Indianapolis Baptist Temple, is founder and director of A.C.U.C., and you may write him at P.O. Box 1224, Indianapolis, Indiana, 46206.

As you know, people in business take advantage of many legal deductions and allowances. If you are a working man or woman still in the slave system, why don't you? You can conduct a legitimate business after work and on weekends right from your home, and enjoy the same tax treatment as General Motors. Again, it's so easy it will astound you, and there are people who can show you how to do it. If you already run a small business, you also need to know that—for you—employees are as antiquated as ownership. The same employees who, fine people though they probably are, nevertheless involuntarily cause you grief by way of unemployment insurance, Social Security, medical and dental, controls and endless paper work, will miraculously be regenerated as unalloyed blessings, when you make them independent contractors.

You can also protect yourself with proper use of the bankruptcy laws, despite what you are told. The Socialist billionaires do it, legally, all the time. Why shouldn't you? Among the financial warriors to whom we have access is one of the nation's half a dozen or so top wizards in every nuance of bankruptcy law, who will tailor a bankruptcy program to your specific needs, if you need it. Shouldn't you use all the help you can get?

Finally, there is the use of foreign insurance, the remarkable possibilities of which our colleagues will be happy to explain.

A word of warning must be said. Remember that, without exception, everything we propose is in strict conformity to U.S. law. We would not even consider getting involved in something that isn't. If you decide to call that number, or write that address, please do not propose that we help you do anything illegal, such as backdating documents, etc. Should you do so, you run the serious risks of hearing a couple of clicks and a dial tone; of receiving no answer to your letters; or of being torn to pieces by several pit bulls trained for the purpose. You also face a visit from several large, impassive men with pistols from the Federal Bureau of Investigation—whom we shall certainly call immediately, pursuant to our duty under the law against misprision of felony. Are there any questions? Please don't waste our valuable time!

Indeed, should you do so anyway, despite everything we have said to deter you, your illegal proposal would be all the proof we need that you are a Special Agent of the Internal Revenue Service. We would immediately lock up our silverware, such as it is, and our daughter.

As we have seen, our friends at I.R.S. maintain expanding records about every aspect of your life; even including some things you may not know about yourself. You may want to know what they know, and you are entitled to that information under the Freedom Of Information Act. To learn how to use it, write the nation's foremost non-governmental expert on the subject: Wayne Bentson, Western Information Network, Star Route, Box 71, Payson, AZ 85541; or call him at (602) 474-3339. For a modest fee, he will help you discover what kind of person our friends at I.R.S. think you are.

Somewhere along the line, you may need legal help. While there are some good, even magnificent, attorneys, most members of the bar association monopoly by far are too terrified of our friends at I.R.S. to provide it—even if they understood what you are talking about; which they probably don't because they are victims of law school. They are victims of their own monopoly, afraid of losing their meal ticket—the license that is the yoke of their enslavement. On the other hand, the legal heroes we mentioned do a good job, but you may not be able to afford it, and they may be too snowed under to take your case. For reliable help (not legal advice) from an independent paralegal who knows much more on the subject than most attorneys—and will pass it on at relatively modest cost—write Leo "The Lion" Masters, 9832 Flower, Suite 103, Bellflower, CA 90706; or call him at (213) 925-7395.

The income tax and the Federal Reserve are of course just two legs on the same bug. The bug is the conspiracy for world government, the goal of which is precisely that. In such a system, the United States would no longer be an independent nation, but a wide spot in the road, not even lines on a map. You would be reduced to a pack animal for the multinational corporations. Among the other instrumentalities of that scheme—the other legs on the bug—is the present disarmament and indefensibility of the United States (yes, even under Reagan); the illegal alien explosion; the war on South Africa; and the consolidation, with Reagan's acquiescence, of Soviet power in Nicaragua. To understand how all these legs, and others, fit together, we recommend that you investigate and join an organization that addresses them: The American Freedom Movement, founded by the late Gary Allen, and run today by Charles Provan, M.D., the distinguished Pennsylvania physician. Write Dr. Provan at the following address: American Freedom Movement, P.O. Box 309, Irwin, PA 15642. On the West Coast, call or write the American Information Network, 2521-F N. Grand, Suite 780, Santa Ana, CA 92701; (714) 385-1776.

Your reporter is available to speak on any of these subjects. For information, write or call us. Indeed, do so in any event, to get aboard the class action suit we are preparing.

Finally, the best protection is total victory. With total victory, protection would be unnecessary. Remember that Samuel excoriated Saul because he hadn't gone far enough—because he hadn't exterminated the enemy as the Lord had commanded. So far, we have been talking about the pressing need to restore the law on the books, the law that is. We have been saying with some prolixity that, since we do have an income tax—assuming as always that the Sixteenth Amendment was actually ratified—it must be administered legally.

However, when that is done, there would still be monumental problems. If our friends at I.R.S. were not confiscating a dime of the working woman's wages, Americans would still be investing substantial time and money in so-called tax shelters and "loopholes"—even under the Reagan "reforms"—the purpose of which is not to produce goods, but to avoid taxes. This distorts and cripples our economy. Indeed, now that investors have been suckered into surrendering many of those shelters with the bait of lower taxes, we believe that the tax increases Congress is muttering about could produce a shelter frenzy unlike any seen before. By now you have probably discovered that the tax "cut" itself is largely a mirage.

Question: Why don't we restore the original American system; the one the Founding Fathers gave us; the one which financed our country for most of its existence, and with which we won all our wars—the one without the income tax? With the restoration of the American system, investors would no longer have the incentive to protect themselves. They would again invest *all* their time and money in production, in profit-making enterprise; in American factories, rather than Cayman Islands banks. The present creeping reduction in your standard of living would cease. Production, which is the key to prosperity and jobs, would explode. That explosion would produce more, not less, business for Certified Public Accountants. How do we arrange all this?

We do it with the Liberty Amendment, which is a proposed amendment to the U.S. Constitution. The Liberty Amendment would repeal the income tax, by repealing the Sixteenth Amendment. It has four short sections:

Section One: The government of the United States shall not engage in any business, professional, commercial, financial or industrial enterprise except as specified in the Constitution.

Section Two: The constitution or laws of any State, or the laws of the United States shall not be subject to the terms of any foreign or domestic agreement which would abrogate this amendment.

Section Three: The activities of the United States Government which violate the intent and purposes of this amendment shall, within a period of three years from the date of the ratification of this amendment, be liquidated and the properties and facilities shall be sold.

Section Four: Three years after the ratification of this amendment the sixteenth article of amendments to the Constitution of the United States shall stand repealed and thereafter Congress shall not levy taxes on personal incomes, estates, and/or gifts.

In other words, the Liberty Amendment would bring to a screeching halt the hundreds of things the federal government does in competition with private business. It is insanity, or worse, to permit the federal government to compete—unfairly—with the people. The abolition of such Socialist "competition" would restore true competition. Our Socialist billionaires no longer would be able to tax away the profits you have accumulated to compete with them, while their own estates are protected in trusts and foundations. There would be no more income tax. No more billion-dollar giveaways to bail out the banks. No more Internal

Revenue Service. Congress would instead control the collection of alcohol, tobacco, and other excise taxes. Socialism for the super-rich would stop.

You may never have heard of it, because the media predictably give it no coverage, but the legislatures of nine states have already endorsed the Liberty Amendment. When the Indiana legislature did so, in 1981, your intrepid correspondent happened by chance to be travelling through the state, on a speaking tour. We couldn't even find anyone in Indianapolis, the state capital, who knew for sure what the legislature had done. We found out only because the man who introduced your reporter at our meeting in that city, was the member of the legislature who had sponsored the Amendment. The Socialist billionaires who control the major media don't want you to know. The address of the Liberty Amendment Committee is P.O. Box 2386, El Cajon, CA, 92021.

When you have set all this in motion, you are ready to do what must be done. If you need any more inspiration, turn the page.

17

WHAT GOD SAYS

As Inquisition police for the satanic cult of government, our friends at I.R.S. worship their own god and dare ours—the real and only—to do something about it; which no doubt He will, when His divine sense of humor is finally overtaxed.

Meanwhile, they attempt to neutralize believers by expounding a perverted version of Romans 13, with a verve that beggars the perfervid energy of the most lunatic punk rocker, and—amazing to relate—many churches support their interpretation. Our friends at I.R.S. say Romans 13 proves we should pay all the taxes they say we should. Indeed, we are told by extrapolation that Romans 13 justifies just about everything government does, because "the powers that be are ordained of God." (Chances are you will find that these same satan-worshippers who swear by Romans 13, also denounce Paul, its author, as a "male chauvinist pig.")

Does this mean we should have excused Nazi atrocities? The question is legitimate, despite the inevitable protestations of our friends at I.R.S. that they speak only of taxes. The principle they invoke says that the government is always right. Well, is it? Is God a Nazi? Does God support the Reds? Should the Founding Fathers have rebelled?

What you and your reporter have to say on the subject could only be laughable and useless. Fortunately, however, we don't need to rely on puny sinners like ourselves. We don't have to guess. The Lord makes the meaning of Romans 13 clear throughout His Book. Remember that all the parts of The Bible fit harmoniously into the whole. Each is related to the others. The "contradictions" the intellectuals claim to see are "contradictions" they *want* to see. They make doubting Thomas look like a disciple of Jim Jones.

What, then, does God say? What is the context to which Romans 13 relates?

Adam and Eve were the government in the Garden of Eden, commissioned by God to obey certain rules. They disobeyed and were kicked out. Pharaoh, the government, told the Hebrew midwives to kill the Hebrew boy babies. They disobeyed; indeed, they lied to him about it, and God "made them houses." Rahab the harlot hid Joshua's spies, and lied to the King of Jericho about it. The conquering Hebrews spared her and all her house, and "she dwelleth in Israel even unto this day; because she hid the messengers, which Joshua sent to spy out Jericho."

In Judges 3, starting at verse 12, we learn that the children of Israel did evil again, so the Lord made Eglon, king of Moab, dictator over them for eighteen years. At last, however, they cried out, so the Lord sent them a deliverer named Ehud. Eglon, who was very fat, was the government, but Ehud stuck a dagger in his belly. The fat closed around it, so that Eglon's people couldn't figure out why he was dead; and Ehud told the Hebrews that "the LORD hath delivered your enemies the Moabites into your hand."

After Ehud died, however, the children of Israel again did evil, and the Lord sold them into the hand of Jabin, king of Canaan, who was the government. Sisera was the general of Jabin's armies, but when he fell into the hands of Jael, Moses's mother-in-law, she "took a nail of the tent, and took an hammer in her hand, and went softly unto him, and smote the nail into his temples, and fastened it into the ground: for he was fast asleep and weary. So he died."

Did God punish Jael for this? On the contrary, Judges 4, verses 23 and 24, tells us this: "So, God subdued on that day Jabin the king of Canaan before the children of Israel. And the hand of the children of Israel prospered, and prevailed against Jabin the king of Canaan, until they had destroyed Jabin king of Canaan." In other words, the Lord worked through Jael and the children of Israel to destroy the government, because it had transgressed.

We're still in Judges, where we learn that Abimelech, a son of Gideon, killed seventy of his brothers in order to become king (government). In Chapter Nine, starting at verse 53, The Book tells us this: "And a certain woman cast a piece of a millstone upon Abimelech's head, and all to brake his skull. (54) Then he called hastily unto the young man his armour-bearer, and said unto him, Draw thy sword, and slay me, that men say not of me, A woman slew him. And his young man thrust him through, and he died. (55) And when the men of Israel saw that Abimelech was dead, they departed every man unto his place."

Now, what did the Lord think about this? There's no mystery (56): "Thus God rendered the wickedness of Abimelech, which he did unto his father, in slaying his seventy brethren: (57) And all the evil of the men of Shechem did God render upon their heads: and upon them came the curse of Jotham the son of Jerubbaal."

Remember that Abimelech was the king (the government).

In First Samuel 8, we learn that when Samuel was old, he made his sons judges over Israel. God tells us this in verse 3: "And his sons walked not in his ways, but turned aside after lucre, and took bribes, and perverted judgment." Needless to say, the Lord was not pleased.

The Lord made Saul king, and Samuel withdrew. In First Samuel 12, starting at verse 3, Samuel asks the people this: "Behold, here I am: witness against me before the LORD, and before his anointed: whose ox have I taken? or whose ass have I taken? or whom have I defrauded? whom have I oppressed? or of whose hand have I received any bribe to blind mine eyes therewith? and I will restore it you."

The people agreed that Samuel had neither defrauded them, nor oppressed them, nor taken any bribes; to which Samuel demanded they testify with the Lord as witness. Notice how important Samuel thought it was to establish that he had conducted his administration in obedience to the commandments of the Lord.

Indeed, in the same chapter (12), Samuel tells the people this, in verse 14: "If ye will fear the LORD, and serve him, and obey his voice, and not rebel against the commandment of the LORD, then shall both ye and also the king that reigneth over you continue following the LORD your God:" Samuel concludes as follows in verse 25: "But if ye shall still do wickedly, ye shall be consumed, both ye and your king."

In First Samuel, Chapter 15, the Lord tells Saul through Samuel to exterminate the Amalekites, man, woman, child and animals. However, Saul preserves the best of the animals and Agag, the Amalekite king. The Lord repents that he ever made Saul king and Samuel cries all night. Samuel takes a sword and cuts Agag in pieces. Saul is out of favor ever after. The Lord chooses David to be king. Today, we not only don't cut off the Soviets, we give them high military technology.

Jonathan and Michal deceived Saul about David. Should they have delivered David to Saul—the government—and certain death?

By Second Samuel 23, David is delivering his last words, and says this at verse 3: "The God of Israel said, the Rock of Israel spake to me, He that ruleth over men must be just, ruling in the fear of God."

Now let's move to First Kings 2, verses 3 and 4, in which David, soon to die, instructs Solomon, his son and successor, on his duties as king: "And keep the charge of the LORD thy God, to walk in his ways, to keep his statutes, and his commandments, and his judgments, and his testimonies, as it is written in the law of Moses, that thou mayest prosper in all that thou doest, and whithersoever thou turnest thyself: That the LORD may continue his word which he spake concerning me, saying, If thy children take heed to their way, to walk before me in truth with all their heart and with all their soul, there shall not fail thee (said he) a man on the throne of Israel."

Still in First Kings, Chapter 9, starting at verse 4, the Lord Himself appears to Solomon and says: "And if thou wilt walk before me, as David thy father walked, in integrity of heart, and in uprightness, to do according to all that I have commanded thee, and wilt keep my statutes and my judgments: (5) Then I will establish the throne of thy kingdom upon Israel for ever, as I promised to David thy father, saying, There shall not fail thee a man upon the throne of Israel. (6) But if ye shall at all turn from following me, ye or your children, and will not keep my commandments and my statutes which I have set before you, but go and serve other gods, and worship them: (7) Then will I cut off Israel out of the land which I have given them; and this house, which I have hallowed for my name, will I cast out of my sight; and Israel shall be a proverb and a byword among all people:"

Further along in First Kings, we run into Ahab, who, as king, was the government. He was also a notorious sleazebag. Ahab wanted a vineyard owned by Naboth the Jezreelite. Naboth refused to sell, so Ahab had a tantrum, "laid him down upon his bed, and turned away his face, and would eat no bread."

Jezebel, his wife, arranged for a couple of hit men to murder Naboth, and told her husband to take the vineyard; after which the Lord, through Elijah, told Ahab in 21:19 that ". . . In the place where dogs licked the blood of Naboth shall dogs lick thy blood, even thine." Indeed, in Second Kings 9, the Lord arranged for the dogs to eat everything of Jezebel but her skull, her feet and the palms of her hands. Whether or not the dogs were pit bulls, we don't know, but inspired by the Lord and by Elijah, they certainly were thorough. "And the carcase of Jezebel shall be as dung upon the face of the field in the portion of Jezreel; so that they shall not say, This is Jezebel." Remember that Jezebel, as queen, was First Lady, but that fact didn't seem to impress the Lord even a little bit.

Now, let's go to First Chronicles 21: 6-8. David, the king, was a man after the Lord's own heart, but was also a murderer and adulterer, among other failings. Now he decides to number the people, and commands Joab, the general of his armies, to conduct the numbering.

"But Levi and Benjamin counted he not among them: for the king's word was abominable to Joab. And God was displeased with this thing; therefore he smote Israel. And David said unto God, I have sinned greatly, because I have done this thing: but now, I beseech thee, do away the iniquity of thy servant; for I have done very foolishly."

The Lord did so, but not before he had destroyed seventy thousand men because of David's transgression.

Shadrach, Meshach, Abednego and Daniel refused to bow down to false gods, thereby brazenly disobeying explicit government orders. Did the Lord punish them? On the contrary, He turned the lions into lambs and the fiery furnace into air conditioning.

In Micah 2: 1-2, the Lord says this: "Woe to them that devise iniquity, and work evil upon their beds! when the morning is light, they practise it, because it is in the power of their hand. And they covet fields, and take them by violence; and houses, and take them away: so they oppress a man and his house, even a man and his heritage."

Remember that Ahab—the government—had the power to do that in his hand, and did it to Naboth. Our friends at I.R.S. do it now.

Indeed, in Zephaniah 3: 3-4, the Lord condemns perversion in both government and church: "Her princes within her are roaring lions; her judges are evening wolves; they gnaw not the bones till the morrow. Her prophets are light and treacherous persons: her priests have polluted the sanctuary, they have done violence to the law."

In short, says the Lord, the government is corrupt, the judges are corrupt and the preachers are corrupt. They break the law.

Finally, in Malachi 3:5, the Lord condemns "those that oppress the hireling in his wages," which needs no explanation.

Please bear in mind that we have given you only a few examples throughout the Old Testament. There are many more. Now, what does the New Testament say?

In Matthew 20, starting at verse 25, Jesus says this: "Ye know that the princes of the Gentiles exercise dominion over them, and they that are great exercise authority upon them. But it shall not be so among you: but whosoever will be great among you, let him be your minister; And whosoever will be chief among you, let him be your servant." In Matthew 23:11, Jesus repeats this: "But he that is greatest among you shall be your servant."

So, what does The Bible tell us here about government and God? Yes, the government, like the church, is ordained of God. Also like the church—and like you and your reporter—the government is required to obey God's laws. God is not a Nazi. God does not authorize government to break any law and commit any atrocity it likes. When government nevertheless does so, it is severely chastised. God designed government to be a servant, not a master.

The Founding Fathers based our system on The Bible. What did they say? Jefferson, for instance, said, "Resistance to tyrants is obedience to God." In other words, when government is bad, evil, our duty to God requires that we resist it. Indeed, in a letter to Colonel Smith, dated November 13, 1787, Jefferson wrote as follows of Shays's Rebellion: ". . . God forbid we should ever be twenty years without such a rebellion. . . . What country can preserve its liberties, if its rulers are not warned from time to time, that this people preserve the spirit of resistance? Let them take arms. . . . The tree of liberty must be refreshed from time to time with the blood of patriots and tyrants. . . ."

Indeed, what did the preachers say? J. T. Headley has the answer, in *The Chaplains and Clergy of the Revolution* (New York, Charles Scribner, 1864, p. 17): ". . . In every quiet little valley and sequestered nook in New England, the pastor had taught the doctrines of freedom, and preached the duty of resistance to oppression."

On May 29, 1771, John Tucker, pastor of the First Church of Newbury, in Massachusetts, preached the annual "election sermon" before the Governor, the House of Representatives and His Majesty's Council. At page twenty six, Headley says this: ". . . While acknowledging that government is the work of man, he declares it derives all its powers from God, and hence its enactments must be in accordance with his will, and boldly asserts that 'the people as well as their rulers are the proper judges of the civil constitution they are under and of their own rights and principles.' When he comes to apply the text in requiring submission to rulers he enters into a full consideration of what kind of submission is due. He says the duties of ruled and ruler are reciprocal, and 'Unlimited submission is not due to government in a free state. There are certain boundaries beyond which submission can not be justly required, and should not be yielded. . . .' Warming with his subject he goes farther, and declares that they not only have a right to complain, but that resistance may become a duty. . . ."

Remember, Tucker didn't preach this on a street corner, but in the Massachusetts Capital, to the Governor, the House and the Council—to the top politicians in office in that colony.

On May 25, 1774, Gad Hitchcock, of Pembroke, preached the election sermon, and took as his text Proverbs 29:2: "When the righteous are in authority the people rejoice, but when the wicked bear rule the people mourn." Hitchcock set forth the history of the grievances of the colonists. Then (p. 30): ". . . 'Let the Governor in his chair of state hear it, we not only mourn, but with groanings that can not be uttered, and all because *the wicked rule*. The castle can not shelter him from that scorching thunderbolt. Families are divided, brother is arrayed against brother, friend against friend. Society is cut from its moorings, and hate and consternation reign on every side, and all because *the wicked bear rule*. King George may say the evils that produce this state of things are imaginary, but I tell you,' says Gad Hitchcock, 'and I tell the tyrant to his face, it is because the *wicked bear rule*.' "

Is it likely, do you think, that Gad Hitchcock would smile insipidly and preach submission to the crimes of our friends at I.R.S.?

In 1776, Samuel West, of Dartmouth, preached the election sermon, and took as his text Titus 3:1: "Put them in mind to be subject to principalities and powers, to obey magistrates, to be ready to every good work." Did he preach blind submission to every excess of government? No (p. 41 cf.). Headley summarizes his remarks as follows: ". . . But the same good will to others and desire for justice, which make us acquiesce in civil government, would oblige us equally to resist tyranny which cares neither for the happiness nor right of the subject . . . ."

Sam West preached that, "Tyranny and arbitrary power are utterly inconsistent with and subversive of the very design of civil government, and all political law, consequently the authority of a tyrant, is null and void." He explained that *any* people, when cruelly oppressed, had a right to throw off the yoke, and be free."

Indeed, starting on page 43, Samuel West preached to the Massachusetts government as follows: "Does not every one know that the King and Parliament have assumed to tax us without our consent? . . . Reason and equity require that no one be obliged to pay the tax that he has never consented to. . . . Can any one suppose it to be reasonable that a set of men, that are perfect strangers to us, should have the uncontrollable right to lay the most heavy and grievous burdens upon us, if they please, purely to gratify their unbounded avarice and luxury? . . . But, if they have the right to take our property from us without our consent, we must be wholly at their mercy for food and raiment . . . . We must turn our plowshares into swords, and our pruning-hooks into spears, and learn the art of self-defence against our enemies. . . ."

West referred to Jeremiah 48:10: "Cursed be he that doeth the work of the Lord deceitfully, and *cursed be he that keepeth back his sword from blood.*" He commented that "God has manifested his anger against those who have refused to assist their country against its cruel oppressors. . . ."

Would Sam West stand still for a government that held children hostage for payment of taxes? Would Sam West preach submission to such an outrage? You know the answer.

Many preachers not only preached resistance, but fought in the ranks as soldiers. Headley writes that the British treated them savagely when they were caught. His book tells the stories of many heroes of the stand.

So, now we have the background to look at Romans 13: "Let every soul be subject unto the higher powers. For there is no power but of God: the powers that be are ordained of God. (2) Whosoever therefore resisteth the power, resisteth the ordinance of God: and they that resist shall receive to themselves damnation. (3) For rulers are not a terror to good works, but to the evil.

Wilt thou then not be afraid of the power? do that which is good, and thou shalt have praise of the same: (4) For he is the minister of God to thee for good. But if thou do that which is evil, be afraid; for he beareth not the sword in vain: for he is the minister of God, a revenger to execute wrath upon him that doeth evil. (6) For for this cause pay ye tribute also: for they are God's ministers, attending continually upon this very thing."

First Paul says that since all power comes from God, so does government power. Not very controversial, unless you are an atheist. If you resist that power, says Paul, you will be damned, because the Lord instituted government precisely to fight evil. That's why you should be afraid if you do evil.

Suppose, however, that the *government* does evil. This shouldn't surprise us, because the government is run by men, wallowing in sin as we are. Does God want us to excuse in them the same sin we condemn in ourselves? Again, is God a Nazi? The question is both pertinent and sober. If you insist on obedience to government, even when it is wrong, you will wind up with Hitler, not with God. Remember that the Lord also requires the government to obey His laws.

In Matthew 22, starting at verse 15, and again in Luke 20, starting at verse 20, the scribes and Pharisees try to trick Jesus into saying something that will cause Herod to throw Him into prison. They ask Him whether the people should pay taxes to Caesar. This question was immensely dangerous.

In *The Life and Times of Jesus the Messiah* (Grand Rapids, Michigan, Wm. B. Eerdmans Publishing Co., 1980, Part I, Pp. 515-16), Alfred Edersheim wrote as follows in 1886: "It is of importance to notice, that the Talmud distinguishes two classes of 'publicans': the tax-gatherer in general (*Gabbai*), and the *Mokhes*, or *Mokhsa*, who was specially the *douanier* or custom-house official. Although both classes fall under the Rabbinic ban, the *douanier*—such as Matthew was—is the object of chief execration. And this, because his exactions were more vexatious, and gave more scope to rapacity. The *Gabbai*, or tax-gatherer, collected the regular dues, which consisted of ground-, income-, and poll-tax. The ground-tax amounted to one-tenth of all grain and one-fifth of the wine and fruit grown; partly paid in kind, and partly commuted into money. The income-tax amounted to 1 per cent.; while the head-money, or poll-tax, was levied on all persons, bond and free, in the case of men from the age of fourteen, in that of women from the age of twelve, up to that of sixty-five."

These are the direct taxes Jesus found, and they are quite modest—especially the income tax—compared to ours. However, Edersheim also says this: "If this offered many opportunities for vexatious exactions and rapacious injustice, the *Mokhes* might inflict much greater hardship upon the poor people. There was tax and duty upon all imports and exports; on all that was bought and sold; bridge-money, road-money, harbour-dues, town-dues, &c. The classical reader knows the ingenuity which could invent a tax, and find a name for every kind of exaction, such as on axles, wheels, pack-animals, pedestrians, roads, highways; on admission to markets; on carriers, bridges, ships, and quays; on crossing rivers, on dams, on licences, in short, on such a variety of objects, that even the research of modern scholars has not been able to identify all the names. On goods the *ad valorem* duty amounted to from 2½ to 5, and on articles of luxury to even 12½ per cent. But even this was as nothing, compared to the vexation of being constantly stopped on the journey, having to unload all one's pack-animals, when every bale and package was opened, and the contents tumbled about, private letters opened, and the *Mokhes* ruled supreme in his insolence and rapacity."

It reads as if he is writing about taxes in America today, but remember that Alfred Edersheim is still talking about taxes in the time of Jesus.

Indeed, Edersheim says this: "The very word *Mokhes* seems, in its root-meaning, associated with the idea of oppression and injustice. He was literally, as really, an oppressor. The Talmud charges them with gross partiality, remitting in the case of those to whom they wished to show favour, and exacting from those who were not their favourites. They were a criminal race, to which Lev. xx.5 applied. . . ."

How Alfred Edersheim could write in 1886 about our friends in I.R.S. today, we don't know, but that *is* what he said.

The question arises: What was the Jewish attitude toward this? For instance, Edersheim writes as follows: ". . . Against such unscrupulous oppressors every kind of deception was allowed; goods might be declared to be votive offerings, or a person pass his slave as his son."

In other words, taxes were so high, so dictatorial, that they amounted to confiscation, to a thug sticking a gun in your back in an alley. Such taxes cancelled law and civility. They justified victims who did whatever was necessary—including lying—to escape, which recalls what Ronald Reagan said in Williamsburg.

Did Jesus, the Jewish teacher, the rabbi, reject this? Well, what was his answer to the question of whether the Jews should pay taxes?

He didn't say, "No." He didn't say it, not because He was an advocate of the hated taxes we have described, but because saying it would have constituted both His application for membership in the Nationalist Party, and His commandment of violent rebellion against Caesar, in which who knows how many of His fellow Jews would have been killed. Remember that Jesus was not at all against violence. He used it—against the money changers in the temple—but He chose not to use it in this situation. He came "not to send peace, but a sword."

Indeed, notice that He also didn't say, "Yes." If He had, He would have crippled the Nationalists, who along with many, noble people of The Book, maintained that to pay tribute-money to Caesar was to acquiesce in his royal authority over Israel, and so to disown the Lord, Who alone was and is Israel's king.

So, what did and does He say? He said and says (Matthew 22:21): "Render therefore unto Caesar the things which are Caesar's; and unto God the things that are God's."

This was a profoundly revolutionary statement, in the sense that Caesar believed himself to be god, and therefore believed that he enjoyed jurisdiction over everything. Caesar believed that *all* things were Caesar's, and that you got to enjoy what was left of your pay after his taxes not because it was yours, but because Caesar magnanimously let you keep it, and could change his mind.

Now, here comes Jesus, preaching that there are things that are *not* Caesar's; thereby restricting Caesar's jurisdiction to that of the government ordained in Scripture; government that has a divinely mandated job to do, but certainly isn't divine—and shouldn't be totalitarian—itself.

Along these lines, consider Jesus's teaching in the sermon on the mount (Matthew 5:25): "Agree with thine adversary quickly, whiles thou art in the way with him; lest at any time the adversary deliver thee to the judge, and the judge deliver thee to the officer, and thou be cast into prison."

In other words, tell your enemy you agree with him while you are travelling with the message—even though you don't—because if you tell him what you really think, he may throw you into jail. Jesus did that Himself in part, in His answer on the tribute, because, according to Scripture, it was not yet time for Him to die.

Finally, assume *arguendo* that Romans 13 does mean what our friends at I.R.S. and in so many churches would like us to believe it means: that whatever the government says is right and must be obeyed, no matter how stupid, cruel or tyrannical. Does Romans 13 tell you which tax to pay? Does it tell you how much? Do you pay the tax on cigarette tubes—even though you don't make cigarette tubes—because Romans 13 says you should be subject unto the higher powers? If you do pay that tax, whether or not the law says you must, does Romans 13 tell you how much to pay?

No, for those purposes we have laws—man's laws—that we must study, which is what we are doing here. Could it be that you pay the income tax, not because Romans 13 says you should, but because our friends at I.R.S. have driven you and millions like you into a state of abject terror?

The churches that preach total government via Romans 13 are slave churches. We have seen what the preachers of the Revolution said. If you are in a slave church, we preach that you should change it or come out. Many free churches—who understand Romans 13—are waiting to welcome you.

18

WALKING TALL

As I write, I look out the window. I see rolling, green lawns, lush with care. I see flower beds, garnishing the airy, modern buildings with color. I see attractive women, fashionably dressed, strolling hand-in-hand with their admirers. If you meet the stringent requirements for admission to this paradise, you could easily be one of them, because there are almost two women here for every man.

Shall I play tennis when I finish this session at the typewriter? No, I have never played tennis in my life, and there is no reason to start now; but if I chose to do so, I could, on one of the two excellent courts. I could also lift weights at a weight pile that would impress Arnold Schwarzenegger, or use the track. In fact, I do use both those things almost daily, which is no doubt one reason I have never been in better health and condition.

There are also baseball, football, soccer, handball, horseshoes, racquetball, ping pong, co-ed basketball, co-ed volleyball, co-ed races and croquet; most sports you can think of except swimming, which would produce string bikinis and chaos.

There are scrabble contests and movies; there are concerts; there are recitals by a professional opera star, who also gives lessons and directs the chorus. There is a drama class, conducted by a man who has worked at various movie studios. There are classes in ballroom dancing taught by yours truly, and many opportunities to put them to use, such as the recent Fifties and Sixties Disco Dance, featuring disc jockey Wolfman Wisehart, and the Latin rhythms of Las Fiestas Patrias Dance, featuring disc jockey La Onda Bajita. Evening wear was not mandatory, but one of the gentlemen wore a tuxedo. There was the riotous, visiting, San Francisco comedy team of Amos and Hill, whom you have no doubt enjoyed on HBO.

There are the bookmobile, which will deliver any reading material you like, the modern dance class and the creative writing class. There was the fashion show, featuring the latest stylings in bathing suits and evening wear.

In this combination of exclusive club, junior high school for adults and fat farm, the food nevertheless is "all you can eat," and compares in quality to what you will find in a medium-priced Las Vegas buffet.

Husbands and wives enjoy each other's company here, along with visits from their children. We recommend it as a haven for the burgeoning army of Americans from whom the government has stolen everything; and we offer this Creative Idea for Retirement at no extra cost beyond the price of the book.

Along these lines, you have probably often complained, like almost everyone else, about the present degeneration in the quality of domestic help. Not so here, where a remarkably attentive staff assiduously keeps track of our requirements. There are even a couple of professionals here daily, whose sole job is to solve unforeseen problems. Have the residence's hair driers disappeared? Simply see your "counsellor," and he or she will make it right.

Isn't security a growing problem these days? Don't you hear all the time about innocent people in good neighborhoods, who are savagely attacked in their homes? Statistics tell us that something like this outrage has already happened to you or to someone you know. When your obedient servant reads about such horrors in the leisure library here, we cannot but reflect that the victims could have prevented them, had they known the secrets of self-protection. We have no such problems here. It goes without saying that my roommate and I have keys to our comfortable room, along with closets that lock. That is just the beginning of a security program that you probably couldn't afford, if you could find it.

There are gates and walls, of course; many fashionable, planned communities have them. However, do they have professional security personnel constantly on patrol? Indeed, have they implemented the novel security technique of several, daily counts of persons on the premises, to make certain that no intruder has penetrated the grounds? As far as your reporter knows, there has never been a robbery here. There has never been a mugging, a kidnapping or a rape. Can your community say the same thing? Could this be at least part of the reason our roommate, a nationally known physician, was so reluctant to leave?

For instance, a word should be said about my schedule. I work on my writing half the day, as we are doing now. For many years, we wished for a Renaissance-type patron to finance it. Now—at last—I have one. That's right; all the wonders we've been telling you about, and more, are absolutely free. Indeed, there is also free and complete medical and dental treatment, including special, pre-natal care for pregnant inhabitants, along with complimentary prescription drugs. There is no deductible. There is no Medicare finagling. The Establishment picks up the entire bill. Who said Socialism stinks? Here we enjoy the benefits of Socialism in microcosm. Our conservative friends have deceived us.

Every afternoon, there is a three-hour computer course, featuring the latest equipment and software. To take it in your expensive, crime-ridden neighborhood—Park Avenue or Palos Verdes—you would have to spend considerable money. Here of course we get it free. Indeed, there is an Education Department here. Residents may take college courses in English, math, algebra, languages and banking. There is a course in financial management and a women's sewing circle. Every afternoon, your obedient servant strolls over there and teaches some of these subjects to people who are trying to get their high school diplomas.

In the evening, your reporter strolls back to his residence, smelling the flowers. Perhaps we spend some time playing pocket billiards or chess, while others play backgammon or cards or watch television in one of the rooms set aside for the purpose. Then, we enjoy a cup of herb tea, perhaps a snack, and drift happily off to sleep on our plush mattress, dreaming dreams of satisfaction. So ends another fulfilling day in paradise.

Where am I? In the Bohemian Grove, near San Francisco? On the French Riviera? In Club Med? In some kind of writers' retreat? No, Pilgrim, the answer is none of the above. Actually, I am an inmate in what we cons call Club Fed: the Pleasanton Federal Correctional Institution, near Oakland, California, where your intrepid correspondent was sent for telling too much truth about the income tax on network radio. Everything we have told you about what happens here is true. This is what you have been afraid of. You have been afraid of a fantasy, of a movie set, carefully nurtured by our friends at I.R.S. as part of the terror campaign they are conducting against the American people.

The clanging bars in your nightmares do exist. They are an important element of the U.S. prison system—in places like Leavenworth—but if you are convicted of a nonviolent "crime" like income tax, especially a misdemeanor, as I was, our Socialist billionaires will not waste such high-powered technology on you. It is scarce. It is reserved for genuine criminals. No, as an income tax "criminal" you would be sent to a co-ed institution like Pleasanton, or to a camp like Boron, where there are no fences at all. A while back, *The Los Angeles Times* interviewed the warden of Boron, and asked whether he was planning to install a fence. He replied, "Not unless somebody tries to break in." Indeed, the U.S. Code says quite clearly that the Bureau of Prisons is forbidden to send someone convicted of a misdemeanor like "willful failure to file" to a penitentiary without his permission.

So the most important message your reporter hopes to leave with you in this book is the fact that there is nothing to fear. Nothing. Roger Olsen says he is trying to "scare heck out of you." Now you know you don't have to be scared. "The only thing we have to fear is—fear itself." The totalitarians have been trapped by their own "humanitarian" hogwash. They have talked themselves into a corner. They are trying to terrify you, but their phony humanitarianism has turned the prison you could visit into the paradise we have described.

Don't misunderstand. This *is* a prison! If your reporter had his druthers, he would druther not be here. We *would* rather be in one of those pleasant places you thought we were when you started reading this. The country is becoming more totalitarian, and this place is more totalitarian still. There are rules here we must obey. There is a "hole" to which we could be sent if we don't. (Your reporter has never been there, and so can't tell you about it.) There are annoyances, some of them picayune to the point of insanity. There are the surprise urine analyses you will have to get used to, in prison or out, as part of the totalitarian fraud called the War On Drugs.

Many of the guards in these places are there precisely because they can't make it in the outside world. In another book, your reporter no doubt will tell you about the guard who doesn't know enough of the alphabet to replace manila folders in a drawer; and his colleague who knows the times table through four, but can't handle five. We'll tell you about routine theft of property from inmates by guards. Your reporter, for instance, lost a rare hundred dollar bill in this fashion. The identity of the guard who stole it is known, but, typically, she is still not in prison. The government allows its own to break the law with impunity.

Along these lines, the man who runs the "hospital" likes to pretend he is a physician, but makes a hobby of mispronouncing medical terms and is a walking definition of incompetence. His title is Physician's Assistant, or P.A., and he is a specialist in practicing medicine without a license. On one occasion, someone with a heart attack was made to lie there for more than four hours without help. On another, the dentist refused to fill a cavity because it wasn't "big enough." Were any clinic in the outside world to operate like this, its operators would be thrown into jail. These are just a few examples of the annoyances you face.

There are more. For instance, your reporter is a space age author, but is writing this on a rickety IBM electric antique, complete with paint spots, which I had to recondition myself. Some of the keys don't work, so I must pencil in the characters. It is ghastly green. A metal sticker on the outside says: U.S. Government Property, AE-02502, Indian Health Service. Inside, a faded label is dated April 30, 1959.

Of course, much depends on your point of view. There were no free computer courses at Yorktown. General Cornwallis himself would regard what you *may* have to undergo as science-fiction luxury unavailable to kings; which recalls a recent wire service story from Stockholm, according to which a man walked out of Communist-occupied Russia, across the top of the world, through the ice, into Sweden. Taken by surprise, the authorities in the small Swedish town where he arrived at first put the refugee up in the jail. However, he didn't know it was a jail. When someone later read and translated a Swedish newspaper for him, relating that he had stayed in a jail, the refugee expressed amazement, explaining that he had thought it was a hotel.

As we said in the Foreword to this book, "You can't make an omelette without breaking eggs." The idea that one could oppose the most pervasive, totalitarian power in history without risk—simply by writing post cards and calling one's Congressman—is a childish fantasy that deserves disgust when entertained by an adult. Add to this the fact that if you are one of the happy many chosen as one of His people by the Lord before the foundation of the world, you will win in the end no matter what the enemy does to you here. What else do you need to know?

Permit your obedient servant to offer an idea that, as far as we know, is novel. Could it be that those of us who have been struggling for many years to restore the Constitution have been on a somewhat wrong track? Some of us have made staying out of jail more important than anything else—to the point at which we have allowed that worthwhile motive to pervert the mission; indeed, to *become* the mission. Suppose Paul had done that? Suppose Paul had not kept the faith, had not stayed the course—because doing so would have required him to go to jail; to become unrespectable. Christianity could well have died aborning, but for the fact that it was ordained.

Some people see the problem, but have a different solution. From time to time, we read of armed groups that are seized in "a right-wing extremist plot to overthrow the government." It is certainly true that in the construction of every dictatorship a point arrives at which the liberty lover is free to do whatever is necessary—because the dictator has canceled the rules, has abolished the laws. When Lenin sent his goons to abolish the Constituent Assembly at gunpoint, he junked any moral constraints against killing them. Solzhenitsyn has taught us in *The Gulag Archipelago* that when Chekist (KGB) goons came at night, the people should have clubbed them to death with anything at hand, instead of cowering in the very terror the goons came to create. By doing so, the people would have terrorized the terrorists. When the Chekist looked at himself in the mirror each morning, he would have wondered whether he would sleep in his own bed that night, or in an alley with a broken skull. Unfortunately, the Russian people did not do what Solzhenitsyn says they should have done.

Again, it was easy to see what was happening in Russia. It isn't always. When Socialist goon Hitler started out, he was careful to do everything legally. He persuaded President Hindenburg to appoint him Chancellor, which was legal. He went to the puppet Reichstag for approval of his Socialist program. When he sent his goons to burn the Reichstag, his Nazi judges backed him up. Obviously, a point arrived in all this "legal" usurpation, "legal" murder and "legal" arson at which the Lord would have encouraged recourse to a higher law, including sabotage of the Nazi economy and bureaucracy, and beheading of any Nazi one could catch.

What was that point? To this day, your reporter still doesn't know. Was it the burning of the Reichstag, or something else? Hitler did not issue an announcement officially declaring the establishment of his dictatorship and the cancellation of law. Had a German liberty lover responded with violence back there at the beginning, his patriotic fellow citizens would have told him that what he was doing was reprehensible, "illegal" and not respectable. And it *would* have been from the point of view of someone who subscribes to the blind letter of the law. No widespread rebellion of "good Germans" would have materialized to back him up.

This is not speculation. There were anti-Nazis, but the people gave them insufficient support.

Today, the destruction of the American system is being accomplished by the Hitler model. Brilliant historians debate the date on which our freedom was lost. Was it 1913, when the income tax and Federal Reserve were inflicted on us? Was it some other incident in some other year? Whatever the answers, notice that there has been no hint of general support for the military action some veterans and deer hunters are thirsting to use to restore our Constitution and the rule of law. Our people are "good Germans."

Without that support, patriot plans have been characterized as the work of dissatisfied kooks by the Prostitute National Press. Indeed, at this point there is nothing the dictators love more than "extremist violence." It offers them the opportunity to ask Congress for more funds to "fight the threat." It justifies more totalitarianism to "fight drugs," et cetera. The time of the Tennessee long rifle could well be approaching, but it certainly has not arrived as we go to press and we pray it never will. Whether it does or not, the traitors and usurpers should be tried under law, with all the constitutional protections. The question for today is: What should worried Americans do NOW?

Here's the answer: Flood the courts! Flood the prisons! Worry no longer about going there. As you have seen, it is nowhere near as bad as you thought. If you go, enjoy the satisfaction of knowing that the government believed your activities deserved it. When the annals are written, you will receive a battle star.

It is important to understand why you are going into court. You are not necessarily going into court to win. It would be good to win, yes. It could happen. It *has* happened. In view of the present, defective condition of popular understanding, however—the predictable result of literal decades of propaganda—any such victory would be a fluke. In order to start winning, we first must keep losing. If you should win one, of course we shall help you celebrate and spread the word. The media won't. However, you are not going into court today because you expect to win. Indeed, it would help your mental balance if you fight as hard as you can in court; keep the trial going as long as you legitimately can, as we did (almost four weeks); fight as if your victory were inevitable—expecting all along to lose.

Again, you are not necessarily going into court to win. At the present stage of the battle for America, you are going into court *to prove you are serious*. A major theme of much patriot literature today holds that the worst thing that can happen is a defeat in court. No, friends, that's not true. The worst thing that can happen is to be considered "frivolous," unimportant, unthreatening, unserious.

Before the Civil War, the Abolitionists went into court—to prove they were serious. In the 1960's, the "freedom riders" of the "civil rights movement" displayed considerable courage for which they honestly won sometimes grudging respect. You may not have agreed with them, but you certainly took them seriously. They were willing to be beaten. They were willing to go to prison. They *wanted* to go to prison. We are perfectly aware that they did so knowing in most cases that their sentences would be a joke and that they would enjoy media support, things you should not realistically expect. However, in India, Mohandas K. Gandhi, one of their heroes, won respect—proved he was serious—by going into genuinely hostile British courts. Now it is your turn to get the people's attention. Now it is your turn to prove you are serious, at least as serious as the anti-nuclear demonstrators who have flooded the jails and crippled nuclear power; at least as serious as the man in northern California who lost his legs under a train, during a demonstration against U.S. weapons.

The people you are trying to reach won't believe you are serious if you are not willing to go to jail. They would not have believed the Founding Fathers if they had not been willing to lose everything.

We shall never win the battle to restore the law in this country, until we flood the courts with people who can take the consequences like men! The point of this book is not to convince you you'll win in court. You probably won't. The point of the book is to show you you're right. Nothing beats the knowledge that you are right. It permeates all your thoughts and activities—everything you do. If you are right, you will win regardless of the verdict.

Along these lines, consider a gentleman named Mark Healy Bonner. Bonner was the prosecutor in your reporter's case, and we have no reason to believe he isn't typical. Before the trial, Bonner invited a close associate of your reporter's to his office, and tried to turn him against us. He couldn't. During the interview, your reporter's dear friend asked Bonner to show him the section of the Internal Revenue Code that requires me to file. Believe it or not, Bonner couldn't do that, either, and we have an affidavit to prove it. Need we add that at this point an honest prosecutor would have withdrawn the charges? Bonner didn't because the orders from the top were to shut your reporter up; or is it down? The reader will recall that we were already under criminal investigation in 1966, eleven years before even our friends at I.R.S. say we did anything wrong. They apparently couldn't tolerate someone talking about the income tax as it really is, every other day on network radio.

Among the other crimes Bonner committed in the process was the illegal use of grand jury subpoenas. No grand jury was sitting to hear the case, so Bonner pretended to be the grand jury and sent the subpoenas out. Again, we don't have to tell you what the judge would do to you if you somehow came into possession of grand jury subpoenas, and sent them to banks and other institutions to collect information on someone you wanted to nail. Indeed, at the sentencing hearing, Judge Consuelo B. Marshall threw out three of the five charges for that reason; but, as of the fall of 1987, we are not aware that Bonner is on his way to prison. The remaining two charges involved the Internal Revenue Service's illegal use of administrative summonses—in which our friends pretend to be collecting information for a civil matter, but then secretly switch it to criminal. The Ninth Circuit Court of Appeal ruled this practice illegal in another case shortly after our own. Bonner denied us "probable cause" by circumventing the grand jury completely.

There was also the lawyer who sent us a letter of advice, for which we had paid. She was threatened with ruin by dignitaries from the Department of Justice in Washington, if she persisted in her opinions, which corresponded with what you have read here. She folded and now wears a saddle and bit. Needless to say, she is a bar association monopolist.

The abiding regret of Mark Bonner's life appears to be the fact that he was born too late to join the Nazi party. He believes most sincerely that the government owns everything, and that what it lets you enjoy of your pay is a favor. He almost said as much at the trial. We would like to quote those remarks from the transcript, but as we go to press *almost a year after the verdict*, that document—for which we paid about $6,000 in advance—still is "not available." The effect has been to delay the appeal until the sentence has been served, offering Bonner the opportunity to argue that the issue now is "moot." No doubt another "coincidence."

We arrived at court to ask for a stay of sentence pending appeal for bond to the U.S. Supreme Court. Her honor was in chambers, so Bonner posed as judge. Like a totalitarian sponge, he usurps whatever power he can sneak. Announcing that our petition for a stay had been denied, he arranged for your reporter to be kidnapped from the courtroom.

Should you wish to write Mark Bonner, and ask him politely what he thinks he is doing, he lives with his wife Ann at 2551 Federal Avenue, Los Angeles, California, 90064.

There is also your reporter's personal Special Agent, Roberta L. Hagopian, who testified that she knew nothing about the law; and that she never answered any of our many letters, because her supervisor told her not to. She lives in Apartment Q224, at 3654 Barham Boulevard, Los Angeles, California, 90068.

How much honest chance would you have against all this? Not much; about the same chance we had. Indeed, even if you do win, you lose in a real sense, because your victory would incite a feeding frenzy among our friends at I.R.S., who are inflamed by any blood in the water, even their own, and would no doubt come after you as never before. So, again, at this stage in the battle for America, you are not going into court absolutely expecting to win, thereby setting the stage for depression when you lose. You are going into court *to prove you are serious*. You are going into court *to educate the court*.

For instance, the ordinary, Soviet-style I.R.S. show trial takes a day-and-a-half or two. We kept ours going almost four weeks. Bonner protested several times to her honor on the record, with most enjoyable consternation, that such trials usually last a couple of days. Also on the record, at sidebar, he complained of exhaustion, explaining that in a daze he had put a pen without its cap into a shirt pocket and ruined the shirt. Her honor replied that the defense appeared to be staying up all night; and that Bonner would have to do so, too. A would-be fashion plate when the trial began, he wound up resembling Renfield after Dracula bit his neck.

He also complained often and bitterly about the fact that we demanded every available right; such as our insistence on complete cross-examinations of his witnesses. He conveyed the impression that our demand for a fair trial was outrageous; and several times lamented the "cost to the government." He really believes that such a trial is an annoying formality. Remember also that we forced our friends at I.R.S. to reveal considerable information about the secret computer codes they use to maintain secret dossiers on you and you and you.

You had better believe that, when the fiasco was finished, incipient Hitlerite Mark Healy Bonner and his bosses at I.R.S. knew they had been in a battle, because they were covered with their own blood. Such "victories" they can do without. Indeed, remember that three of the five charges in our case were thrown out, and, as we go to press, there is good reason to believe the remaining two will be thrown out as well. If they are, the government's "victory" would turn to gall; while ours would be even sweeter than it would have been at trial. However, even if none of this happens; even if we "lose," we've won, for the reasons already stated.

By vote of Congress and signature of the President, "nonviolence" has been made the official public policy of the United States, via the national holiday for Martin Luther King. So, your intrepid correspondent used it. When one of Bonner's storm troopers came running at me in court—as I stood flabbergasted, looking in vain for the judge—I simply lay down, went limp and offered no resistance whatever. Your reporter now can testify that "non-violence" works. The civil rights leaders are right. Bonner's minions went berserk. On the way down to the lockup, one of them whispered in my ear that he would break my wrist. (He didn't). It was marvelous!

More than anything else, the storm troopers would prefer that you fight them physically. Violence would allow them to do what they are lusting to do all along: maim you. Less satisfying to them than violence would be your acquiescence in what they are doing. On the other hand, non-violence tells them you know you're right, expresses your disgust and contempt for what they are doing—for their usurpation—and underlines the fact that they can't retaliate, but must stew in frustration.

Now, imagine such a trial multiplied a hundred times around the country. A thousand times! Indeed, later, in the lockup, a couple of marshals told your reporter with some wonder that they are seeing more and more people like him lately. Imagine such trials taking place before jurors educated to their own powers. How much such pressure could our friends at I.R.S. take? You can be sure that, faced with these new Abolitionists, the sissies in Congress typically would protect themselves by dismantling the monolith and taking credit for the change. Your alternative is doing nothing, thereby condemning your children to life as drones in an international Socialist dictatorship.

The Bible teaches that you will go into captivity if you have no knowledge. Knowledge is the solution. Knowledge is the ultimate tax shelter. The more Americans who know what is happening—who know how Taxscam is taking them—the better the chance we have to win. The more Americans who understand what you have just read in this book, the better the chance we have to stop the extortion and restore the law.

Now that you have read this book, pass it on. Buy copies by the carton and sell them, to anyone who will listen, to anyone who can read—especially to registered voters; to anyone who will *serve on a jury.* If you really want some action; if you are seeking a new hobby, and have become somewhat jaded by sissy sports like hang-gliding and shark hunting; why not sell *Taxscam* on the steps of your local, federal courthouse. You will be preparing the electorate to cast their most important vote. At the end of the book, we'll show you how to order.

This entire book boils down to one simple question. The reader will recall that it is dedicated to Ruth Studley and Nancy Brodie. Both these distinguished ladies were inmates with your reporter at Pleasanton. Many of the ladies there use language that makes General Patton sound like Little Miss Muffet. Not Ruth and Nancy. Both immensely genteel, they are Christian grandmothers and will be sixty when you read this.

Nancy Brodie is a Registered Nurse. She and her husband, Doug, a physician who specializes in degenerative diseases, live near Reno. In 1977, federal judge Thomas J. McBride sentenced them to six months in prison for "willful failure to file." His honor told them: "Although no crime has been committed, I sentence you as a deterrent only to others." Mrs. Brodie was thereupon taken right off the floor into Sacramento jail.

McBride was saying, in other words, that he was throwing an innocent woman into prison, to teach someone else a lesson. Of course, McBride himself should have been jailed and thrown off the bench, but he wasn't. Indeed, Mrs. Brodie reports that his statement, made in open court in the presence of the reporter, somehow did not find its way into the transcript.

In 1987—still right—they were sent back to prison for a year for the same thing. Nancy says her C.P.A. figures that if they owed anything at all, they owed $900. That's right: $900! Yet, their C.P.A. was not allowed to testify.

Ruth Studley in real life is a real estate broker in Redding, California. Mrs. Studley was also in Pleasanton for "willful failure to file." Sacramento federal Judge Milton Schwartz gave her the option of reducing her prison term with probation, but, "Probation is a contract, and I don't sign government contracts." Grandma Ruth had no attorney and refused to waive any of her rights.

In fact, she explains only half in jest that she doesn't want to go home. There she would have to cook, clean, et cetera, for various individuals—including sons—whose knuckles drag on the ground. Here, she is having the time of her life, and people do those things for her. Indeed, both grandmas say with tongues in cheek that the one thing they fear most is that "someone will find out how much fun we're having." Now you know.

It looks as if the government is going to outsmart Ruth. As of August, 1987, she has been told that they will kick her out in September—although she won't sign the probation papers—no strings attached. In the probation system, one must trade a relatively short period of time outside the institution, for years of supervision. In this case, she would have to trade six months of liberty for five years' probation. Ruth won't. When she walks out of here, she will be a free woman. Reassigned from office work to landscaping—outside the fence—Ruth gets herself transferred back. "They might have been planning to lock me out," she wisecracks. "They'll do anything to get me out of here."

As this manuscript sets out for the printer, the Judge is threatening to throw Ruth Studley back into prison, because she is still refusing to sign the probation papers—and Ruth cheerily is ready to go. Show me a Hemingway character with more "grace under pressure."

So, now here's the question we have been waiting to ask you. You are being fooled, humiliated, taken to the cleaners, folded, spindled and mutilated. Your estate and country are being ravaged. Your *grandchildren's* estates have already been spent. You are losing your liberty. You are well on the way to becoming a farm animal. What are you going to do about it?

Washington's barefoot troops at Valley Forge left bloody tracks in the snow. Many of the Founding Fathers lost everything. We are not asking you to leave bloody tracks in the snow. We are not asking you to lose everything. We are asking you to have the time of your life in court, and, if necessary, in prison. We are asking you to take the free computer course at Pleasanton, or a place like it; to enjoy the free concerts, fashion shows and movies. We *are* asking you to do some of the things you have always wanted to do, but have never had the time for, such as learn a foreign language via Señor Berlitz or lose weight.

We are asking you to take a risk. For me, this time in prison has been a minor inconvenience; minor because, as you see, I have been able to keep doing what I would have been doing anyway, what God created me to do. For you, it could be a major inconvenience.

Question: Are you willing to suffer a major inconvenience to restore the Constitution and the law? Are you willing to suffer a major inconvenience to restore your liberty? Are you willing to suffer a major inconvenience to preserve the property you hold so dear? William Gordon, pastor of the Third Church of Roxbury, preached the first election sermon in the Massachusetts House after the Declaration of Independence, and said, ". . . [H]e that does not mean to bear a part in the public burdens of the day, *but to escape wholly unhurt in person and property, is no patriot*" (J. T. Headley, *The Chaplains and Clergy of the Revolution*, op. cit., p. 39).

Are you as much of a man as Ruth Studley? Do you have as much American guts as Nancy Brodie?

If your answer is, "No," then let me tell you, Pilgrim, that you are in the wrong game. You shouldn't even be reading this book. We invite you to close it now and slink away. You're a parasite, a windbag. You are living off the sacrifices and accomplishments of others and are trying to impress yourself. You don't deserve your liberty and property, and you shortly won't have them. You deserve to be a slave and shortly will be one. Don't come up to me after meetings and tell me what you think *I* should be doing. Just get out, go home and wait for the knock on your door. Years from now, when America has been restored, and your grandchildren ask what you did in the Great War, you can say with some nostalgia that you shovelled bleep in Louisiana, or somewhere else, while the women did your fighting.

The Founding Fathers did not risk their lives, their fortunes and their sacred honor in order to establish a nation for wimps. As you will recall, Judge Leventhal thinks you *are* a wimp. Well, Pilgrim, *are* you?

If you are ready to do what must be done, we invite you now to walk tall with Ruth. We invite you now to walk tall with Nancy.

As David told his son Solomon (I Kings 2:2): "I go the way of all the earth: be thou strong therefore, and shew thyself a man." And Paul tells us this (I Corinthians 16:13): "Watch ye, stand fast in the faith, quit you like men, be strong."

We'll see you in court.

DISCLAIMER

Nothing you have read here should be considered legal advice. Only bar association monopolists, so certified by license, enjoy the legal privilege of giving such advice, and your reporter is not one of them.

Also, please do not go into court with anything you have read here, unless you have expert assistance. If the material is presented incorrectly, it could establish bad precedent, which would give our friends at I.R.S. the opportunity to claim that the arguments have been considered and rejected.

For the expert assistance you need, see, for example, Lowell H. "Larry" Becraft, Jr., Esq., 209 Lincoln Street, Huntsville, Alabama 35801; (205) 533-2535. Although he is a bar association monopolist, Brother Becraft has a monumental understanding of the law, and can present your case in the mystifying manner that will more than satisfy the courts.

KUDOS

When our friends at I.R.S. decided to attack the Murdock family, of Salt Lake City, one of them decided that wife Billie was the "weak link." We don't know who made that decision, but we're confident that he or she will never make Commissioner, because Billie Murdock since has demonstrated an uncanny capacity for research. It was she who dug up many of the documents on which this book is based, which required a descent into archives as dusty as the vault where Jack Benny used to store his money.

So, our gratitude goes to our friend at I.R.S.—wherever he or she is locked up—who gave us this "weak link," and kudos goes to Billie the Bulldog.

TABLE OF AUTHORITIES

(The final number[s] is not part of the citation; rather, it refers to the page[s] in this volume on which the case is discussed.)

INDEX

ABOUT THE AUTHOR

Alan Stang has been a journalist for thirty years. He was an original Mike Wallace writer, before Mike went to CBS. More than two hundred of his feature magazine articles have been published by national magazines. Alan Stang exposed the alien conspiracy to seize control of New Mexico; the conspiracy behind the attempted assassination of Governor George Wallace; the terrorist FLQ in Canada. His exposé of OSHA brought the excesses of that agency to a halt. He has lectured around the country and the world. His lectures in the Sixties prevented race riots in the South. He has been a network radio commentator and a preacher. His novel, *The Highest Virtue*, won five stars—highest rating—from the *West Coast Review of Books*. He has won awards from the American Academy of Public Affairs of Los Angeles, and the Pennsylvania House of Representatives, for journalistic excellence.